Buffalo County:

A Native Son Speaks

Historical writings of and about E. F. Ganz

Compiled by The Buffalo County Historical Society

TABLE OF CONTENTS

Foreword

Several years ago, soon after starting at the Buffalo County Historical Society, I came to realize that when I look at the large collage of pioneers in the courthouse stairway, there was something missing. I am not talking of the women that are not pictured, though they are certainly a part of it, but the many, thousands upon thousands of men, women and children who were not rich enough, famous enough or even bad enough to warrant newspaper articles, lavish biographies, larger than life portraits and the like that some of the pioneers in Buffalo County have been blessed with.

In working with genealogists and other researchers, I have found a kindred spirit that we all share in wanting to hear the stories of everyday pioneer life, how the crops for that year couldn't pay the mortgage, how miraculously Aunt Ida was only in her mother's womb for six months instead of the usual nine, or how deeply the loss of a loved one not only affected the family, but the entire community.

This is when I found that a certain man, by the name of Edwin Ferdinand Ganz, had spent nearly his entire life trying to capture those minutiae and make each person's story known. If you never have had the opportunity to read an obituary written by this man, then this book will impress upon you his heart for his fellow man in all things good and bad. E. F. Ganz had the innate ability to find the best in any situation, no matter how dire the circumstances.

Another very exciting aspect to Mr. Ganz's writings was his history of growing up in a pioneer home from soon after his parents arrived in America. This afforded him the unique opportunity to not only see firsthand the conditions pioneers experienced, but also to become friends with many of Buffalo County's true pioneer families. This allows him to write not only about what the prominent families in Buffalo County were like, but also to delve into the depths of everyday life in early Buffalo County.

This compilation includes a collection of Mr. Ganz's writings from over the years that he owned or worked with the Buffalo County Journal. Some articles were requested by the State Historical Society of Wisconsin as well as some being written for other publications such as the 1919 Biographical History of Buffalo and Pepin Counties. His proficiency in writing memorials and obituaries is exceeded by none here in Buffalo County, but we felt including one of his would be worthy to this subject, and fitting with the historical theme, we have included that of Lawrence Kessinger, author of that well-known History of Buffalo County, written in 1888 as the first comprehensive history of this county. The articles have been reproduced with the same spellings and punctuation of the original to help the reader get a feel for the writing style of Mr. Ganz and the others included.

Our hope for you, the reader, is that this compilation of E. F. Ganz writings will allow for a better understanding of not only the general history of Buffalo County, but to be able to finally close your eyes and imagine the pioneer struggles of a pioneer farmer having to carry a plow on his back across the bluffs, a pioneer wife waiting at home with six children and a farm to care for while her husband walks for a week to Alma to register a land sale, or a pioneer child celebrating the blessing of a swollen water hole after a summer rain.

Mr. Kelly Herold
Executive Director
Buffalo County Historical Society

Autobiography of Edwin Ferdinand Ganz; Written For and Addressed To His Children

January 1, 1934

My Father, Johann Kasper Ganz, was born March 19, 1812, at Embrach, in the Canton of Zurich, Switzerland. His father died when Kasper was but four years of age and he went to live with an uncle, a Mr. Bodmer, at Wuelflingen, in the same Canton. This uncle was the owner of Bodmer's Mill and a general factor in that village, owning practically every business enterprise in it. This was not unusual in those days when, of course, the enterprises were of a rather primitive nature but the miller was an important personage nevertheless. My father well remembered the famine of 1817, which seems to have been almost world wide owing mostly to the cold summer of 1816. I say cold because cool will really not begin to adequately describe conditions since practically all crops were destroyed and it is recorded that here in America there was such a severe blizzard during the month of June that whole flocks of sheep perished and the same weather conditions prevailed in Europe. Father did not suffer from the consequences of this calamity for in the mill and store houses of his uncle there was abundance of food but he remembered how his schoolmates, running through the mill while playing with him, would scoop up handfuls of bran from a bin and eat it. He, of course, did likewise but when his uncle told him that the boys did this because they were hungry, the big piece of bread which his aunt always had ready for him on his return from school was never again neglected but always given to the other boys who eagerly fell upon it.

This uncle owned the village butcher shop and traded in cattle which were bought in the Canton of Bern and other regions among the

1

mountains, Zurich not being a cattle country, the land being fit to grow grain and other like agricultural products, besides fruit. When quite young father had to help with the driving of these cattle and besides often had to carry the money for their purchase in a belt suspended by shoulder straps. When he used to tell us about this we thought it was great but when he further told us that the straps made open sores and the coarse shoes blistered his feet we did not so much begrudge him that task which was arduous indeed, the money being all in silver coin. His uncle drove back and forth in a chaise or sleigh but feared that a Herr, driving in state, might be waylaid by robbers while a poor little boy, plodding along under a load of silver was comparatively safe from such attacks as was the silver which was, of course, the main consideration. This Uncle was a stern man who exercised his power but that was considered the privilege of the well-to-do in those days and father never laid it up against him for did he not house, clothe and feed the poor orphan boy? The butcher in his uncle's shop soon made friends with the boy and he became his helper, acquiring a fair knowledge of that trade which he exercised on the farm after coming to this country, doing the work not only for himself but for the neighbors, gratis of course, for one neighbor was supposed to help out where the other was stuck, that being all in the day's work. One of the tricks of that trade was the making of that excellent "Country Wurst", to which no factory product can be compared.

His trade, however, was not that of butcher and after serving an apprenticeship of five years and some years as a journeyman he became a fully licensed saddler. A saddler was a man who made saddles, harness, collars, and upholstered mattresses, coaches, furniture, etc., therefore the term harnessmaker would hardly be adequate. As a journeyman he traversed a large part of southern Germany and every canton in Switzerland except Graubuenden. This being the case, he always seemed to think that Graubuenden was not so much. His children, however, seemed to differ with him for three of them were married to people coming directly and two more to descendants of emigrants from that canton, so it seems that set opinions do not last through more than one generation.

In 1844 father was married to Maria Magdalena Meier of Buelach in the Canton of Zurich and there he established himself as harness maker or saddler, cultivating some land on the side. To them four children were born. Rudolf Arnold, born October 26, 1844, who

2

during the Civil War enlisted in Company K, 48th Regiment Wisconsin Infantry, and died at Fort Scott, Kansas. Anna Maria (Nanetta) who was born November 25, 1845, and was married to Fred Beck who died leaving three children: Fred, Arnold, Louisa. She was then married to Joel Doenier, six children being born to them, namely: Christina, Anna, Alwina, Anton, Casper, and Emma. She is also deceased. Barbara Paulina was born September 17, 1847, and was married to John Farner, a veteran of the Civil War. The children born to them are Emma, John 1st, Emil, Rosina, Elisa, Alwine, Amalia, William, Henry, Albert, John II and Louise. This good and kind sister died since I started to write this at the age of 86 years. Alfred was born January 18, 1849, and was married in 1887, to Mrs. Joseph Keller, nee Dorathea Christ. The children born to them are Arnold, Elfrieda, Edwin, Emil, and Alice. Alfred died in 1930. Mrs. Maria Magdalena Ganz died in 1855 after a protracted illness.

In 1857 father was married to our mother, Louise Kuederli, of Buelach who was born at Schwamendingen June 29, 1835. Together with the above named children they came to America the same year, crossing in a steamer and landing at New York. Thence they came by rail to Dunleith, Illinois, passing through Chicago which was but a straggling town in the mud-flats. A steamboat brought them from Dunleith (now East Dubuque) to La Crosse where they were met by John Bosshard, father of Otto Bosshard, who took them by team to the home of our uncle, Henry Utzinger, who lived on a farm on what is known as Dutchman's Creek, near Bangor. Here they remained for about two months during which time father went to Waumandee where he bought from Jacob Bosshard of Bangor 160 acres of land in the heart of Waumandee Valley, most of it virgin prairie, a fourty-acre tract of woodland, belonging to it being five miles away in the town of Glencoe. The hills in Waumandee Valley, now covered with timber, were then all bare owing to the annual ravages of prairie fires.

When the family first came up from Bangor, they lived in a little log cabin which stood on the little knoll, a short distance northeast of where the mill is now located. This was over two miles from the farm and every morning father and Arnold walked to the farm and back in the evening but that was not all, logs had to be cut for the house and then for the barn and that meant another five miles to and from the woods. Finally the house was built and the furniture made and they moved in. The table, bedsteads and benches were made by a carpenter, some other things by father and a good cookstove was bought. All tools and implements had been brought from Switzerland also household utensils of all kinds. This was done on the advice of some friends who had come to America a year previous. While the folks lived near the mill site, about two hundred Winnebago Indians camped on the prairie near where the schoolhouse is now located. They stayed about two weeks and while they were peaceable they scared mother and the children and pestered the settlers by their persistent begging which was not very successful since the settlers had very little themselves.

A good yoke of oxen and a very good cow were bought in Bangor and this gave them a good start in farming. Their first crop was cut with a cradle and some of the grain was trampled out by driving the cattle and a neighbor's horses back and forth over it. It was then winnowed by letting it drop from the roof of a lean-to and taken to the mill at Mishamokwa. Four oxen drew the wagon and father and Captain Jake Richtman, the latter a mere boy, drove the team. I have never been able to figure out the route they took but there were hardly any roads and only pole bridges across the creeks, while the Beef River must have been forded. The rest of the grain was later in the season threshed by a machine that made the rounds.

I can remember when we first got horses. One of the oxen broke a leg while hauling logs and father bought a fine team from Mr. Richtman. A year or so later all the oxen were sold and another team bought.

Then came the Civil War. I can, of course, not remember the first year but soon the word "drafted" assumed horrors. There were no exemptions but anyone could hire a substitute for $300.00 but many could not raise that amount and had to go, often leaving the farms and a family in not very prosperous circumstances. Many also volunteered, the notion that volunteers got better treatment than drafted men prevailing. On the wedding day of my sister, Nanetta, to Fred Beck, Sheriff Beeli drove in and a near panic ensued among the women (and I followed suit) for it was the duty of the sheriff to serve papers on those who had been drafted. Mr. Beeli had, however, driven in to say hello, offer congratulations and drink a couple of beers with his friends and thus the gloom was dispelled for the time being at least.

In the early spring of 1865 a volunteer company was formed and our oldest brother, Arnold, enlisted in Company K, 48th

Wisconsin Infantry. This made us short handed on the farm and father greatly reduced the wheat acreage, fearing that he could not secure harvest hands and thus in a year when wheat went to three dollars a bushel we did not have much of it. Arnold died of typhoid fever at Fort Scott, Kansas, August 19, 1865. All this I remember very vividly.

During the next year Louisa and I started school. School was held in a private house belonging to a village blacksmith and the teacher was a Polish refugee who had spent many years in Switzerland and was quite a scholar but not so much of a teacher yet we got a good start. I had learned to read German very well from mother and had read the school books she had brought from Switzerland which were very far ahead of those then in use here; in fact, on a plane with those used now. Next year the new schoolhouse, near Ochsner's, was built but not completed until the first of January, I think, because it was too close to the saloon, the workmen spending their time there instead of pushing the work to completion. On the first of January over a dozen of us, including four in our family, were baptized by the Rev. Mr. Struve (Lutheran) of Fountain City. There being no protestant churches, outside of the villages, the ceremony was performed at our home and in a very primitive manner, as was everything done in those pioneer days. Next day, off to the new school house two miles down the valley. We were a little late in arriving but instead of meeting an old Polish bear we were greeted by a friendly, smiling girl who helped us off with our wraps and after warming us up near the big box-stove showed us to our seats and started us in our work which was very pleasant indeed. We had not learned much English from our former teacher who always spoke German to us but it was not very long before I knew enough to say to the pretty school marm "I like you". This she told her landlady and she in turn told my mother who proudly announced it at home where I was teased until I cried, being quite a sissy that way. The friendly relations, however, continued and since the one at the head of the class was allowed to stand on the little platform on which the teacher's desk was placed and share his book with the teacher, I stoutly maintained that honorable position to the end of the term. When in spring Miss Peeso returned to her home at Mondovi, many of the girls cried and at least one little boy felt like joining in the chorus. She was married to Mr. Charles Harvey of Mondovi and I met her a few times later on and one time during a Grand Army reunion at Alma we had the honor of entertaining her at

5

our home, and I told her that I still liked her in the same old platonic way, of course.

Our next teacher was George Harper, a graduate of Oxford, who while sojourning in some British province in the tropics, had contracted yellow fever and although perhaps in the thirties when he arrived in Wamandee was an old, old man with silver locks but a kindly ruddy face. Poor Mr. Harper's life history would make an interesting volume in itself but I can here but briefly refer to him and his work as our teacher. With his family Mr. Harper was the first to occupy the teacherage which, according to a Swiss custom, had been provided in the second story of the schoolhouse, being the first and perhaps the only one of its kind in the county. Mr. Harper was a man of erudition and affability and his kindness to us knew no bounds but I am proud to say that we never took advantage of his absent-mindedness and other weaknesses, partly because we liked him so well and largely because the Swiss maxim "The will of the teacher is the supreme law", had been drilled into us by our parents, most of whom were of that nationality. Mr. Harper was a good teacher. He told us many enlightening and interesting stories, some of them perhaps above our heads and being an eminent scholar taught us much which was not in the curriculum. Mr. Harper later on taught in most of the schools in that part of the county but almost everywhere his pupils took advantages of his kindness and his failings but I think he never realized this, was always cheerful and happy. He was also, for over a quarter of a century, town clerk of the town of Waumandee.

Our next teacher was Anton Cajoeri, a graduate from the Contonal College at Chur, Switzerland. He was not a brilliant man, not even bright, but a tireless worker and good reasoner. His English was defective but he translated every lesson from English into German and vice versa, so that he became a good English scholar, all except orally for having no one to guide him through the intricacies of English pronunciation his spoken English was simply impossible and what is more his oral German was quite ungrammatical being by birth a Romaner whose language comes closer to Latin than any other living tongue. Thus it is not surprising that although most of us learned to write an article or letter in fairly good English, our pronunciation was bad and both the advantage first mentioned and the last mentioned disadvantage have remained in a measure with us to this day. However, we wrote correctly from the grammatical point of view, knowing neither slang nor such idiosyncrasies as slighting the "ing", double negatives, plural nouns with singular verbs, etc., and very few, if any, Germanisms. In fact, I did not know the slang meaning of "kid" until after I was of age. Mr. Cajoeri was a bachelor but kept house in the teacherage. He was strong in mathematics and having mastered the fundamentals before I went to school, it was easy for me to stand in on that score. He also taught vocal music technically and practically and while many of my schoolmates were good singers I fell down woefully in that branch.

Mr. Cajoeri taught four years, always attending summer school at the Whitewater Normal to perfect his English, when he was superceded by a German teacher named Haussner. He was a fairly good scholar but his personality was against him; in fact, he was a weak sister and too fond of his beer. He lost control of the school entirely and even the pupils, who had their own way with him, were glad when the year was up and he left. He had a family and also lived in the teacherage.

Paul Casparis, another of Mr. Cajoeri's Romanish countrymen, came next. He went about the work in the same manner as the former, being as deficient in oral English and German as Mr. Cajoeri but much quicker witted and outside of a few minor lapses a very good teacher, being a graduate of the same college. He liked his beer but was too tight fisted to buy much of it so that did not interfere with his work. He taught vocal music in the same manner as Mr. Cajoeri and also started a mixed choir outside of the school which was kept up long after he left. He was a very good teacher and after five years with him I became far more proficient in written English and German than most of the teachers of that day but while I was a good German speaker my pronunciation of English was still simply awful. I attended teachers' examinations and got a third grade certificate, standing high in English composition and perfect in German and Arithmetic. Mr. Casparis had a family and lived in the teacherage.

On the fourth day of June, 1875, our father died from blood poisoning, resulting from the removal of a wen on his forehead, the necessary precautions having been neglected. This left mother alone with most of us quite young but she encouraged me to go to the Platteville Normal for the winter. Our county superintendent, Mr. Kessinger, advised the same and good advice it was, for although I had well mastered all the work I took up there, under Mr. Casparis, there remained my wretched English to be brushed up and that very thoroughly, and what was more I needed contact with other young people in order to get rid of my provincialisms and to learn how to behave among strangers. I stayed all winter and although all the defects mentioned were not remedied, I got a good start which helped me a great deal in the self-education which I had to depend on from then on. The fact that John Ulrich, one of my Waumandee classmates, was a student there induced me to go to Platteville and he helped me a lot to partially overcome my morbid bashfulness, at times not in the most sympathetic manner, but it was most necessary and effective. I got to Platteville Saturday and waited until I caught him coming out of the schoolhouse Monday noon, being afraid to inquire for either him or Prof. McGregor, to whom Superintendent Kessinger had given me a personal letter of introduction. Such cowardice is really pathetic and no one can realize what a handicap it is. Of all this I was, in a measure, cured at Platteville and that without ever being subjected to any indignities by my fellow students who always treated me like a normal being instead of like the greenhorn that I was.

Before I continue with my personal story, I will mention my sisters and brothers and much as I would like to enlarge on this subject. I must need be brief since this is written in response to a request to write my personal biography and despite the omission of many essentials, that has become too long already, then again all that I have said of my schooldays in Waumandee applies to them also. My childhood companion and sister, Louisa Emma, was born April 9, 1858. As far back as I can remember she was my mentor, in a subtle way influencing my every action. She did not boss me around and yet made me do, say what and act about as she did or thought. She never took advantage of me but always played the roll of big sister and I would have been lost without her when first we went to school. It was indeed a case of "Everywhere that Mary went the lamb was sure to go." And always "the lamb" was satisfied and is to this day. As we grew up these relations faded away but always we remained the best of chums. About the time that I left home to go teaching she went away to work out in different neighboring towns and went with a family for whom she worked at Arcadia, to California. She was married to John Schmitz of Fountain City, a veteran of the Civil War. To them a daughter, Edna, now Mrs. Henry Haase, was born. She died when Edna was but a few years of age.

Edwin Ferdinand (subject of this sketch) was born June 13, 1859. Alwina Rosa was born April 7, 1861 She was one of those children who got along with everybody, at home and at school. She was a favorite with our teachers and schoolmates and never quarreled with the rest of us as we sometimes did amongst ourselves. She was married to Conrad Farner and with him moved onto a farm in Gilmanton. They had the following children: Otto, Ella, (Arthur and Lydia who died as children), Edna, Arthur 2nd, Walter and Wilma. She now lives with her daughter, Edna, at Seattle, Wash.

Jacob William Casper (who did not fancy so many names and now goes by the name of J. C. Ganz) was born November 11, 1862. He was always a husky lad and never afraid of anything or anybody (in the daytime). He spoke to everybody and made friends with all who came to our house and especially with the hired men and the harvest hands of whom there always were five or six. Thus he was always a favorite and preferred to me, who was shy and shrinking and prone to cry and whimper at the slightest offense. He was never teased and always stood his ground. Being so different, we had many a tiff but are now, I hope, the best of friends. He was married to Rosina Knecht, went to farming but has for years enjoyed the fruits of his labors living happy and contented with his good wife at Arcadia.

Lydia Selina was born April 10, 1867. She was a most loveable child and retained an affectionate disposition throughout her short life. She worked for others after mother left the farm and was very popular with her employers as well as with everybody who knew her. She died at La Crosse, having taken ill while working there. Arnoldina Elvira was born February 27, 1869. She was a little live wire and always contrived some baby trick that kept us in good cheer. She was very fond of music and often sang and played on some primitive instrument. She was also very fond of dramatizing incidents in her contact with her playmates and her pets. She was a favorite in school and on completing her work in the district school took up teaching and made a success of that work, keeping at it up to the time of her marriage to F. L. Mattausch. They resided on a farm in the town of Lincoln and in 1915 went to Rosalia, Wash., locating on a farm in the Palouse country but are now retired at Rosalia. Their children are, Edwin, Louisa, and Lenora, all born in the town of Lincoln.

John Adolf was born October 9, 1871. Being the baby and of a jovial disposition, we got a lot of amusement out of playing with him and sometimes teasing him. I went to teaching before he went to school and was not so much with him until he became my pupil and then when things did not go to suit him he found solace in telling his tales of woe to his sister-in-law who always lent a sympathetic ear. Those occasions were, however, neither numerous nor serious. He took up teaching which he practiced for a number of years but after his marriage to Christina Bruegger, he moved to the home farm, leaving the same when he was elected clerk of court, a position which he held for four years and was then elected register of deeds for the same length of time. His wife died after a lingering illness and his devotion to her and sacrifices for her, during that trying period, deserve approval from all and the undying thanks of his children who are Jay and Peter Roy. He has been for a number of years in the hardware business at Alma.

Now to return to my biography. On my return from Platteville I spent the summer on the farm and in the fall after waiting for someone to ask me to come and teach. I drove to Alma and my friend Superintendent Kessinger quite peremptorily placed me in charge of the Mill Creek School. There in the new schoolhouse, after waiting a week for the seats and desks to arrive, I started out with about sixty pupils, some mere beginners and a few a year older than I was. For about three or four years they had had Yankee teachers and yet nothing but Swiss was spoken and when an ultimatum was delivered that nothing but English should be spoken in school or on the play grounds, silence reigned supreme whenever the teacher hove in sight. Now but few of the children of those pupils know a word of either the German or the Swiss dialect. Things seem to go by extremes and contraries in this world of ours.

To go into details on the subject of my ten years of teaching in that district would fill volumes, suffice it to say that those of my pupils who were qualified acquired some of the knowledge which helped to fit them for the tasks which confronted them in after life. School was kept but six months in the year and until I rebelled, I had to teach every other Saturday but even the children began to resent Saturday school so that custom had to finally be abandoned. During the first few summers I worked at home but in the spring of 1881 your uncle Ulrich and I went to track's end of the Northern Pacific Railroad which was then on the boundary line of North Dakota and Montana just west of Sentinal Butte. We intended to locate somewhere in the "Golden Northwest," but after a couple of months' roughing it out there we returned and in August went to work in the harvest fields in the Red River Valley which was more congenial work for us. For three summer seasons I also drove the peddle wagon for the Bangor Woolen Mills and thus gained much experience and acquaintance with Buffalo County roads and people. I must not leave Mill Creek without mentioning the fact that I had a pupil who during all her school years was never absent or tardy, never whispered or broke any other rule and, of course, was head and shoulders above all the rest in achievement, never failing in a single recitation. Was there ever such another girl?

During the summer of 1886 I attended business college at La Crosse and finished all but the practice course in six weeks. I learned the rudiments of bookkeeping but my main object in attending was to improve my penmanship and to learn how to teach it, in which I succeeded very well for it is an established fact that you are best qualified to teach those things which are hardest for you to learn. About this time I concluded to change schools. Ten years was rather long to stay in one place and six months was rather a short term and last but not least a certain young lady whose opinion I valued above all others agreed that it was better that I should seek fields and pastures new to which she some time promised to follow me. Thus encouraged I applied for the principalship of the state graded school at Waumandee, my home district. To secure this position was very easy for I still had many friends there and it was inferred that a fellow who could stay for ten years in a Swiss community might fit in another of that kind. The term was nine months and I stayed at home, walking the same two miles back and forth that I had traveled every day as a boy. There were some big boys, in fact about eight or ten of them, who had years ago gained somewhat of a reputation, but my friend, George Schmidt, who preceded me, had taken the pep out of some of them and besides I made friends with most of them in the start by visiting and discussing congenial subjects in the morning before school, as I had to be there early to start the fires. The primary department was up stairs, the old teacherage having been fitted up for a school room. This department was taught by Mathilda Waelty but had always been kept up for six months only, both schools being thrown together for the spring months. This was a most unsatisfactory arrangement and I was not disappointed when, at the annual meeting, it was decided to return to the one-room system of a dozen years ago.

One of the reasons why I welcomed that move and undoubtedly the main one, was that I had my eye on that teacherage, for the two miles that were so short when I was a boy seemed quite long now when I knew that there were unoccupied dwelling rooms upstairs. Therefore, on her birthday, September 1, 1887, I was married to Kunigunde Wald, of Mill Creek, the ceremony being performed by Squire William Ulrich at his home, and witnessed by my sister Louise and my brother Casper and that was all there was to it. The custom at that time, especially in the community on the Beef River, was that a wedding meant a big spree as they called it, and a real spree it generally was. There were hundreds of guests, and abundance of food and drink and much dancing and merrymaking and subconsciously, if not really, everybody considered this spree the wedding and without it there was no wedding. Thus when we so radically departed from this custom it aroused not only consternation but indignation and by many was considered an outrage. In fact, one of my old friends stated publicly that I had simply stolen that girl. Well if I did, it was a mighty good theft and required no violence, both she and her mother being apparently willing, for if your grandmother liked me half as much as I did her, everything was lovely and as to your grandfather, who had been dead for almost three years, he was my best friend and I know he was always on my side. Therefore, it was not so much of a theft after all. Well, after a few days we moved into the teacherage and lived there for three years. The first winter was very cold; the snow was so deep that it covered up all the fences, and it was frozen hard as a rock, the temperature often being 40 or more degrees below zero and, of course, our habitation was not any too warm. Well, we lived here for three years and your mother made many friends, especially was this the case with "the little ones" who, of account of the overcrowded condition in the school, got long recesses especially in summer. These intermissions were taken advantage of, by them to sneak upstairs and visit with "Mrs. Teacher" and later on when there was a baby that of course, was the main attraction. Both Rosalie and Olga were born in this teacherage.

The details of my school work here, as in Mill Creek Valley, would fill a book but I will mention but a few outstanding incidents.

The people here, occupying one of the most fertile tracts in the state and being thrifty and frugal, some of them decidedly so, were quite prosperous and felt their oats. To this I was used from my schoolboy days when this was often forcibly impressed upon me. Now it was in command and by some, this was resented, although not openly, since the old adage that the teacher was "the boss" in school still was a tradition but not so religiously lived up to as during my school days. Then there was one incident which I could not ignore but must recognize which caused a little dissatisfaction or jealousy. There was a genius among the pupils and I knew it from the start. Rather than cheat that boy out of his opportunity, I would have thrown up my job. It never came to this pass, but the situation at times was perhaps more strained than I realized. This boy advanced by leaps and bounds and soon became the classmate of his schoolmates who were much older and had been several grades ahead of him at one time. This they naturally resented and I know not but what I was partially to blame for this myself since I exulted in the progress of my protege. Yet he soon proved that it was not owing to any favoritism on my part that he made advancement for he passed through the Alma High School, the State University, Rush Medical and Johns Hopkins with flying colors. While taking post graduate work at the last named institution, he was stricken with typhoid and died. Just think of it—died at Johns Hopkins of typhoid when but a decade or two later immunization from that scourge became general. Had he been spared, Dr. Henry Ochsner was destined to become a national figure among physicians and surgeons. In this assumption I am not alone, for at the time of his death the President of the University of Wisconsin said, "Henry Ochsner was the brightest man ever graduated from this institution." Thus I must not have been entirely wrong when I picked him for a genius and gave him a fair start. I could easily have had the school back but my friends, George Schmidt and Edward Waelty, tried to persuade me to buy the Buffalo County Journal which was said to be for sale. This proposition at first appeared preposterous to me but Edward soon convinced me that it did not require so much to put it across and I became reconciled; in fact, it soon became an obsession with me and when Mr. DeGroff after much hedging and scheming finally accepted the proposition which he himself had made me, not without raising the price a couple of hundred dollars, I felt very happy. The deal was made on the day that the Sea Wing disaster on Lake

Pepin took place but being convinced that the first of September was my lucky day, I waited about six weeks before taking charge, in the mean time doing some work in the office. The man who aided me financially and otherwise in this venture was my friend George Schmidt which kindness I will never forget. Others offered me money when they saw that I was making a go of it but then I did not need it. The office was located in a building owned by Hunner and Ginzkey as was the dwelling house that we occupied. In the second year, P. E. Ibach proposed to me that we buy the building on the S. W. corner of Main and Pine owned by G. M. Reinhardt. This done, we rebuilt it and fitted it up for store and printing office with office rooms upstairs. This roused the ire of Mr. Hunner who lost two good tenants and together with the booze element and others induced my foreman, Earl Farlin, to form a partnership with Frank Kempter. In the building vacated by Ibach they started "The Mirror." Mr. Farlin withdrew after about three months and Mr. Kempter discontinued the paper when the year was up. Mr. DeGroff, who was postmaster, hung around for several months and discouraged me where he could, even telling me that he could not see how I increased the circulation and kept getting more and more job printing, etc. This, of course in spite of the fact that I had no stand in with the saloons.

Shortly after we came to Alma, a son whom we named Armin Arnold was born to us. He was a bright, lovable child; and early displayed unusual affection for his parents often clinging to me when I left the house. When about a year old he got a piece of a nut shell into his windpipe. We took him to St. Paul where he was operated upon by Drs. Schimonek and Schwyzer but died one day before he was a year of age, his birthday being October 29, 1891.

Before we came to Alma, I was for years a delegate to Republican county conventions and now took a more active part in politics, becoming first secretary and then chairman of the county committee and attending state, congressional and senatorial conventions, also by personal effort and through the paper bringing the towns south of the Beef River into the Republican fold, they having previously been on the other side. This activity entitled me to consideration at the hands of the party and as my convictions were sincere I enjoyed the work. On the change of the administration, I was made postmaster but not without encountering opposition from parties who coveted the same position. Without attempting self-laudation, I think it is not out of place to mention a few things which I tried to accomplish. My aim was to serve the public and whenever the mail train was late we kept the office open after 8 p. m. When I took the office over some of its patrons were Jacob Braem and neighbors, at the head of Little Waumandee Valley, the Michaels, Volmers, etc., up Hutchinson Creek, for although there were offices at Tell and Cream they preferred to get their mail here since they never passed those places except on their way to Alma. The postoffices at Regli in Jahn's Valley and at Praag and Whelan in the upper Little Waumandee were established through my efforts and served these people until Free Delivery was introduced and in this I was also very active, having the sincere cooperation of my friend, Congressman J. J. Esch. The mail service by train which was very insufficient was after much pegging away made exceptionally efficient, almost every train handling mail. I called the attention of the department to the fact that the farming out of mail contracts to individuals by corporations who bid in hundreds of star routes was a menace and finally this was stopped. Rural carriers were first forbidden to deliver mail within corporate limits, but I from the start, had mail boxes served to every one outside of the plat. I also informed the department that small cities and villages often extended for miles beyond the platted area and that this ruling worked hardship and discriminated against residents of such sections. All these petitions were prefaced by the remark that those at headquarters could not be aware of these conditions unless their attention was called to them. How much credit I deserve for bringing about all these reforms I do not know but I know that I started something which brought results. I took office in 1897 and resigned in 1913 when Wilson became president although my term did not expire until 1915.

When Mr. Farlin, my foreman, left me, Andrew Lees, who had worked for Mr. DeGroff and myself, took his place and more than filled it. He consulted with me and offered advice freely and thus helped me a lot. Later Chris. Fuoter and Frank Stroebel, both of whom worked under Mr. Lees, took his place and were faithful employees.

Among other offices that I was elected to was that of school district treasurer, Mr. Hunner being city treasurer and when his bank was closed in 1898, after the mill was burned, I was caught with over $2300 in that institution and this set me back almost $2000, the dividends not amounting to much.

I went to the World's Fair in 1893, going on Saturday night and intending to stay a week but got so homesick that I came home Friday. In 1898 your mother and I went to visit her uncle and family at Carbondale, Colorado. We were there but one day when we received a telegram, telling us that your uncle, August, had been killed by falling onto the revolving cylinder of a threshing machine. We returned home at once but did not get here for the funeral.

Armin Edwin was born August 26, 1893 and Alma May on May 18, 1896. Our first house which we first rented and then bought we sold to Mr. Ibach and we then bought Mr. Schmidt's house where we lived until we moved onto the farm in 1913. The farm was bought in 1901 from Julius Wilk. When I resigned as postmaster, I also sold the Journal to Stroebel and Buehler, having almost trebled the number of subscribers since I bought it.

In 1901, when County Superintendent Eberwein began to agitate the establishment of a Teacher Training School here, I took a very active part and we carried the day. I also favored the introduction of the waterworks system and opposed the building of a new city hall. In those days the Journal took a decided stand on every public issue and there was no trimming and hedging. I was a member of the Training School Board from the establishment of the school to January 1, 1934. I also was for one term a member of the city council and for five years represented the second ward on the county board, being its chairman the last of those years.

In the early nineties, Judge Helms appointed me a court commissioner and that office I still hold. In that capacity I performed many marriage ceremonies but not one since I left town. When the war broke out in 1917 Gov. Phillip appointed me on the selective service board and that was the most arduous and trying task ever imposed on me. During the same time I was made chairman of the county council of defense. In 1918 Rosalie and Olga left for Camp Grant to serve in the Army Nurses Training Corps, serving until honorably discharged in 1919. In the fall of 1918 I was elected to the state legislature and served in the lower house for two years.

As stated, we have lived on the farm since 1913 and carried on general farming and breeding of pure bred live stock. In 1927 your mother and I undertook a trip to the coast. We stopped off at Bowman, North Dakota, going thence to Yellowstone Park and after touring that to Spokane, spending a week there and at Rosalie, visiting

16

relatives and friends. Thence doing the same at Seattle, Portland, San Francisco, San Jose and San Luis Obispo. With stops at Los Angeles and Salt Lake City we set out to visit mother's relatives in Colorado. The pleasure of this visit was clouded by the news of the accidental death of your mother's cousin Conrad which had reached us while at Rosalia. We visited with Edward Wald at Glenwood Springs and with Uncle Peter, Ursula and the boys at Carbondale. Uncle Peter was blind and died that fall. We also called on Carrie up on the Messa and on Leo. Leonhardy's but everywhere we missed Conrad.

In 1930 I was made a Master Farmer and your mother and I attended the recognition meeting at Milwaukee in 1931 as well as in 1933 and also 1934 when I was president of the association and she was made a regular member of the organization together with all Master Farmers' wives, yours truly making a motion to that effect. What the annual picnics of that association are you well know and I hope you may be able to attend many more of them.

The following, which appeared in The Wisconsin Agriculturist and Farmer, of August 22, 1931, gives some of the reasons why they selected me as one of their Master Farmers.

Edwin F. Ganz, Master Farmer.

Buena Vista herds of Aberdeen Angus cattle and Duroc Jersey swine make a convenient trade mark for a cozy farm home, standing on a towering hill above the Mississippi River, near the city of Alma, Buffalo County. The farm is operated by E. F. Ganz and his son, Armin. Mr. Ganz was born of Swiss parentage, at Waumandee, Wis., in 1859. After attending the public school there he entered the Teachers' College, at Platteville and then taught in the county for fourteen years. Then he bought the Buffalo County Journal, at Alma, and published it for 23 years, greatly increasing its circulation because it advocated the interests of agriculture.

Because his son Armin did not care to spend his life in town, Mr. Ganz bought the farm nearby consisting of 360 acres, of which about 130 acres are in plow land. He built a new house the necessary outbuildings and secured a herd of Aberdeen Angus cattle from W. L. Houser, of Mondovi. In 1913 Mr. Ganz sold the newspaper and moved onto the farm.

"Conservation of soil fertility and the building up of a worn out farm has been my chief aim," says Mr. Ganz. "I realize that I am only

17

the temporary custodian of these lands and that it is my duty to leave them in as good or better condition than they were when I took possession."

Manure is conserved and spread promptly. The soil has been tested without much sign of acidity and no lime has been needed to get alafalfa or clover established. There are about 20 acres of alfalfa and 12 acres of clover, 10 acres of corn for silage, 12 acres of corn for grain and about 25 acres of small grain such as spring wheat, oats and barley plus about 20 acres of succotash feed mixture. They work four horses and employ one man to help them. They use a 10-20 standard tractor. Usually the second crop of clover is plowed under but in 1930 it was cut for seed, yielding 40 bushels. These fields, however, have received an extra application of manure to make up for the harvesting of this seed crop.

All the cattle on the farm, except a couple of milk cows, are pure bred Aberdeen Angus. The present herd bull is an Enchantress Trojan Erica, bought from Fay Bros., of New Richmond. He is a double grandson of Earl Marshall on the dam's side. On the sire's side he is from Ensign of Page. This bull has been first at the Wisconsin State Fair and has stood high at the Minnesota State Expositon.

The Durocs on which the herd is founded were secured from some of the best neighboring breeders and in turn, from the Ganz herd many hogs have been sold for breeding purposes. They buy feed for supplementing the rations only, as silage and legumes together with home grown grains furnish the main rations.

"I am a crank on conservation, and care more for my land and upkeep than I do for my pocketbook," says Mr. Ganz. His records of receipts and expenditures are kept carefully and he does his business through the local bank. Farm buildings are modern and in good repair. Originally the farm was overrun with wild mustard but today there is hardly a plant of that variety on the place. Quack is kept down by cultivation and there are some thistles and quack to cut out.

The barn, built in 1914, is 36x96 feet, the stalls facing outward, of which there are 16, including pens for calves, young stock, etc.

There is no dairying done on the farm, concerning which Mr. Ganz says; "Perhaps we haven't so much steady income with our breeding and stock beef cattle as we would have with a herd of milkers but the labor bill is cut in half for us."

"Yes we probably could do well in dairy farming, if we chose, but as usual I would have to depend on my wife for leadership as she has always been an expert dairy maid since her youth on her farm." Mr. and Mrs. Ganz have a pleasant home with a warmth of hospitality awaiting strangers.

The three daughters of the family graduated from high school and the son is a graduate of the La Crosse County Agricultural School. Schools have been a hobby with Mr. Ganz all his life. He has been a member of the school board at Alma and since 1902 has been a member of the Country Rural Normal school board. As editor of The Journal he helped establish that school and for 23 years he constantly upheld educational betterment for the community. Mr. Ganz was chairman of the County board and for 16 years was postmaster, at Alma.

In 1919 Mr. Ganz served as a member of the state legislature and at that time introduced the bill which increased the number of county agricultural agents. He also introduced a resolution to limit the time of legislative sessions but it failed to pass. "I voted for the eighteenth and also for the nineteenth amendment, and am proud of it, adverse criticisms to the contrary notwithstanding." declares Mr. Ganz in his usual upstanding manner.

The Ganz Aberdeen Angus herd was the first accredited herd of that breed in the state and the first of any breed in Buffalo County."

When I was made a Master Farmer I received many complimentary press notices from different local papers and although all of them were appreciated no one pleased me as much as the one that appeared in the Spooner Advocate, written by its editor "Eddie" Bardill, one of my boys, who "grew up" in my office.

"Ten farmers of the state were honored as Master Farmers, by the Wisconsin Agriculturist and Farmer, at a banquet given by that publication at Hotel Pfister in Milwaukee, February ninth. Similar honors are accorded each year to a class of ten citizens of high standing in their respective communities. Among the ten thus honored this year, we were happy to find the name of Edwin F. Ganz, of Alma. This gentleman is undoubtedly a stranger to most of our readers, but to the writer he has been a personal friend and benefactor for years. It was under his guidance that we were first initiated into the mysteries of a printing office, quite a few years ago and we trust that the kindly discipline may have left lasting effects upon our subsequent efforts in our chosen field of work. E. F. Ganz was a successful publisher, a gifted writer and a man who possessed the sincere desire to lend a helping hand to such youths in the community in which he lived, who sought employment in his office. Deserting the editorial desk nearly twenty years ago so that he might devote himself to agriculture and thus satisfy his yearning for such pursuit, he built up a fine farmstead, known as Buena Vista, where he spends all of his time with the exception of that demanded by public office. Although engaging in farming when a man of mature years, his success has been such as to merit the proud honor bestowed upon him as Master Farmer and we take pleasure in extending our humble congratulations."

Since this is to be *for* you and not *of* you, I have refrained from saying anything of any of you except what refers to you as related to your mother and myself. I may have forgotten some things that should have been mentioned but not intentionally and as this is too long already much had to be and will have to be omitted. However, having given my father's biography, it is proper that I briefly refer to your other grandparents and that will close the sketch. First I will however state that your mother was born in the town of Alma, September 1, 1861, and Rosalie Agnes was born September 28, 1888, and Olga Louise December 22, 1889.

Your grandmother, nee Louise Kuederli, was one of a large family, owning a hotel in the City of Buelach, in the Canton of Zurich, Switzerland. Her life history in this country is closely interwoven with that of our father until his death. She then carried on with the farm which was deeply involved, more so than most of the members of our family realized or perhaps know now. Thus it was a hard struggle throughout and mother made many sacrifices to keep things going. She had received a very good elementary education and in that respect was far above her contemporaries. She had her dreams and one of them was to visit the scenes of her childhood and view some of the historic and scenic spots of her native country, so rich in both of these, all of which had been denied her during the time she lived there. I am glad that this opportunity was afforded her. Her brother, Jean, died without leaving any direct descendants and she inherited a sum of money which enabled her to realize this dream and she spent a happy summer there. On her return she lived with her children but not as a dependent, having sufficient means of support and besides making herself useful and especially so in entertaining and educating her grandchildren to whom she was very much devoted and who in turn all loved her dearly. Your mother was always very kind to her and I am glad that this kindness was appreciated for she in turn loved her dearly and was proud of her. To her step-children she was loyal as she had been most sincerely to their father. They had a considerable claim on the estate of our father which although fair and equitable had been long outlawed but in the restoration of which I insisted and in this I was strongly supported by our mother. For this and many other things that she did, I am proud of my mother. It was the right thing to do and I am glad that it was done.

Your grandfather, Ulrich Wald, who came to America with his parents, Conrad von Wald and his wife, nee Ursula Margreth, in 1852, was married to Agnes Ruedi, who with other members of her family came across in the same sailing vessel. On leaving his home at Parpan, Canton Graubuenden, your great-grandfather sold it to Mr. Bruegger, father of your aunt, Christina Ganz, hence she and your grandfather were born in the same house. Sauk City, Wisconsin, was in those days largely settled by Swiss emigrants and there this contingent arrived after a tedious voyage and journey. Here they expected to meet John Ruedi, brother of your grandmother but learning that he had gone to Grant County, they all followed him and took land in the town of Wyalusing, coming from there in 1855 to Buffalo County and locating in Mill Creek Valley on land which has ever since been the home of the Walds. Conrad von Wald was a remarkable man of powerful physique, honest and firm but of a very kindly disposition and withal a leader among the early pioneers. I did not have the privilege of his acquaintance but come to this conclusion from what others, among them your grandfather and the elder David Jost, a close friend and ardent admirer of him, told me about him. He was a plain man, very democratic and on coming to America dropped the handle to his name so that his descendants always have answered to the plain cognomen of Wald, while his distant relatives who had come here before him retained the title of nobility and their descendants go by the name of von Wald. He died prematurely from an attack of strangulated hernia. His wife lived to be over ninety years of age.

Your grandfather Wald was the most lovable man that I ever knew and I am proud to have had him for a friend. He was of an

21

extremely kind, hospitable and generous disposition and never bore anyone a grudge. Naturally there were those who would impose upon a man so disposed but he never resented it nor bore them ill will. He delighted in being of service to others especially in time of need or stress and while many in the community appreciated this, others came to look upon it in a matter of fact way. He was the community butcher, thresherman and veterinarian also pathmaster and sexton and for all these services the compensation was in most cases nominal but that never bothered him and he was always happy and contented for it is indeed more blessed to give than to receive. Although not a man who wore his religion on his coat sleeve and made loud and violent professions, I claim that he led the life of a true Christian. He was always cheerful and as he liked the world and everything in it he got more satisfaction out of life than those whose only aim is the acquisition of worldly goods. I cannot here refrain from relating an incident which corroborates what I have said. When your uncle Anton was yet a boy he once asked me whether I liked a certain fellow who was somewhat of a pest and when I replied in the negative he said. "I hate him, everybody hates him, except father and he hates nobody." That was the truth; he really hated no one, was absolutely unselfish and led a pure, simple and useful life.

During the summer before he died, he was kicked in the stomach by a horse which he was leading. This led to a hemorrhage which was aggravated when in the fall of that year while returning home from town he picked up a poor fellow mortal who had fallen by the wayside and helped him, to his shack. He was then confined to the house and later to the bed with repeated hemorrhages but made light of it until near to the end which came December 26, 1884. It is needless to say that a man so kindly disposed as he was towards others was more so in the home and his loss was most keenly felt there as well as in the entire community.

What shall I say of your Grandma Wald for what I could say would again make a book. The best thing I can think of is that I am thankful that all of you have had the privilege of knowing her personally and thus reaped the benefit of her companionship, her benign influence, her inborn kindness and her untiring efforts for the welfare of others and especially toward those near and dear to her. She endured untold hardships without ever being aware of it. She experienced deep and bitter sorrows but always seemed to find solace in, if possible, redoubling her kindly efforts in behalf of her dear ones who had been spared to her. She truly led the simple life and like her life companion she found her greatest delight in being of service to humanity and in her simple way she succeeded admirably. It was my privilege to pay tributes to the memory of both of your grandmothers at the time of their demise and since each of you has a copy I will come to a close.

Thus I will close this sketch and only hope that it will be received in the spirit in which it is tendered with malice toward none and charity to all. I have no excuses to make and no apologies to offer and as nothing has been said with unkindly intent. I trust it will be thus accepted.

Autobiography of Louisa Ganz

I

I was born on June 29, 1835 in Swarindingen on a small estate near an ideal village only 3/4 hour distant from the historical city of North Zurich, the twelfth child of my parents, Wm. Kuderli and Barbara nee Meister.

There with my parents I spent the first eight years of my life and with my many brothers and sisters attended the school. The teacher, an elder man, was the children's friend in the true sense of the word. The school was the model school of the Zurich district. There were six classes.

I shall always remember these school days and the teacher. He always tried to give pleasure to the children. When the weather was good, he would take the whole group of children to the near by Buchenwald, in the midst was a large meadow which we named the "School Meadow". All kinds of games were played there, and he schooled the older pupils in nature and her wonders, and so the children had happy outings as did the teach.

Naturally everyone brought alone some food, and after we were through eating, a lovely song was sung and we returned to school to be dismissed. On the last day of school he took the younger children and their parents on a trip, either to the neighboring hills or some other place of interest nearby. The older pupils made a day of it, leaving in the morning and riding a distance of several hours, returning in the evening. It was a big jubilee.

II

My parents sold our lovely home to a "Romanischer Schweutzer" who owned bakery in France. Because France was again

25

in a turmoil, he wanted it for a refuge and had a caretaker in charge. I do not know if he ever lived there himself.

My parents then bought a hotel in the lower part of the Canton of Zurich, one hour distant from the Rhine, and the family operated it. It was in Bülach, which was a district like our county seat. There I continued my education. After I was confirmed, I had to help in the hotel as most of the older children were married and the younger ones had to take their turn.

Early in 1853 my father died after a short illness. Henry, the youngest brother was only 12 years old. My mother, older sister, and two oldest brothers then took over the business in their name. They operated it until in the sixties when they sold it and the family parted, each going his way until they got married. Mother and sister stayed together till a year later when my sister married a widower with two children.

Mother then went to her youngest son in Hargen on the Zurich Sea where he was at the head of the school, highly esteemed. When upon request of his father-in-law, this son assumed the directorship of his silk factory in Wainlingen, Germany, mother did not want to go along. She wanted to die in Switzerland so she went to stay with her oldest daughter Verena in Schwaningen where she used to live. She had a good home there until she died.

III

In 1857 before my folks sold their hotel, there was in Bülach and the neighboring countryside a great movement of migration to North America. Two men from Bülac had come back to get their families after having spent one and a half years in Wisconsin, U.S.A., having bought or acquired land there.

Many from aroud Bülach wanted to go back to America with them, one of them being Daddler Ganz (harnessmaker) from Bülach. They told him at once that a widower with children should not attempt to go to America, because women were scarce, even a young single man would have a hard time to get a wife. Now, good advice was dear, at any rate he now wanted to get a wife before selling his business and home. Now he often came to our hotel which he had never done before, and so we became acquainted. He asked me in the presence of others if I would like to go to America too. I said, "Yes, certainly," but I knew beforehand that my folks would not permit it.

26

"How old are you then, if I may ask?" he said. I answered, "Not quite 22 years old." He said, "Well, then, you are of age and can make your own choice."

So it came to pass that by spring, I was his wife, even though he was again as old as I, and my folks were opposed to it until they saw I was firm in my decision which I never regretted, for he was a righteous and sensible man and always treated me with kindness and love though there were some difficulties, which was to be expected where there are two sets of children, but this situation had to be accepted.

My youngest brother who was very close to me, liked by my husband and a good friend of his two oldest children, helped win mother's approval for us. When my sister and her husband visited us in spring and met my husband they said they were not opposed to it since he seemed to be a sensible man and knew what he was undertaking and I'd be well taken care of and so it came to pass.

Then an auction was held – first the business, then the house and furnishings and the barn. We got a fair price for everything.

The in-laws of the first marriage managed to get one of their sons to go with us; though he didn't favor it, they won out. I was really against it but could do nothing. However, since so many of our friends went along it was not too bad.

IV

Now the time was set when we must leave our old home, the rest of the party left for Zurich on Sunday, but we, my husband, four children, and I left the next morning at 5:00 A.M. My oldest brother took us to Zurich in a coach. We stayed there several days, visiting relatives and tending to many other things.

On the tenth of April, 1857, we left Zurich with the first train, 4 hours to Baden, Argew, from there by coach to Basel where the head agents were. An agent went with us from there to Antwerp, Belgium, where he had to present his papers. We had gotten our pass in Zurich.

From Basel we went through the beautiful German countryside by train to North Nanheim where we stayed over night. The following day we had to take a passenger boat on the Rhine to Cologne. We saw the beautiful vineyards again. We had to spend a day in Cologne. We saw the city and the great unfinished cathedral, a beautiful memorial of the ages. Various centuries were represented in the building, also various types of architecture. It was completed only a few years ago in 1880.

From Cologne we went through the lowlands to Antwerp, Belgium, where we were delayed a week because the painting of the boat was not finished. It was one of the first steamboats taking immigrants to New York. It was the Leopold of the Belgian Line.

On the trip from Cologne to Antwerp, we could see the capitol city of Brussels with its many cupolas and towers very well. While we were in Antwerp we had time to look over our supplies and shop for more necessities – straw mattresses for the boat and tin dishes to get our food from the Provision Masters stock room. Fish and "speck", and barley soup cooked so thick a cat could nicely have slept on it, and naturally always burned – the pea soup was good and not cooked so thick; mornings we had coffee without milk – fortunately we had taken sugar along, and green tea. We could hardly force ourselves to drink the water. Potatoes were poor because it was late in spring.

Good fresh bread was taken aboard at Southampton. It was lovely bread, fresh from a bakery and still warm – a whole room full, but in a few days it was so moldy it could not be used. We had packed ham, bread, dried apples and other foods in one of our trunks which we wanted to keep near our sleeping quarters, but which was thrown into the hold and it took two weeks before my husband could get it by paying money and using persuasive methods. By then the bread and ham were somewhat moldy.

Next to our quarters was a large family – husband and wife, seven children a grandfather, maid, and hired man. They had a large chest of wine, and often a flask was sampled. We shared and exchanged food with them. They had a few gallons of sweet cream cooked with sugar which was even better than milk and they were very generous with it. Sometimes my husband could get better fare for a price, and so we could endure it.

One night we had a terrible storm. We were much concerned. Two masts were broken. My husband worked all night fastening chests for us and others. He threw a child in bed with its parents and calmed those crying for their relatives. Finally toward morning the storm abated, and also the terror.

On the 15th day of May we landed at Ellis Island, landing in New York.

A pilot with a small boat came to meet the steamer the day before. It was in the evening and we had to stay on our boat over night. Several small boats circled the steamer and hailed "Meier and Miller", the two men who came to our homeland to get their families. Whether in passing through or by letter, they had asked the keeper of the Frutli in New York to send some one to meet the Leopold at the landing. Meier and Miller had ordered beer, bread, sausage and cheese to be delivered on board ship. Then the landing really was celebrated, there being about 60 Swiss people in the group. Lovely evening songs were sung and there was music till ten o'clock, then all retired. The last night on board was a happy one. Everyone was given a good piece of bread and a good drink. Many had been seasick on the voyage, but in our family only Arnold, the eldest of the children, was sick for a few days but recovered quickly. Families with small children suffered more with it.

After the first night in this promised land, unloading of the passengers and their belongings began the next morning. We were met by a Swiss hotelkeeper at whose establishment accommodations were made for us by Meier and Miller. We had to stay in New York three days before we could pass inspection. Immigrants were not treated well in those days. We could only travel nights when no express trains were going and day times we had to spend in the station, so it was slow going: first Albany, N.Y., then Detroit, Mich., then Chicago, Ill. which was then an unsightly city with muddy streets. In the winter of 1856-57 which was a severe one, starting in November, there was one snowstorm after another, and the cold was severe, too. Deer would get stuck in the snow and were easily caught, being weak with hunger.

When we left our old home in April everything was green and in bloom. Spring flowers were blooming in the garden and in Baden everything was in bloom, but when we arrived in New York, May 7th, there was still snow on the side streets. Niagra Falls, where we spent a day, was still in ice and snow and we saw the great waterfalls.

In Ohio water covered many places and also in Indiana and as I said before in the city of Chicago one could hardly get through the mud. Then we came to the Mississippi where we had to wait again for a steamboat. At that time and for many years later, the boats were the mode of travel to the north. He waited at Dunliht opposite Lubane, and went by boat to LaCrosse which at that time was just starting to be a city with few large houses, sand piles, and streets that left much to be desired. From La Crosse to Bangor, where Meier's parents and a brother had their home, and where my sister Selina and her husband had come the year before, it was twenty miles.

Their trip to America was a very hard one, having three small children, two boys and a girl and three small children aged five, two and one-half and one year. I still remember when they left, for the children were so dear to me, having stayed with us the last week. They came in a sailboat, so it took six weeks before they arrived in New York. A plot among the sailors was discovered in time so the rebels were punished and put into chains.

My sister had much concentrated milk for the children but sad to say not enough for such a long time. The boat was plagued with storms and during the fourth week, within two days the two little ones died, and had to be disposed of in the ocean in the presence of their father. They were naturally not strong and could not endure the hardships of the trip. I was deeply moved when we received the news and could hardly get over it.

Many Zurchers from Overland and Graubunten had settled in the vicinity of Bangor and they met us and with horse and wagon took us that long distance with our chests and trunks to our folks where we arrived the next day. They had settled farther up in a valley and built a house, and so after six weeks we were again under a roof and could rest.

Besides Gustav who was now six years old, they had an eight month old daughter named Paulina, which made our girls very happy, and me, too.

V

We helped as much as we could, my husband and Arnold the oldest boy, help plow the virgin soil. Soon we had an opportunity to buy a pair of large, heavy oxen but not till the grass grew. It took several weeks before the cattle could eat enough to satisfy themselves. My folks had only one cow and later on we got to buy one, too. During this time my husband and brother-in-law, Conrad Meier, and our oldest son Arnold, looked for land for us but could find none that suited them. The best homestead land had been taken, and cultivated land with some buildings was too high priced. So they passed and in June they plowed land for my brother-in-law (Utzingers). Much of the land being treeless and in large tracts could be cultivated and prepared so he could plant wheat, corn and potatoes for family use next spring.

A Mr. Boshard advised us to go farther north where a colony of Zurichers and overlanders from his homeland had settled. His brother Jacob owned 160 acres of land there which he would like to sell because it was too much of a wilderness and moreover, he did not want to be a farmer.

So they started out having to go to LaCrosse to take a steamboat up the Mississippi River to Holmes Landing, now Fountain City. From there they had to walk 17 miles into the country where they were well-received by his countrymen. The next day they went to Jacob Bosshardt's land which was three miles from there. There was a small log cabin without a floor, made of rails laid crosswise, with a low door. It had been the first house in this area and had already served several families as a roof over their heads. A Henry Oertli from Jars Bulach bought this land from a Theodore Meili but saw at once that with the high rate of interest he could not hold it, so sold it to Jacob Bosshardt when he had the chance. My husband bought this land from Jacob Bosshardt who wanted to go back to Bangor and therefore sold at a lowered price. At LaCrosse my husband bought a wagon and other necessary supplies and after that we packed to leave.

Our brother-in-law, Utzinger, and his brother-in-law Meier and our eldest son Arnold then undertook the trip over hill and dale to Waumandee with two pair of oxen, the cow, and all our belongings. They had a cover over the wagon and provisions so they could camp, and sometimes stayed overnight at farms. Bosshardt took the rest of us and several chests to LaCrosse where we took a boat to Holmes Landing, and the next day we were on the way to our new home.

One of the Ochsners sent a yoke of oxen and wagon to get us, and so we came to Waumandee. John Ochsner promptly said to my husband, "You cannot keep your family in that hut which is on your land so I am offering you the new log house which I built on my land until you can build a house of your own, since I have no wife yet". We accepted gratefully.

Manz, John Ochsner and Henry Waelty all were brother-in-laws and lived close to each other. John Ochsner boarded with his sister, Mrs. Manz. So we, too, lived near by. Our house or the house was a log house with a living room and bedroom, an open porch in front, and in back a shed to store things. We lived there eleven months. Mrs. Manz who had a 16 month old child was a true advisor to me in everything.

One is still so "green" when newly arrived and she had already been in this country for five years, having come to Sauk Center with her parents. Her oldest brother, Henry Ochsner, had come over before and taken a homestead and finished a home for himself. He then went to the old homeland and in dear Zurich found a life companion. A younger brother still was teaching in Zurich.

VI.

Now our pioneer life really began. My husband and Arnold had a hard winter. The cow we had could be kept where we stayed but we had two yokes of heavy oxen for which we had to find shelter. Our land was 3 miles up the valley. Had threshed some there so there was plenty of hay and straw and they made a shanty for the oxen beside the haystack, or strawstack. Every morning they had to go up to feed the oxen, then with them went several miles farther to cut and haul wood for fence rails so the cultivated land could be fenced in spring. Had raised some potatoes which we kept in a pit.

Fortunately the winter was not as severe as the previous one but it was hard just the same. When spring came we had survived it all. On the 9th of April we had an addition to the family being blessed with a healthy little daughter. All went well, young and old rejoiced. She was one of the first babies in this settlement and all the men came to see this wonderful child. We stayed in John Ochsner's house eleven more weeks till our house on the farm, which a carpenter had been busily bulding, was far enough along so we had a roof over our heads for which we were thankful.

VII

Now the real pioneer life began. We managed to get a hen that hatched a flock of chicks and we raised vegetables in the garden which helped and we were satisfied. Finally in winter we bought a skinny pig. Flour was still very expensive and after we had our own wheat my husband threshed it with the oxen. He then took the wheat to a faraway mill which took several days. One day when he came back

32

from the mill he said he was glad to get his sacks back. After that two farmers would always go to the mill together, one driving out of the mill on one side, and the other on the other side.

In 1851 John Ochsner with great diligence built a large mill which still is in use (1910). The stream which powered the mill had enough flowage but in spring it often overflowed causing much damage. Once the mill burned down but everyone was always ready to help him restore it so it would be ready for use as soon as possible. He also had a farm, and in spite of all the trouble and losses, became a rich man.

Naturally, as time passed other mills were built and farmers did not have to come so far but this first mill is still a good one and is operated by his son though the father is still living.

VIII.

So time went on, we experienced good years and bad years. The Civil War began, and it was hard to get laborers for the harvest. Reapers and binders were not in use yet, only rakes, and $3.00 a day and good board had to be paid to hire them and everything was so expensive. After three long years they were still drafting and enlisting men, and our son Arnold decided to enlist rather than be drafted. The war could not last much longer he felt and he could come home again, but sad to say, it did not turn out that way. He had been in service scarcely four months when he contracted malaria and was confined to the hospital at Fort Scott. We sent him money but he never received it, nor was it returned to us. He was buried in unfamiliar soil. It was a hard blow to us, especially for my husband to whom he was a great help. The other son was not so dependable and left home before he was of age. We had to hire strangers as our children were too young and still going to school – so it was hard, and very hard for me, too.

My stepdaughters were both married – the eldest married twice. Fred Beck to a Berner, her first husband died after a short illness. Their first child died, and the fourth was not born when he died. Later she married Joel Doenier, a Graubuntner, to whom were born six children. After a long illness Joel died, leaving the family in good circumstances.

Paulina, the second stepdaughter, married a Zuricher from Stamheim, John Farner. They still live in Waumandee where they began farming. They established a prosperous home, and raised eleven children, two dying in infancy. (John, the first died when he was about sixteen and one baby died at birth.)

Alfred left home early, going out west where he married. After a short time his wife died and he returned to Wisconsin where he bought a farm on the Fountain City bluff. He married a Mrs. Keller, a widow with three children, and two unfortunate brothers and a sister who made their home with them, two dying in childhood. Through hard work and thrift, they now have a comfortable home and a good farm.

After the war, hard times continued. My husband was getting older and the children were still going to school, having to walk three miles in the morning, and three miles back in the evening. We were building a new barn. My husband had an operation. He had a growth on his forehead caused by the irritation of a military cap years ago, which was growing larger. This he could have prevented if he had been faithful in rubbing it with a finger during the waning moon, and I know full well this was the case – having neglected it several times it grew fast to about the size of half an egg. Later he said that it always embarrassed him when strange children stared at him, and that the doctor had always told him to have it cut off, saying there would be no danger. I myself believe that it would not have been fatal if he had rested.

One day he went to Alma with a load of wheat and came home with his head bandaged saying he had had his operation. Dr. Zeiler and McGee had urged him to have it done. I was worried about it because it was deep and bled profusely and he had the long ride home alone on the lumber wagon. He could have fainted on the way but he felt well and the next few days did much easy work and went to Buffalo City to get a load of lumber. The doctor told me afterward that he had ordered him to take it easy for a few days, but everything piled up. That evening he went to bed and slept well all night but when he wanted to get up in the morning he was dizzy and lay down again. Soon he became delirious and never came out of this state dying a few days later.

So I was left a widow with seven children, the oldest seventeen and the youngest not yet four years old. It had always been his wish that I could stay with our children till they could fend for themselves, as his children now were all self-sustaining.

But God did not forsake me. He gave me good help by means of the older children. Edwin, my oldest son was a great comfort and help to me, and like a father to his younger sisters and brothers, and he cared for them and for me, too.

Superintendent Kessinger had helped him to get in the Normal School at Platteville after he finished the public school. Later he taught eleven terms in the same school. Between terms he helped me on the farm and never neglected me.

There were poor crops, too. The cinch bugs caused much damage and we had no luck raising horses whereas others could raise and sell horses and free themselves of debts. We did better with the cattle.

My son Casper stayed at home after he was through school. Louisa learned to sew and often sewed for others. Alvina married Conrad Farner a brother of Paulina's husband. When he came to America he worked for us and later at other places. Then he went out west and was gone for twelve years. He had made up his mind to save enough money to buy a farm, and with industry and persistence he reached his goal, and returned to Waumandee. A year later he bought a farm in Gilmanton from the heirs of a man for whom he once worked. It was badly neglected after the death of the owner and he got it cheap but it took a lot of work to get it back in good condition again. Now they have a nice home and family of seven, most of whom are grown up, three having died.

Edwin took a course in business college at La Crosse and after that he taught four years in the home district in Waumandee. In the meantime I had rented my farm to a neighbor's son for five years.

When everything was sold, my son Casper took some horses he had bought at the auction out West and my youngest son Adolph, who was through school went along, for a time.

Lydia, the second youngest daughter stayed with me for a while. I had rented a small house with a garden and two acres of land and pasture for a cow from Miller Ochsner. It was near the schoolhouse where Edwin taught and lived with his young wife nee Kunegunde Wald. Lydia often worked for others, also in La Crosse where at the time an epidemic of typhoid (Note: the sentence was not finished; grandma evidently found it hard to write of Lydia's death from typhoid, of going to LaCrosse to care for her, then bring her home for burial.)

Edwin got a school for Arnoldina, the youngest daughter, as soon as she was through public school. She taught several years in three different districts till she was married to Frank Mattausch. They now live on a good farm and have three children aged 13, 11, and 9 years.

After teaching in Waumandee for four years Edwin bought the newspaper in Alma, the Buffalo County Journal. He published it with good success, and is still doing so. He was also appointed as postmaster of Alma and later bought a large farm on the bluff above Alma, which he still operates. Now he bought a large farm – rather a whole section of land – in North Dakota as an investment.

Louisa who (Note: again grandma could not go on with telling of the sad loss of this other daughter, my mother, and at this point the writing ended. Grandma died three years later at the home of her daughter Alvina in Gilmanton.)

This autobiography was translated from grandma's native tongue by her grand-daughter Edna Schmitz Haase, and typed by her great-granddaughter Joyce Louise Ganz.

FAMILY

Husband:	John Casper Ganz
Wife:	Louisa Kuderli Ganz
Step children:	Arnold Ganz (died in the Civil War)
	Nanetta Ganz Beck Doenier
	PaulinaGanz Farner Alfred Ganz
Their children:	Louisa Ganz Schmitz
	Edwin F. Ganz
	Alvina Ganz Farner
	Lydia Ganz
	Casper Ganz
	Arnoldina Ganz Mattausch
	John Adolph Ganz

Historical Articles on Pioneer Life in Buffalo County

Foreword

My first incentive for writing these articles, was a request from the State Historical Society, to write on a number of subjects and to these I have added a number of others that I thought might prove of interest to Buffalo County people. Briefly, I have attempted to depict some of the trials and struggles of the early pioneers together with their brighter experiences, the joy of achievement, the satisfaction of self help, the generous exchange of neighborly assistance and above all that independence and self respect won through Industry, thrift and economy, making of them upstanding men and women who having hoed their own row, were beholden to no one whose wants were always kept within their means. Often have I heard the remark "Those fellows had easy going for they got their land for the asking". Land before the homestead act of 1862, became effective, was fifty dollars for forty acres. Many a man worked and slaved the greater part of a year to earn that sum and many a one signed a note for one hundred dollars, bearing interest at ten per cent and then got sixty dollars from the loan shark, before he could go to work grubbing giant oaks on that easily acquired land. Therefore my second and chief incentive for writing these articles, is to arouse an interest in the present and coming generations in the work and lives of our ancestors and to awaken in them a realization of what they have done for us, as well as that feeling of gratitude which we owe those courageous and intrepid men and women and to remember the Command of, "Honor thy Father and thy Mother."

"A Son of the Middle Border."

Reminiscenses of Activities on the River in the Early Days, when Transportation by Water was the only Means of Communication with the outside World

This is not to be a history of early day navigation and activities on the upper Mississippi, for that work has been performed by historians much better qualified for this task than I am. In fact I can figure in that capacity as an onlooker only, having never been directly connected with any phase of steamboating or other river work.

As one of those who sixty-five or seventy years ago used to come to town hoping to see a "Niggerboat", I take more than a passing interest in these projects for improving navigation and controlling and regulating the vagaries of "Old Man River". These attempts at reviving navigation bring back memories of the days when the river meandered, at will, through the bottom lands and among the islands, nothing obstructing its course. In other words nothing had been done or attempted to improve navigation or to aid it, in spite of the fact that the river was our only means of transportation and communication with the outside world. There was no aid provided or given by the government until some years after the Civil War, when dams or jetties were being constructed with a view of confining the waters of the river to the main channel, the object being to make it self-scouring. This however did not work out as it was planned for the silt washed down by the tributaries, in time of high water, soon filled the channel and dredging had to be resorted to. In this somewhat makeshift way the channel was kept open most of the time. Insufficient as this may have been, without this work, navigation during the greater part of the summer, would have had to be abandoned. Before these improvements were made, the main channel of the river was on the west side of the island above the depot, generally known as Harry's Island. Away back when I was a small boy, I remember coming to town with my father in quest of harvest hands, when we saw at least half a dozen steamboats stranded on a sandbar which had formed across the channel west of this island. How they ever managed to get off, I do not know but I am sure there was no government aid tendered or rendered, before or after the fact simply because no provision had been made for it.

At this time when the first systematic attempt at permanently improving navigation, by means of dams and locks is being made, it may not be amiss for a mere landlubber to reminisce on conditions as he observed them, when he was a small farmer lad on whose mind those visions, experienced but once or twice a year, made a lasting impression.

There were, at that time, neither buoys nor lights to mark the channel and navigators were guided by landmarks only. Prominent among these, was Twelve Mile Bluff, at the foot of which is now located Alma's public cemetery. This promontory was so named because it was visible from the mouth of the Chippewa, the distance between the two points being twelve miles. When a settlement was made at the foot of the bluff, it was first named Twelve Mile Bluff, but soon the name was changed to Alma, both shorter and more euphonic.

As already stated, the boats being the only means of transportation and communication with the outside world, they not only brought in all the necessaries for the settlers but they also carried away all their surplus produce. This consisted mainly of wheat brought in by the farmers who had located in the Chippewa, Beef River and Waumandee Valleys and their tributaries and later on, on the bluffs dividing them. Wheat was brought to Alma and Fountain City a distance of thirty or forty miles over roads that were little more than trails and the wagons bearing these loads were drawn by oxen, in the majority of cases.

All the wheat grown in the Trempealeau valley was brought either to Winona, Fountain City or Trempealeau, prior to the building of the Green Bay Railroad. Before the Chippewa Valley road was built from Wabasha to Eau Claire, most of the wheat raised in the Beef River valley and far up the lower Chippewa valley came to Alma, while from the Big and Little Waumandee valleys part went to Alma and part to Fountain City all of it being loaded onto barges and boats at these distributing points during the season of navigation. The towns on the banks of the Mississippi had an advantage over larger inland towns like Eau Claire and much wheat was brought to Alma by farmers living beyond Mondovi, even. When the Valley Road reached Durand that town absorbed much of the trade of that region, the building of the Green Bay road absorbing much of the trade that formerly went to Fountain City; Arcadia, Independence and even Whitehall serving those who formerly had to drive thirty miles or more to market.

In the days before these railroads were built the river banks at both Alma and Fountain City were lined with large warehouses for storing the grain preparatory to its shipment. Almost all the merchants had auxiliary warehouses of this kind, this being a connecting link between them and the farmers and all wheat checks, or tickets as they were called, were cashed in the stores, the merchants paying a small premium to the wheat buyers for this privilege. Among those who operated warehouses and bought wheat at Alma, I remember: R. R. Kempter, C. A. Boehme, M. Polin, Henry Rabbas, Phillip Phillippi, Schaettle & Kempter, William Hoefling, Tritsch Bros., Balthasar Carish and Harry Bros. Fred Laue also had a large warehouse, which I think was generally operated by others. After the railroad was built and the Alma Milling Company began to operate, most of these gradually went out of business but Paul Huefner, of Fountain City, the R. E. Jones Co. of Wabasha and William Heise continued for some time after the burning of the mill, the bulk of the trade finally being carried on by Mr. Heise but the grain shipped was then mostly barley, the introduction of dairying having crowded out wheat. At Fountain City, I remember Bohri Bros., Schuster Bros., Fugina Bros., Huefner Bros., Henry Teckenburg, Carish Bros., a Mr. Schank and others.

Contact with these early day grain buyers is what brought me and other farm boys to town where one of the great sights that we enjoyed was the grand side wheelers and stern wheelers, "The Niggerboats", that carried downstream our wheat. I remember driving a team with a load of wheat following across the Sand Prairie, wallowing in six inches or more of sand or up the Lincoln Dugway, in the heat of summer, the teams straining in their harness all the time and the sun beating down on them unmercifully. Often we walked by the side of the load but the wheat had to be taken to town to meet bills incurred in harvesting and threshing it and the compensation was that

41

at the end of the trip I might see a "Niggerboat". This may not be river history and yet it is all incidental to that period and may re-awaken memories in the minds of my few surviving contemporaries and to those of the present generation may depict things as they were in those by-gone days.

The wheat was practically all shipped in sacks, carried from the warehouse to the boat on the backs of the deck-hands, mostly Negroes, former slaves of southern planters but now slaves of a brutal mate, who drove, kicked and cursed them unmercifully. This was neither an elevating nor an enjoyable sight but the landing and pulling out of the majestic craft was compensation to a boy whose mind was starved for new and unusual sights and experiences and then all the abuse of the mate was met with a shrug and derisive smile by his "slaves" who seemed to consider it all part of the day's work.

Not all deckhands, however, were Negroes. Occasionally there were those among them who had the warning, "Hands off" engraved on their countenance and the brutal mate wisely heeded it. Many of the pioneer farmers, especially those who opened farms in the timbered sections, were abjectly poor and took time off from their digging and grubbing to earn enough to carry them through the winter. While their women carried on at home, as best they could, these sturdy pioneers took berths, as deckhands on steamers. I can not but recount an experience related to me by one of that group many years ago, a man who was physically disabled by the ravages of rheumatism, brought on by hard work and exposure but whose mind and memory were as clear as a bell. I refer to the venerable John Wilk, late of Herold. John, Henry, Fred and William Wilk, John Korb and Joachim Erdman, six sturdy farmers, who pioneered on the Belvidere Bluff, were among the deckhand on a big steamer plowing up the river with barge loads of rails, for the continuation of the Milwaukee Road into Minnesota. The bright mind of John Wilk conceived the idea that here was the opportunity for those six farmers to make history. He therefore told his companions that those were the first rails to enter the State of Minnesota and they were to be the ones to carry the first one onto shore. This proved an easy job for none of the other hands had ambitions of that kind nor had the significance of the act occurred to them nor intrigued them. Thus it happened that the first rail taken off the boat was carried by those six "Low Dutch" Belvidere farmers, and thus a bit of local river history was made. Right here let me state that everything that I am about to relate will be strictly local in its nature.

The main activity, on this part of the river, however, was rafting. The vast tracts of pine along the Chippewa and its tributaries were being exploited by the lumber barons and the mills along the Mississippi were clamoring for their share of the logs, while those along the Chippewa were bound to hog all of them in order to create a monopoly of the lumber business. To facilitate the transportation of logs to the down river mills it became necessary to assemble them into rafts and Beef Slough, extending from the mouth of the Chippewa to the mouth of the Beef River, was an ideal location for the proposed rafting works. Therefore, in 1867, a company composed partly of local business men and partly of down river lumbermen, was organized at Alma and styled Beef Slough Manufacturing, Booming, Log-driving and Transportation Co. The lumbermen and mill owners on the Chippewa, at once began to fight this organization and crippled it to the extent that the first year only five or six million feet were rafted, while in its heyday that company rafted that many in a single day and one season's output was often from five hundred to six hundred million feet, employing all the way from five to six hundred men at the Beef Slough rafting works. The corporation soon expanded and all the stock holders were lumber and mill men, the local parties retiring from the company after it became fully organized and the name was changed to The Mississippi River Logging Company. Buildings for offices and for the accommodation of the workmen lined the banks of the slough and a beehive of activity prevailed on its waters. The local representative of the company was Thomas Irvine, an executive and business man of rare ability and withal a thorough gentleman, liked by both the employees and the citizens of the community. As a sideline he bought and bred purebred horses and cattle and at one time brought a fine herd of Holsteins from New York State, offering the produce to local farmers for improving their herds. This met with no response, perhaps because time was not yet ripe for this step and perhaps because they did not fancy white collar farmers but the assumption of this attitude was a great mistake. Personally and through the columns of this paper I advocated the acceptance of this offer but to no avail. Mr. Irvine then removed his herd to a farm near St. Paul. He also owned and bred some fine driving horses and a herd of splendid Jersey cattle.

Beef Slough Scene in the Logging Era

In the beginning rafts were floated down river without the aid of boats, being steered by the aid of huge oars at both the stern and bow and propelled by the current. Soon rafts were being pushed by steamers and later on they were steered by so-called bowboats. To those of us who had witnessed the back-breaking work of the oarsmen at the bows and sterns of the oldtime rafts, this evolution seemed worthwile indeed.

The operations of The Mississippi River Logging Co. were carried on at Beef Slough until about the middle nineties, when it became almost impossible, especially in time of low water, to get logs into the slough, the water at the mouth having become low on account of silt from the Chippewa being deposited there. A snug little village, with a postoffice and railroad depot, had been built up, at Camp No. 1, at the entrance to Iron Creek, all within the city limits of Alma and for some reason or other this was long overlooked by both the federal authorities and the railroad company and it was perhaps the only case on record where two postoffices and two railroad stations were maintained in one municipality of less than fifteen hundred population.

The postoffice and the depot were closed before the removal of the rafting works and with them the village for the removal of the works meant the doom of the village and it was a common sight to see building after building towed on barges to the new site at West Newton, about eight miles down river. The filling up of Beef Slough with silt as well as the fact that the new rafting works were eight miles nearer to the down river mills were both inducements to make this change.

"Ottumwa Belle" Tows Last Raft, 1915

To steer the logs, that were floated down the Chippewa, into West Newton Slough, a sheer boom was strung across the main channel of the river above Harry's island and a government dam, across the mouth of the slough, mysteriously disappeared during the night, an investigation of this matter revealing nothing and nothing being done about it. At Little Falls, up on the Chippewa where Holcombe is now located, The M. R. L. Co., maintained a dam behind which the logs accumulated. This dam was opened ever so often and a flood of saw logs would descend upon the Mississippi, so closely wedged in that a riverman could easily cross the stream by stepping from one to the other. This taxed the capacity of the sheer boom which guided them into West Newton Slough and often it could not be opened, thus when a steamboat happened along at such a time it was compelled to wait for hours but there was no complaint made, the company paying handsomely for the delay caused, in fact, they made more money while being delayed than they did in their regular course of progress. Rafting at West Newton was carried on until all the timber on the Chippewa was exhausted by the wasteful system employed by the lumber barons.

Just a line on what folks used to think of this long vanished timber supply. A few years after the terrific forest fire of 1871, we had a man working for us on the farm, who had been badly burned in that fire and in a conversation bearing on this wanton destruction of resources, I deplored the fact that our supply of pine was thus being despoiled and could not hold out much longer. In a rage, he raised the fork that he was using above his head and dashed it to the ground, shouting; "It beats h......l to hear some d.......d fools who think they know something, talk about the pine giving out. Why there is enough up there to last a million years." He honesty believed this and so did most of those who lived among the timber and yet it was less than a quarter of a century thereafter that the last raft was taken out of West Newton Slough and at the same time occurred the closing of the largest sawmill in the world, at Chippewa Falls, because the last tract of pine had been cut or destroyed by fire.

The activities on both the Beef Slough and West Newton rafting works were a great aid to both the business men and farmers and the boarding houses or camps of the company afforded a ready market for all kinds of truck. The large crews employed were good customers in the adjoining towns but as is always the case with so-called floaters, most of their earnings were spent for liquor yet taking it by and large, their behavior was always fairly orderly.

From what has been stated it is evident that the business men in the river towns had things pretty well their own way but that they could not serve their customers but had to put them off until the next day, may surprise my readers and yet that is just what often happened. When farmers had to drive a long distance, especially in winter, they would drive in groups of a dozen or more and when they came to town in the evening, after unloading their grain and stabling their animals, they would hasten to a store to make their purchases so that they might be able to start back home early next morning. When several of these groups happened to arrive at the same time, it became next to impossible for the merchants and their help to wait on them and often it happened that some one would beg to be waited upon before closing time but when it got to be about midnight, it was physically impossible to do this, considering that everyone in the store had been busy since early morning and the eager customer had to either wait until next morning or go home without his supplies. Thus you see that, at times, it actually became necessary to turn customers away.

To come back to the steamboats and packets, I can remember the names of but a few of the most popular ones, among them the Quincy, the Centennial, the War Eagle, Minnesota, Mary Morton, Pittsburgh, Sidney, Libbie Conger, Josephine and Josie. There were then two different lines operating on these boats. The Diamond Jo line and the Keokuck Northern Line. I do not remember to which particular line these boats belonged but think that most of them were Diamond Jo boats and their landing signal "Two long and two short", was familiar to everyone. Some of these boats were regular floating palaces, often being 250 feet long 35 feet wide, with over fifty staterooms and over 350 tons burden.

After the Milwaukee road had been built on the right bank of the river, it became desirable to establish connections locally with the Minnesota towns located on that road: namely between Winona and Fountain City and between Wabasha and Alma. Fountain City was served, first by a small boat named Express of Fountain City and then for many years by the Robert Harris, both being owned by Schneider & Heck. Service between Alma and Wabasha was first established by Captain Levi Deetz with the propeller Comet, which he sold to Captain Hiram Wilcox, who in 1873 replaced it by the steamer Lion, that boat remaining in the mail, passenger and freight service until the Burlington road was built. These local boats performed a much needed service in their day, for by giving us connections with the railroad both passenger and freight traffic was greatly expedited. This is about all the old time steamboat lore at my command but this sketch would be absolutely incomplete without a mention of my old friend and neighbor;

Captain Jacob Richtman

Jacob Richtman was born in Rhenish-Prussia and came to America, with his parents when a mere boy. They were pioneers of the Waumandee valley, settling in 1855, on the farm across the road

47

from the store just above where the creamery is now located. The place is now, I think, owned by the Henry Rosenow heirs. When quite young, he left home to work as deckhand on steamboats but during the Civil War, enlisted in Company L, Second Regiment of Wisconsin

Captain Jacob Richtman

Cavalry. Some time after returning from the war, he rented a farm, joining his father's and again became one of our neighbors. About that time I began to take notice of "Jake" Richtman and to look up to him with a small boy's admiration for he was different, in fact he was a remarkable man. I always felt, that like many others, he was naturally quick tempered but exercised such wonderful self control that he was always cool and composed and never allowed his emotions to get the best of him. Denied practically all educational advantages, he was possessed of a well developed intellect and always seemed to be able to do the right thing at the right time. I specifically remember this because at different times he helped with work on our farm when we were pinched and this was always performed in a workmanlike and masterly manner but being as modest as he was self-composed he never boasted of his superior ability or even mentioned it. He was different in another way. He was an absolute total abstainer, using no beverages but water and milk. That, in those days and in that community, would have brought scorn and criticism upon the head of anyone else, for of all the terms of contempts in common use, that of "Temperenzler" was about the last word but never did I hear Jake Richtman criticized for this inconsistency with public opinion and had there been criticism he would not have cared for he knew he was right. Calm and careful as he appeared, he was never afraid to venture and take a chance but that also was done in such an unostentatious manner as to cause no comment. Some of the things that I have said may appear to be personal and I might be accused of taking undue advantage of intimate knowledge of facts gained by close observation but those who knew Jacob Richtman, will also know that every act of his was open and above board and he did and said what he considered right regardless of what others might say or think. Thus I feel that in saying those things, in order to establish a proper background to what follows, I am not transgressing and need offer no apology.

After a few years spent in farming, as an expert thresherman and in small business ventures, he bought a store that his father had been nursing along, at Fountain City, for a number of years. He started in a small way for his capital was limited but by smashing war prices and devoting himself to his business with that calm determination of his, he soon secured more than his share of the trade and when he took into the firm a Mr. Henry, a retired Waumandee farmer with little capital, things were apparently coming his way. Then he had a vision. The speculative side of his nature asserted itself. Uncle Sam was letting contracts for building dams or jetties to improve navigation and he was bound to secure some of those contracts and do some of this work. He got the contracts, hired men, opened quarries, bought tools and implements and built barges. This meant going head over heels into debt and edged on, as I have been told, by envious parties, his creditors became alarmed and one day peremptorily called upon him, for an accounting. In his calm, calculating manner he is said to have told them that he was too busy to discuss that matter but asked them all to call on him at nine o'clock that evening. When they did that, he calmly and deliberately laid all his cards on the table before them. He told them – and I have it from a fairly reliable source – that if they forced his hand, there would be little or nothing left for either him or them, while if they allowed him to carry out his plans they would all be paid in full and he would be able to branch out. His frank statement reassured them and Mr. Richtman, as he had told them, made good on his contracts, paid his creditors in full and expanded his business. By this stroke of business Fountain City got the inside track on river improvements, others following in Captain Richtman's footsteps and making good but indisputably he was the pathfinder and trail breaker, the others benefiting by his leadership. This was the first step toward the many stone and brush contracts that followed, as well as toward the establishment of the boat yards, at that place.

Captain Richtman had now become river conscious and the store became but an adjunct to his business, in fact. I doubt whether to him it was ever more than a means to an end. He therefore formed a

49

new partnership, taking Albert Kirchner, one of his former Waumandee neighbors, in with him. Mr. Kirchner first took over the management of the store but soon familiarized himself with all phases of the business and in time became a real steamboat man and navigator with the title of captain. He was conservative and careful and the business management soon developed upon him, the senior partner giving all his time and energy to the executive department, his chief aim being to achieve and create.

The ambition of every riverman seems to be the ownership of a steamboat and soon after taking his first contracts, Captain Richtman became the owner of the steamer Penguin. As river contracts were of an ephemeral nature the boat had, at times, to be otherwise employed and a triweekly freight and passenger service between Alma and La Crosse was established. But the ambitious captain craved something more than ordinary, therefore he had a steamboat built, for this service, that was calculated to outstrip anything of its kind. It was modern in every way and all its appointments were the best that money could buy, including a steel hull and thereby hangs a tale. The boat was decidedly a deep water craft and during times of low water navigated with a serious handicap. With a tenacity, bordering on stubbornness, the captain stuck to his pet but finally had to give up and sell his craft, which he had named the City of Alma. She plied on the lower Mississippi, where like most steamers she met her fate in a watery grave. Thus ended one of Captain Richtman's fondest dreams. The Belle of Bellevue, a most serviceable craft took the place of the City of Alma and was for years navigated by the firm of Richtman & Kirchner. More and more Captain Richtman devoted his time to steamboating, leaving the contracting and construction work to his partner, who finally assumed full control of that line of the business as well as of the store. The purchase of the Steamer Libby Conger, if I remember it rightly, was Captain Richtman's last venture in these waters. Two of his sons were now full fledged masters of the packets, thus attaining the height of their father's ambition. With the Libby Conger the old veteran drifted down river establishing himself at Nauvoo, Ill. He continued in his chosen vocation on that part of the river and I think, on the lower Missouri until he joined the innumerable hosts of the Grand Army beyond. Being, at that time far from home the event was barely made note of locally and that is one reason why, at this time, I see fit to pay a humble tribute to one of

Buffalo County's most remarkable citizens, who fired by an untiring zeal and ambition did more than anyone else to make local river history. Repeatedly when I took passage on his boats, I was struck by his untiring energy and attention to details. At that time wood was being generally used as fuel on boats and Captain Richtman, early in the game, acquired timberland in the bottoms near what is now the site of Whitman Dam. Here he erected buildings for wood cutters and Camp Richtman was a busy, bustling place. As a deckhand he had evidently been impressed by the tyranny of the brutal mates and on his boats that practice was reversed. Whenever a landing was made he was the first one to take a hand in disembarking and loading freight, the same being true when the boat stopped at a wood yard. Always the captain was the first one out and the first one to grab a big armful of cord wood. Here was no driving or cursing but simply the setting of an example that no one could dodge. Others may have aided in making local history on the river, among them Captain John Harry and Captain F. J. Fugina but as pathfinders and trail makers the names of Captain Jacob Richtman and Captain Albert Kirchner stand out in bold relief.

A heroic attempt at reviving navigation on the upper Mississippi is at present being made and it is hoped that it may succeed as it has on the Ohio and on the Rhine where all heavy freight is conveyed by barge lines but the floating palaces, the packets, the Niggerboats of our boyhood days, will never return but with their historian the immortal Mark Twain, have passed on.

Amusements, Sports, Games, Recreation and Diversions of Children and Young People in Pioneer Days

Much has been said and written of the trials and hardships, the work and sacrifices, of pioneers and their families and yet not half has been told, for everything of that kind was, by them, considered part of the day's work. To a greater or lesser extent the children shared in all this and often do I hear the remark made that ours must have been a drab existence. Measured by present day standards, this may have been true but then it must be remembered that contentment and enjoyment are relative concepts, depending largely on circumstances and environments. No, the days of our childhood and youth were by no means drab and devoid of pleasures and satisfactions. True we did not have many of the things that today are considered necessities even in the way of toys, games and amusements but not knowing of them we did not miss them and necessity, although a harsh taskmaster is withal a stimulant to resourcefulness, and was then as now, the mother of invention.

Thus we provided our own means for enjoyment, assisted by our parents and older sisters and brothers who often provided the crude toys and taught us games and plays, some of them practiced by them in the old Fatherland across the broad Atlantic or in the East where some of them hailed from. Most of the outdoor games were played during intermissions in school or at home when neighboring children gathered on a Sunday afternoon. In summer there were the primitive ball games like two old cat and ante ante over, together with others but all with balls made by mother or sister of old yarn. Then there was prison base, pull away, hide and seek besides improvised games, invented by ourselves as well as many foreign games above alluded to. Then, of

53

course there was the swimming hole, sand slides and primitive clay modeling, mud pies etc. Indoor games were practically out of the question during the long summer days, when early to bed and early to rise, was not only practiced by the elders but also enforced as regards the youngsters, for there were, in those days no "kids" except four legged ones and I was a grown up boy before I ever heard children spoken of as "kids". This I mention but to illustrate the changes that time brings about and not in a spirit of criticism. We had swings made of a rope dangling from the branch of some tall oak and merry-go-rounds consisting of a plank that spun on a wooden pin inserted in a wooden post but those were luxuries and did not come until later on.

Winter sports were about the same as today but primitive in the extreme. Coasters were hand made affairs but answered the purpose and skates were few and far between. We enjoyed running and playing on the hard snowdrifts that formed along the rail and board fences, much to the chagrin of the traveling public the drivers of horse and ox teams. There was snow balling and games of fox and geese, also snow forts and battles, especially the Civil War, when playing soldier took our fancy and it was always arranged that those to the South (the rebels as we called them) lost out. It was also a treat when on our way to or from school we got a ride on the sleighs of farmers hauling grain to town or going after firewood, fence posts or fence rails, the latter being a necessary piece of work, for rails and posts were the only available material for the construction of fences and fences they had to have. In the evenings we played "mill", checkers and like games, the necessary figures often being drawn on a slate. We had a set of dominoes, that father whittled from shingles, the points being marked with a red hot wire but this was soon superceded by a set brought us by Santa Claus. We also had jumping jacks whittled from shingles, rocking horses made of inch boards and all kinds of home made wagons, both large and small, the wheels being disks, sawed from a log. At our home we always had a Christmas tree, the ornaments being apples, popcorn, candy, cookies and sometimes tinsel cut from any kind of colored paper. All this bounty in honor of his natal day, from the Christ-child directly, according to the custom generally prevailing in Switzerland, where the Christ-child (Christchindli) in person descends to this Earth on His natal day to reward all good children. Easter Rabbit would hide colored eggs for us in the most inaccessible places but they were always found even if the aid of our elders had, in an emergency, to be invoked and wonder of wonders, they always seemed to know where to look.

Soon after Easter came barefoot time. Oh, the glory of that event. To be allowed to doff our cowhide shoes and woolen stockings was indeed a relief. I say allowed because not many things were done without permission, in those days but the permission once given it became permanent for the spring and summer or until cold weather again confined our feet to "the prison cells of necessity – not of pride". With barefoot time came flowers and strawberries and later in the season rasp-berries, black-berries, goose-berries, wild plums and hazel nuts, in profusion and to pick and gather them was not considered work but great sport.

The creeks and brooks abounded with trout and as we grew older fishing became a favorite sport, the tackle being rather simple, while the catch was usually limited by the demand, the supply being ample whenever the conditions were right. Hunting small game was also a favorite diversion, for boys who had any kind of fowling piece and were that way inclined and most of them were. There were prairie chickens, partridges and quail in profusion, to say nothing of the wood pigeon, the bird of whom a book could be written. For days and days in the springtime cloud after cloud of these passengers would appear on the southern horizon to pass over us all day long without cessation, almost obscuring the sun as they passed. They often swooped down upon a freshly sown field of wheat, which lay exposed while the farmer went after his oxen and drag to harrow it in, and in less than a minute's time cleaned up every kernel of the grain. A roost of them would extend for miles and cover hundreds, aye thousands of acres, the branches and twigs bent and weighted down so as to form a veritable thatch. People would poke long poles up into this thatch and pick up the squabs, carrying them home in sacks or baskets. It is said that in some places vandals even hauled their hogs to those roosts and fed them on the young and eggs that they got down in this shameful manner. I am glad to say that nothing of this kind was ever practised in our neighborhood. Their was also an abundance of waterfowl and the migration of wild geese with the accompanying "honk" "honk", was almost as interesting as the passage of the pigeons. There were ducks in profusion and mudhens by the thousands but in those days only Indians would take the latter. Jack-rabbits, cotton tails and squirrels abounded in the woods also raccoons, foxes and timber wolves but the last named were very wary and boys seldom managed to bag one of them. Deer were banded in flocks and some boys managed to get one or more of these fleet footed animals frequently but as a rule they were hunted by those who were older, only.

Trapping was another sport indulged in by boys who could afford a trap. Muskrats, in profusion, inhabited the creeks, ponds and sloughs, also mink and martin. Musk-rats brought from five to ten cents a piece and a good mink from fifty to seventy-five cents. Thus, although it may have been good sport, trapping was not very remunerative.

Of course, there were pets and among them the wild animals and birds kept, not in captivity, but tamed so that they remained on the premises, where they were the chief source of pleasure and enjoyment, if not of pride. A few, who lived remote from neighbors in some secluded dale, captured young bears but they never became real tame and had to be kept chained. Fawns were the favorite pets and I remember a pair kept by a country store-keeper near our schoolhouse that enjoyed the freedom of the entire neighborhood and were never molested by the dogs of the community. For about two years they roamed about and came to the schoolhouse and to neighboring farm houses to pick up discarded scraps of food, preferably molasses bread and sweets of any kind. These pets were not uncommon in the early days and were generally protected by young and old. Then there were raccoons, badgers, and often foxes but all these, like the bears had to be kept chained. Squirrels and other small animals were also tamed but they were so common that they did not arouse much interest.

Among birds the crow was perhaps the most interesting pet that we had. This is a most intelligent bird, very clever and full of tricks and besides it learns to talk almost as easily as the parrot and its deep voice sound more agreeable than the raucous screech of the tropical bird. We had several of these pets and all were good talkers but extraordinarily mischievous and often destructive, so that they were not always in high favor with the elders and had they not been so clever and amusing might have been taboo. Prairie chickens and partridges were sometimes domesticated, as well as wild geese. Occasionally some boy would have a pet trout in some hole in the creek or in a spring near his house but those pets almost invariably became the victims of poachers.

Then there were the barnyard pets, colts, calves and lambs trained to follow you around and often perform tricks. The domestic fowls, including the doves were often trained to eat out of our hands and perch on our shoulders and heads. All this was sound diversion and the owner of the pets would proudly exhibit them to his playmates.

What did the girls do to amuse themselves? They took part in some of the things that boys did, like berrying and roving in the woods but as soon as they grew old enough they learned that, like their mothers, they were to consider certain occupations as play. They partook of the indoor games but often it was crocheting, stitching, working on samplers and even knitting that counted for recreation. They gathered long strings of friendship buttons, attempting to get a string of as many different ones from as many different persons as they could. They had few, if any parties, outside of the informal Sunday afternoon gatherings, already mentioned and until they were grown up did, as a rule, not attend any of the few dances that were given.

Girls, of course, had dolls but these too were mostly homemade, so was the doll furniture and dishes. Clam shells and acorn cups often serving in the latter capacity. Homemade kites, bows and arrows and willow whistles all figured as toys for both boys and girls. Colored pebble and sand and even sticks of the red dogwood fascinated us for there were few if any colored pictures to be seen and nature furnished about all the color schemes that delighted us. The gold and crimson sunsets, the gorgeous wild flowers, the green hillsides and the sparkling brooks furnished us the color schemes that no artist could duplicate.

There were spelling matches between the pupils of neighboring schools and in some communities there were singing schools, sometimes sponsored by the school or church or community. There may have even been husking bees and even red ears but in our community there were none, partly because there was very little corn grown in the early days and partly because New England customs did not prevail among the European emigrants. There were quilting bees and raising bees but in these only the older boys and girls joined the grownups. There was horseback riding but no buggy rides until later when the country was well settled and most of us were pretty well grown up. For many years the lumber wagon and the bob-sleigh were the only means of conveyance for both freight and passengers. A trip to town was an event never to be forgotten. There was a chance to see steamboats and white painted houses with green blinds and a hundred and one sights in the stores and shops all of them interesting and new.

Different customs prevailed in different communities but these, in short, were some of the things we did to amuse ourselves and I will not enumerate what we did not do and did not have time for that would take time and space infinite. Let the present day youngsters compare what we had with what they have, in the line of possessions and opportunities and they will know what we did not have but it would be useless to waste sympathy on us for we "The Sons and Daughters of the Middle Border", were really contented and can look back upon a happy childhood and who can tell but what some of these experiences, this going without some things, has not better fitted us to cope with many of the things which confronted us in after life.

The Part of Buffalo County Women in Pioneering

In the courtroom at Alma, hangs a picture. It contains the photographs of a couple of hundred men and ONE woman. Everyone of the photographs is the likeness of one of Buffalo County's pioneers. Why should there be hundreds of men and but one woman? Were there not more women here in the early days? Of course there were but it never occurred to anyone, connected with the making of the picture or to anyone depicted thereon that woman had a place on it. By this I do not mean to say that woman and her work was not appreciated by any of them but the idea that the man of the house was its representative prevailed so undisputed that the only consideration woman got was as the wife of Mr. so and so. I do not think that any of the pioneer women resented this attitude on part of the Lords of Creation but that they acquiesced in it as a matter of course. Was not that the way it was in the old country and did not Eve pluck the apple of which poor Adam ate without protest? There was one thing to which every woman was entitled and which was always conceded to her without dispute and that was the right and privilege to work. This was as it should have been or rather as it had to be for in those days it was absolutely necessary that everyone should work but I feel that everyone should also have had credit for what was done and therefore this article. Whenever I stand before that picture in the courthouse, my head is uncovered in honor of the men whose pictures I contemplate but even more so in honor of the women whose pictures are missing.

Far be it from me to criticize anyone for conditions prevailing and opinions predominating in those early days regarding the rights of woman and I will try as fairly as possible to present the part they took in building up this county. It can not be denied that in many instances, the burden heaped upon them was heavier than necessary but that was

59

to a large extent due to traditions and conditions prevailing in the homeland, where partly from dire necessity and partly due to the injunction that man was woman's superior, the lot of the so-called weaker sex became unusually hard.

Allow me to digress by illustrating this with a short story. In the early seventies, we had a man working for us who came from an Alpine valley in Switzerland, from one of those isolated districts where the people provided for practically all their own wants and needs, independent and almost cut off from the outside world. This young man came fully equipped with all necessary clothing and all of it was made, by hand, by his mother and sister. He had at least, three full linsey-woolsey suits and at least half a dozen all linen shirts, the size and length of night gowns, besides a full quota of long woolen socks and a sweater. I said that all this was made by his mother and sister and he told me that they provided for two of his brothers in like manner. Now briefly what did this mean? Those two women planted and cultivated the hemp or flax that went into the linen then they harvested it, soaked it, dried it, retted it, combed it and spun it, weaving it on hand looms into linen cloth or using it as a warp for the linsey-woolsey, the wool being woven into this warp on hand looms. To get this wool the women sheared the sheep, carded and washed the wool and then spun and wove it by hand. This cloth was then made into clothing, every stitch being sewed by hand. This was not an exceptional case but the regular routine in every family, in that and many other parts of Switzerland and that was only one branch of the work that women performed regularly and in most cases of necessity, but they were also required to do much outside work of a mental nature. I am quoting this instance because I have my information at first hand and because most of our neighbors were Swiss as were most of the very early settlers of the county. By this I do not mean to say that the lot of woman in other European countries was less hard, in fact, some stories that were told me by emigrants from Germany and Poland, where many of the tenants were actual serfs of the landlords or nobles, depicted conditions bordering on slavery, especially as concerns the treatment of women. Thus it will be easily seen that these pioneer women, most of them emigrants from Europe, were well prepared to take up the burdens awaiting them in their new homes. This you may remark is neither American nor Buffalo County history.

It is not really but it establishes a background to what I am about to relate.

All pioneers, in order to succeed, men, women and children alike had to work unusually hard and endure privations of a more or less serious nature but no more than their share of burden. Work in the fields and in the woods and necessary travel on the roads, such as they were, kept the men folks away from home the greater part of the time and many tasks that were not women's work, fell to their lot without any blame falling on the men folks. Outside of the multitudinous household duties, cooking, baking, sewing, spinning, knitting, washing, mending, churning and many others, these women virtually became hewers of wood and carriers of water. When I speak of sewing and knitting, let me remind you that there were no ready made clothes, suits shirts, overalls, socks or stockings underwear or anything whatever of the kind but all this was made at home and by hand and of course, all by the ladies of the house. By hand they sewed every garment worn by man, woman and child as were knitted by hand all socks, stockings, mittens, sweaters and comforters and all of it at home and by the women. Yes absolutely by hand, for sewing machines were too high priced and in the beginning were not quite satisfactory. Straw hats were also made at home and at that, some fancy ones from June grass, that were more flexible and pliable than the finest Panama.

There were a multitude of other jobs that fell to a woman's lot but I ask you to pause and ponder for a minute and figure out how and when they did the things that I have already enumerated. Yet that was not all for besides all this most pioneer farm women did a lot of work that is now rightfully considered man's work. Carrying the water from the spring or creek, often a long distance and always up-hill was almost always a woman's job. Milking, in many European countries, was entirely a woman's job and that custom was easily transplanted to our shores. Planting, hoeing and harvesting corn and potatoes was all in the day's work for women. Often they were only helping the men with this work but in the spring and summer when the latter were clearing and breaking land or in the fall when they were following a threshing machine this work had to be done and the performance of it fell to the lot of the women and children. Harvest time was the crucial period. First of all grain was cut by hand but with the coming of the reaper, that machine cut it but the binding was left to be done by hand. More land had been broken and hardly any crops but small grain were raised thus the problem of harvesting this grain became a serious one and there were few grown-up farm girls who did not stand up with the men and bind their station uncomplainingly. In many instances mothers, besides doing their housework, went and bound their stations, regardless of babies who were cared for by their sisters at home, often mere children themselves. Grain must be garnered or it would go to waste yet I could never figure why the father of those babies, present and future, should have to sit on the reaper, while their mother should have to stoop and toil in the burning sun. Such instances were rather the exception than the rule but I have personal knowledge of them and I farther know that these women were satisfied and contented with their lot, although I am glad to say that my mother was never required to do this.

I spoke of carrying water from the spring or creek but what did the women in the bluffs, who had neither spring nor creek to go to do? In summer they set barrels, tubs, pans, cans, basins, pails and other vessels under the eaves when it rained and in winter they melted snow on the cookstove and that again was no imposition for the busy husband who had to clear the fields from giant oaks by hand found no time for other work and in the winter he was busy cutting cordwood or hauling water up from the valley.

It was no uncommon sight to see a woman who was walking along a path or road, busy with her knitting. Among the Norwegian emigrants this was rather the rule than the exception, for they seemed forever to be knitting. One of the first possessions that they aimed to acquire was a few sheep. The wool from these was spun and knit, first for home use, the surplus to be sold or traded in neighboring stores and many of us wore "Norwegian socks", even after pioneer days were supposed to be past. Always remember that knitting was a form of recreation. If you do not believe it, try it for a change.

This seems like work enough but as most of it was necessary, it was all cheerfully performed. Besides this routine work one woman was active in one way and one in another. The girls must be taught to sew, spin and knit and mother looked after that when they were at home from school, in the evening. Often she also helped both the girls and the boys with their school work and in case there was no school she often shouldered the task of teaching altogether.

The tasks that I have so far mentioned, although arduous, were mostly dictated by dire necessity and therefore cheerfully performed but there were some tasks that imposed upon women that I would rather not mention but facts are facts and should be told. First let me mention conditions prevailing during the Civil War. A young farmer, who had just about gotten a start and was able to eke out an existence for himself and family was drafted into the army. He had to answer the call for there were no exemptions either for farmers nor for heads of families. He could pay three hundred dollars with which to hire a substitute, that being the only alternative but few, very few could, at that time raise three hundred dollars. The woman with her flock of little ones was left to shift for herself. She had her fields, her cattle, a few meager implements but no help, in fact owing to the war, it was almost impossible to get help even had there been money to pay for it and in most cases that was also lacking. Yet those women managed somehow. Study this picture and ponder on it for a while. There was no relief, federal or otherwise. It was simply help yourself and help themselves they did. It was from such stock and conditions that independent, capable and thrifty men and women sprang.

Sad to relate, then as now, there were women who were imposed upon and required to do and endure things that bordered on the inhuman but being out of the ordinary those instances do not go to make history and the less said about them the better. The typical pioneer can not be accused of any of these things for it was his aim to as much as possible make things easier for these plodding women and gradually he succeeded. Not all the hardships of pioneer life were, however, physical for oftentimes there was mental torture as well. Just think of those soldiers' wives and mothers who for weeks and months, waited for some word from the front and all the time living in fear and trembling that when word came it might be the saddest news ever told.

Then there were the women who remained at home while the husband was absent trying to earn a few dollars to keep the wolf from the door or when on his way to or from town he was detained by bad weather or bad roads, without being able to send word to her. Think of the woman who day after day shoveled a path to the road from her cabin, so that her husband, who was chopping cord wood on an island twelve miles from home could reach her on his return home, before the arrival of her first born. Then contemplate the plight of those women in Gilman Valley, whose husbands and sons had driven to Alma, after provisions and did not return home for a whole week, the trip having taken them just that long. What fears, what longings there must have been and what fortitude and what courage this must have required.

Therefore when I say, "Hats off to Buffalo County's pioneer women", I feel that I can do so without detracting from the deserts of their men for both the men and women deserve our unstinted gratitude but the latter should, at least, be placed on an equal footing with the former, therefore this article.

Activities of Swiss Immigrants and their Descendants. Their Influence in the Development of Buffalo County

In speaking of the development of Buffalo County, why should I single out any special group or nationality? Admitting that this development was brought about by the combined efforts of different groups and nationalities it is not necessary, at this time, to dwell on a subject which has been extensively treated elsewhere, notably so in Kessinger's History. Therefore I deem it right and proper that the nationality to which my parents, as well as an overwhelming number of the very first settlers of the county belonged, be given the credit and recognition due them. Owing to the fact that most of these pioneers came from the part of Switzerland where German is spoken they were roughly classed as members of that nationality. This classification was always practiced by the German papers published and circulated in the county although the publishers were mostly Swiss themselves. Much of this was perhaps done unconsciously and in fact there was no particular harm done and far be it from me to say that anyone is better for belonging to one nationality than to another but facts are facts and as such should be adhered to. It is no more proper to call a Swiss a German or vice versa than it is to call a Norwegian a Dane because he speaks the last named language. Therefore when I took over the publication of The Journal, almost half a century ago, I made it a point to call a spade a spade. Natives of Germany were spoken of as Germans, natives of Austria were spoken of as Austrians and natives of Switzerland were spoken of as Swiss and the same rule was adhered to as regards their descendants. Thus also, a postoffice established in a Bohemian community was named Praag and one in a Swiss community was named Tell, at my suggestion. Again allow me to state that this was not done because I felt that preference should be given to one nationality over another but on the contrary that each be give its fair deserts. This is offered not as an apology but as an explanation. The fact that I have chosen to write about the nationality to which my parents belonged, does not prevent others from going and doing likewise. The fact that in four different sections of the little Alpine republic known as Switzerland, four different languages are spoken, is a farther reason why its citizens should not be classed as belonging to any one of the nations represented by one or the other of these languages.

Not all our Swiss pioneers came directly from that country for extensive settlements of that nationality had been made at Highland, Ill., and in and near Sauk City, this state. From those places as well as from Galena and Nauvoo, Ill., came many of the early Swiss emigrants. Galena, although situated several miles from the banks of the Father of Waters, was at that time a kind of port of entry to the Upper Mississippi valley, the steamboats, even the large packets, being pushed by long poles up a stream, known as Fever River. Pushing these boats up river must certainly have kept the deckhands at fever heat.

Among the actual settlers, who permanently located in this county, before 1850, only two, John Adam Weber, who located at Holmes Landing and Madison Wright, who located in the town of Nelson, were not Swiss, according to Kessinger's History. This story might perhaps be made more interesting by mentioning names, in connection with the facts related but that might make it too long and omissions that might occur would be embarrassing. I will therefore mention, by name, but a few of the very earliest ones.

Andrew Baertsch and family came from Galena in 1847, their son Anton being the first child born to white parents in this county. Andrew Baertsch left a family of ten children, all growing up to be useful and respected members of society. He located first at Holmes Landing, then moved onto the farm now occupied by his grandson, Oscar Baertsch, in Eagle Valley.

Nicholas Liesch, his wife, son Anton and daughter Magdalena, came to Holmes Landing, from Galena, in 1848. Mr. Liesch, later on, became one of the founders of the City of Belvidere, on Pomme de Terre Slough. This venture was not a success, not a trace of the erstwhile city remaining outside of a few caved-in cellars. Mr. Liesch and his son both joined the army and served in the Civil War, the first named dying near Helena, Ark. The daughter became one of the foremost of the county's pioneer women and later, as Mrs. Martin Polin, removed with her family to San Luis Obispo, Cal., where she died a few years ago.

Christian Wenger came to Holmes Landing, from Highland, Ill., in 1848 and platted part of what is now Fountain City, in the following year and later on he also platted part of the City of Alma. He then located on a farm in the town of Alma, where he died over fifty years ago.

Victor Probst came to Twelve Mile Bluff in 1848 and entered a tract of land which he platted and which is now a part of the City of Alma. Here he lived in comparative retirement until his death.

Joseph Berni, a veteran of the Mexican War, came to Twelve Mile Bluff in 1849 but subsequently entered what is now the Klein farm, near Cochrane, selling it later on to Henry Klein and returning to Alma, where he died.

John C. Waecker came in 1849 and settled on what is now the Henry Brinkman farm, in the town of Belvidere, going later on to Ada, Minn., where he died.

Casper Wild, another veteran of the Mexican War, came in 1848 and located on the river bank, three miles below Fountain City, at what is to this day known as the stone house. He was the first settler in the town of Buffalo and died there years ago.

John Buehler came a few years later and went first into the wood business, furnishing employment to a large number of his countrymen who worked for him, as wood-choppers on the islands, getting out wood for passing steamboats. He built the first mill at Fountain City, was one of the leading, pioneer hotel keepers and held different official positions, serving as sheriff, at three different times.

Jacob Wald came up from Grant County at about the same time that Mr. Buehler came and located with his parents and their family, in what is now known as Mill Creek valley. His untiring efforts and the unlimited hospitality extended by the family are, in a large measure, responsible for the fact that the lower Beef River valley became a veritable Swiss colony, without any organized attempt at colonization. He chose the post of acting as a guide for all prospective Swiss settlers and his folks offered them food and shelter all this being done without accepting or expecting remuneration of any kind, outside of the expectation of securing congenial neighbors and rendering them a service.

Christian Bohri, who with his sons, Christian, Fred, Jacob and Gottlieb formed the vanguard of the Swiss settlers in what came to be known as Bohri's Valley, deserves mention as the Swiss pioneer of that region.

There are scores who, later on, performed yeoman's service of this kind in different localities but suffice it to mention a few of the very early ones not with the intention of slighting anyone but simply for the reasons, already stated. The homes of those mentioned, naturally became nuclei of the Swiss settlements that soon were formed in the county. In the south end, Bohri's Valley and Eagle Valley were largely settled by immigrants from that country. In Rose Valley in the town of Belvidere, and from there along the river to Alma, as well as in that village itself the Swiss predominated, while the town of Alma was a veritable Little Switzerland. The upper part of the Waumandee Valley, including that part which later on became part of the town of Montana, was also overwhelmingly Swiss. Other groups of Swiss settlers were scattered here and there but there were very few to be found in the northern part of the county in the early days although there is a fair sprinkling there now. Of those tabulated as early settlers, in Kessinger's History, 220 of the 705 enumerated, came from Switzerland, eighty-one coming before 1855; fifty-eight between 1855 and 1860; seventy-six between 1860 and 1865 and seven immediately after that period. Thus it can be seen that over thirty percent of the pioneers of the county came from that little republic, less than half the size of Wisconsin. Is it surprising then that people of that nationality should have wielded a powerful influence in shaping the destinies of this county? Of the three hundred and eight soldiers from this county, enlisted in the army during the Civil War, eighty were natives of Switzerland, or about one fourth of the whole number. They not only took a prominent part in the defense of their country's honor but they also led in advancing the civic and social affairs of the county. In each of these groups there were leaders, outstanding men who led, advised, helped and encouraged others but there were so many and perhaps some that I may not know of and I will therefore refrain from mentioning names.

Among the pioneer merchants, hotel keepers, millers, mechanics and professional men, the Swiss were well represented, both at Alma and Fountain City as well as in the rural towns. One firm, in Alma, was by one of the prominent New England pioneers in the northern part of the county, designated as the fathers of that section, for said he, "Without their aid in extending credit to the pioneers of that region, the latter could never have held out and developed that fertile region". The development and up-building of the prosperous Village of Cochrane is almost entirely the work of Swiss pioneers and their sons. To this day, in all of the cities, villages and towns of the county, men of that nationality occupy prominent places in the business and professional line as well as in the mechanical occupations. Among the physicians and surgeons of the county, both past and present, are numbered prominent members of that nationality as well as those of Swiss descent. Among those who have gone abroad and made names for themselves as doctors, lawyers and educators are many whose parents were Swiss pioneers or members of Swiss pioneer families.

Perforce the inhabitants of a rocky and hilly country like Switzerland, acquired habits of industry, frugality and thrift and as people of that nationality were pioneers in the introduction of the dairy industry, in this state, so were they leaders along that line in Buffalo County. When the fertile lands in the valleys and on the bluffs began to rebel, at the continued cropping of small grain, they were among the first to introduce and patronize the co-operative cheese factories and creameries, thus aiding in the prevention of soil robbery and redeeming the waning agricultural interests of the county, when almost at their ebb. True, others fell in line but almost in every instance the Swiss dairymen took the initiative and many of the leading dairy institutions were and are now headed by men of that nationality, men who descend from a country where milk, cheese and butter are truly and perforce the staff of life.

The common schools of Switzerland, were at that time already, among the very best extant and it follows that in the advancement of education, the immigrants from that country should take a leading part. Although the official language of their adopted country differed from their own, they were anxious that their children should become well versed in English, as well as in American manners and customs, not however forgetting the traditions they brought over with them from the oldest and most stable republic. Right here allow me to state that the most loyal and trustworthy citizens of our country are those who bear in their hearts a love and respect for all that is good and noble in the homeland. No foreigner who does not cherish these sentiments ever becomes a good citizen of his adopted country all contentions to the contrary notwithstanding. In many instances the first teachers in the Swiss communities, were graduates of Swiss colleges and the sons and daughters of Swiss pioneers took a leading part as teachers of the schools in this county.

Socially they were no less active and partially by themselves and partially in conjunction with their German neighbors, they organized singing, shooting, turning and literary societies, such as they had been members of in the old Fatherland. Such organizations were perfected at both Fountain City and Alma as well as in some of the farming districts. These organizations are fully described and dwelt upon in Kessinger's History. I will therefore speak of the activities only of such organizations that were purely Swiss or in which members of that nationality predominated. Foremost among these is The Buffalo County Saengerbund, composed of about half a dozen singing societies, of whom the Arion, of the Beef River, the Frohsinn, of Alma, the Columbia, of Montana and the Harmonie, of Waumandee were almost entirely composed of members of Swiss descent. The county singers' festivals, held by this organization, alas now extinct, were an annual event ever fondly remembered by those who participated in them, either as principals or as part of the audience. There were two or three other societies in the Bund, who are no less deserving than those mentioned but in this article I shall confine myself to the activities of the Swiss only and as already stated Mr. Kessinger has done justice to all these organizations as a whole.

The Arion, one of the earliest organizations, of this kind, although mainly devoted to the culture of vocal music, at one time had a considerable library of books by German and Swiss authors. The Frohsinn and Columbia directed their efforts to the cultivation of vocal music only and in a social way did much along those lines.

In the variety and extent of its social and community activities, although this may not be generally known, The Harmonie (not Harmonia, if you please) of Waumandee, took a leading and important part. Although originally organized as a singing society, it catered to non-musical members from the outset and early in its history a library was acquired. This contained full editions of the works of Schuller, Goethe, Heine, Zschocke and other leading German and Swiss authors

70

besides bound volumes of the leading current magazines published in the German language in this country and some published abroad. None of the members were well versed in English and forgetting, for once, the needs of the rising generation, no works in the official language of the country were provided. Although we did, at the time, not realize it this oversight, neglect, slight or whatever it may have been was a serious set-back to the educational advancement of the children of these pioneers. The attitude of the German-American press, actuated perhaps by the spirit of self-preservation, was very hostile toward the English language and American traditions and institutions and this undoubtedly had much to do with this act of omission or was it perhaps an act of commission? Although this society is still in existence no library, of any kind is maintained nor is the practice of vocal music continued, its activities being of a purely social nature.

What about other activities of this society? It was largely composed of wide-awake, progressive men, holding monthly meetings, alternately at the homes of its various members. At these meetings, primarily social, matters of common interest were freely discussed. The affairs of the community and the town were weighed and considered and often projects approved of there, were acquiesced in at the annual town meeting and it is not stretching the truth to say that the government of the town and the management of its affairs were often decided upon by that body. Matters pertaining to the advancement of education also often had their source there.

Horse thieves had been more or less active in the county and in that community and a society for the prevention of that crime had its origin due to the moral effect it had upon the perpetrators of that crime, some of the suspects having hideouts at a none too great a distance from the location of this organization. Purebred sires were bought, not by the society as an organization but by a combination of some of its members with other progressive farmers.

The most important and far reaching project that was however sponsored by this society, was the launching of a project to form a farmers' mutual fire insurance company and although few if any of its members, outside of myself may know it, The Fountain City Mutual Farmers' Fire Insurance Company was, if not officially but actually, born there. The problem of fire insurance had become a serious one and was very unsatisfactory in its operations. Premium notes, signed

71

by members of so-called mutual fire insurance companies, became both irksome and burdensome when they had to be paid and this together with other causes of dissatisfaction brought up this subject at the monthly meetings of the Harmonie society. The matter was then discussed with interested parties, at Fountain City their leading market town and a meeting, for the purpose of effecting an organization, was called at that place. It was effected and from a small beginning has grown to be the most powerful and beneficial organization in the county. Its first secretary who put the company on its feet and the present one, who ably follows in his footsteps, are by the way, both of Swiss extraction.

In 1890 the society built a hall, amidst a grove of white pines previously planted by its members but the monthly meetings, I understand, are still held in the homes of the members and although it has strayed far from its early traditions, I trust that the organization is still a factor in the promotion of the welfare of the community. I have devoted this space to this society, not because my father was one of its charter members and I, later on, one myself but because its activities have resulted in real good to the county at large.

Officially the Swiss have also done their part. In the cities, villages and towns they have done more than their share in administering the often unthankful job of home government. Many of them have served as mayor of their city, president of their village or chairman of their town board and in other official positions. In the county government, during the prevalence of the commissioner system, many of the nationality represented their districts as county commissioners and after the return to representation by local units, many of them have acted as chairman of the county board. The position of postmaster, in the county's larger offices, has repeatedly been filled by men of that nationality and at Alma, uninterrupted for almost half a century. The office of county clerk has been administered by the Swiss, for a longer period of time than by those of all other nationalities taken together and that without counting the services of Nic. Weinandy, who is Swiss only by adoption, or shall I say by adaptation. In the other county offices especially as sheriff, treasurer and register of deeds, persons of Swiss extraction have also served with distinction, in fact there is not a county office that has not at one time or another been filled by persons of Swiss extraction.

Likewise in both the upper and lower branch of the state legislature have men of that nationality served our county.

In the advancement of agriculture, business, industry, the profession, as well as in the social and official activities the people from that little Alpine republic have exerted a salutary influence on the development of Buffalo County and without any attempt at detracting from the deserts of others I present to you the facts gleaned above.

How Farming Began in this County And Its Development

The statement that a pointed, bent stick was the first agricultural implement is undoubtedly true but I am inclined to think that long before the idea of cultivating the soil was ever thought of, the Neanderthal man garnered his crops as they were offered to him by mother nature. Or, in other words that the practice of agriculture began at the receiving end, man garnering the fruits, berries, seeds, roots and leaves that went toward furnishing him sustenance without the least effort on his part toward their production.

This is going back rather far and yet the advancement made in agriculture during the last hundred years covers a period embodying as great changes as those wrought from the very beginning to a period only a century ago. It is true that in those parts of Europe, whence most of our pioneers came, intensive cultivation and liberal fertilization were the watch-word but outside of hauling, most of this work was hand work, the same being true of harvesting the crops.

The first proposition that confronted the pioneer was the selection of a site for his farm and home. The valleys, even the narrower ones, were practically bare of timber of any kind, even along the creek bottoms. Prairie fires, set regularly by the Indians, had brought about this condition. Timber was to be found only in shady gulches on northern slopes and on top of the bluffs, where snow lingered long in the spring, thus protecting the timber from these fires. The grass lands in the valleys although not always level, were designated as prairie land. Mother nature although lavish in the producing was nevertheless rather step-motherly in the distribution of her favors. Where there was plow-land for the asking, there was timber and where there was no timber the plow-land had to be fought for literally by the sweat of the brow. Transportation with ox teams

75

was slow and cumbersome, for there were no roads leading to this timberland. To get even a small load of logs onto the prairie farm – as I shall designate the broad fertile tracts in the valleys – was an arduous day's work for both man and beast. This is undoubtedly the reason why, in 1851, the wide-awake Daniel Schilling forsook the prairies to locate at the head of that valley back of the Henry Brinkman farm. For the same reason that hospitable pioneer Johannes Mueller (Engelhans) the ancestor of perhaps more former and present Buffalo County people than anyone else (are you one of them, dear reader?) made his home at the head of Rose Valley. For the same reason Joseph Rohrer, that pioneer of Buffalo county dairymen, a few years later made his home there also. Of course, the fact that in the "Engelhans" family there was a capable, young lady who fascinated him, may have been a special inducement. Be this as it may, in both instances he chose wisely. Here all these pioneers found bubbling springs of clear, pure water, timber close at hand, hay meadows, pastures and farm land so rich and fertile as in their old homes in Switzerland. They had never dreamt of. When the Wald family came to Mill Creek Valley they first squatted in "War Eagle's Hollow" (The present Andrew Mueller farm) being attracted by that bubbling spring and not deserting it for the broad acres, now owned by their descendants, until they found out that the tract which they had selected for a home, was owned by a clerk on the ill fated Steamer War Eagle, hence the name of the hollow. On their new location there were springs in profusion but they were across the creek and for years they had to lug all the water up the steep hills that bordered on the creek, for they had spring water in Switzerland and would drink nothing inferior to it in their new home and they drink it to-day. Thus pure water, that boon of mankind, was the greatest inducement to most early pioneers. Of course proximity to the river, that only source of communication with the outside world was an additional inducement.

The site for the home and farm being selected and acquired, the next step was the erection of buildings and the breaking of the sod for a crop. Some had ox teams and a very few had horses but others had neither and exchanged work with their neighbors who, in turn, plowed a few acres for them. Where the plowing was done early enough in the season, wheat was grown, only enough for home use in the start. Land plowed or broken, as we called the first plowing, too late for a crop of wheat, was planted to potatoes, corn, root crops and vegetables and the fertile soil produced most abundantly, furnishing feed for the oxen, a cow or two, a couple of pigs and the means of sustenance for the family over winter.

The hardest problem that faced the "prairie" farmer was getting material for the necessary buildings, all of which were made of logs, some hewn or squared with the broad-axe but most of them unhewn as they grew in the woods. The chinks between the logs were closed by blocks of wood wedged in between them, this being plastered or rather smeared over with a mixture of wet clay and chopped straw or marsh hay. Doors and windows were often very primitive and most roofs were covered by a kind of clap-board, made by splitting a straight grained, red oak block and hewing them into the desired shape. These were nailed onto poles that ran parallel from gable end to gable end. They shed water when wet or moist but the sun warped them so badly that often a shower was over before they were soaked sufficiently to shed water. Soon shingles were split from pine blocks and shaped with a draw shave and what shingles they were. They were the size and shape of the regular shingles used now and I know of an instance where they were still serviceable fifty years after they were put on. After the advent of saw mills both shingles and boards for floors, gables and doors became available but the log house still survived, on the farm. Barns were made in the same way only, if possible more crude, the roof often being a heap of straw, piled into the top. Some of those who came from northern Germany had real good and serviceable thatched roofs of rye straw, on their buildings. After the herd grew larger, cattle and sheep were often housed in sheds made of a frame work of poles, covered by a straw stack.

Farming implements and tools were both simple and few and far between. The most perfect and efficient implement in use was the plow. The breaking plows were practically the same as those in use today, while the hand plows were much the same as those now in use only they had wooden beams, like the breaking plows, instead of steel beams. The sod that was broken in the spring was either seeded to winter wheat the following fall or to spring grain the next spring. The seed was scattered by hand, a good man seeding twenty or more acres in a day. There was little cultivating done to cover the seed. A crude five shovel cultivator and a harrow, often one with wooden teeth, were about the only implements used but the virgin soil, free from weeds, produced abundantly both as to quantity and quality.

77

The harvesting implements were equally simple, the grain being cut with a cradle (a scythe with a long fingered rake attached to it.) With this the grain was laid in a neat even swath, the heads all pointing in the same direction. This was raked into sheaves and tied by hand with a band fashioned out of a handful of the grain. How many of you can make a band and tie a bundle? Cradling was an art, an expert cutting from three to four acres of grain a day, but two acres was considered a good stint. Then came the reaper, a clumsy affair, at first, requiring the service of a man to rake off the sheaves, then the self-rake, with an attachment for doing this work. With the coming of these machines the acreage was greatly increased but during the harvest season, the force on the farm had to be trebled or quadrupled and everyone, young and old was pressed into service for all the grain had to be tied by hand, as heretofore. This was grueling work, since the time for doing it was limited by the ripening of the grain. The coming of the self-binder in the seventies, was a boon indeed. The first machines used wire but they were soon superceded by the twine binder, in use today.

Haying implements were equally simple and crude, consisting of a scythe, a rake and a fork. Marsh hay was considered to be the only hay available and many a farmer went eight or ten miles after it, often carrying it by hand onto small stacks to be hauled home after the marsh froze over, when some of the straw which they burned, would have made better fodder or when they might have broken up an additional ten acres and seeded it to oats, yielding hay that was much superior to what they got. The introduction of timothy and later on, clover put an end to this drudgery for that could be cut with a mower and raked with a horse-rake and did not have to be hauled any considerable distance. The side-rake, hay-loader and the horse-operated hay fork are rather recent inventions.

Threshing was first done by trampling the grain out with cattle and winnowing it by dropping it and letting the wind blow the chaff away. The threshing machine was however one of the first labor-saving machines, introduced on the farm. The first machines were crude affairs fanning mills and straw stackers being soon added to them. They were all operated by horse power, in fact oxen often performed that service. Today we would sing, "And the ponies went round and round, Gedapp", but then it was "Hop, hop there" accompanied by cracks and cuts from a stout whip. Gruelling work indeed. There were, in the beginning, not many of these machines and often they were kept busy away into the winter, while some farmers were compelled to keep their grain in the stack until next spring. The introduction of community threshing rigs remedied this, to some extent and then came the steam threshers, first operated by portable engines and then by steam tractors, simplifying this arduous task for both man and beast.

What has been said so far refers mainly to the conditions that prevailed on the valley farms, where no clearing had to be done, in the early days but what about the timbered farms on the bluffs? There were huge oak trees to be felled but in this vicinity hardly an acre was ever plowed before the stumps were removed, hence those trees were never chopped down but literally dug out of the ground, before cultivation was attempted. Some of the wood was made into cordwood and sold to the steamboats but much of it was burnt on the spot. What a gigantic undertaking that must have been and when it is farther remembered that many a farmer cleared his first acres on a diet of sour milk and potatoes, the story becomes more remarkable even. After the first crop of corn etc. was raised a few hogs and chickens were added and there was a change in the diet. After this hard start the routine on these farms was about the same as in the valleys only that the task of clearing the land remained. The most serious proposition, however was always the question of the water supply. By this condition they were sorely handicapped until near the close of the last century when the problem was solved by the deep drilled well and the windmill.

After the plow, the wagon was the most important utensil but very often it was a crude affair. Many pioneers, among them "Engelhans" made their own wagons with wheels of disks cut from saw logs, the pole, axles and the rest of the gear being shaped with an axe. These vehicles served for the conveyance of both passengers and freight. Soon lumber wagons, made by local mechanics, came into general use but it was a long time before any farmers sported buggies and reference to the much ridiculed "top-buggy days" would not take us so many years back in Buffalo County history.

In connection with the wagon we naturally think of roads and it would not be amiss, in referring to conditions in the pioneer days, to use the slang phrase "There were no such animals". If plodding through knee-deep mud in the spring and fall, through sand and dust in the summer and through shoulder high snow in the winter means roads, well then we had them but that was all. In the valleys the roads were usually laid out so high up on the hillsides as not to interfere with any farming that the owner of the land might plan on in the future but year after year his ambition grew and soon there was land cleared above the road, where he had first not intended to break any ground. This created an intolerable condition not only as concerned the so-called road, for water falling onto the upper field would run along the road and over the lower field in ditches causing more damage than a road on the level land below, would ever have caused. The road had eventually to be moved to where it should have been originally laid out but usually not without the payment of damages to the owner of the land.

Fences were a serious problem, for they were a dire necessity. The only fence, in use, was the worm-fence, (A stretch of this fence is – I think – still in use along the road that leads from Cochrane to the Buffalo City cemetery.) A load of rails made but a few rods of fence and often they had to be hauled, with oxen, five or more miles. Later on, fences with rails nailed to posts came into use, also board fences. The coming of the barbed wire fence was a kind of two-edged sword. It cheapened and facilitated fencing but many poor beasts suffered from wire cuts before they got used to this novel restriction of their liberties. This and the woven wire fence however constituted a great boon to the farmers.

When those pioneers, many of whom came from rocky, hilly neighborhoods in the old homeland, beheld that rich, black loam in the valleys and that chocolate brown clay, underlying the humus and leaf mould, on the bluffs, they were awe-struck and told each other that this soil must be inexhaustible. Alas, only too soon were they to be disillusioned. For two or more decades it was wheat and more wheat with, of course, enough oats for feed and some barley, to supply the needs of the local breweries, besides a little corn for the hogs that supplied the pork for the family larder. This one sided method of farming was bound to deplete the soil but owing to the fact that their grain was often badly lodged most of the farmers complained and believed that their land was too "fat", meaning rich, forgetting that when it was first put to crops their grain was seldom, if ever, lodged. The fact that the soil had been robbed of certain elements or plant foods that took the stamina out of the straw, occurred to few if any of them, at the time.

You ask, why was this one-sided method of farming practiced? The answer is that there was little choice. They had cows but absolutely no market for dairy products of any kind. They had hogs and could have fed more of them but what could they do with the pork? The same was true of poultry and eggs. The local market absorbed what they had, at starvation prices and often that failed them. You may have perhaps heard me tell of the two little boys, later prominent citizens of the county, who carried a big basket of eggs from Waumandee to Holmes Landing and after trying hard to trade them off, finally succeeded in getting a couple of straw hats for them. The nearest railroad stations were Winona, Wabasha and Eau Claire and from none of these was live-stock shipped. Many from the central and northern part of the county, took dressed pork and sometimes salted butter to Eau Claire, whence it went to the lumber camps. The price obtained was a mere pittance but they could, at least, sell it. Often they took home with them, from Porterville or Shawtown rough lumber, the price of which corresponded with what they got for their produce but thereby hangs a tale. Such a trip could not be undertaken by anyone alone and they had to band together so they could take turns in breaking the drifted roads and often they had to shovel or drive oxen ahead to break a road for the horses, the former being much better fitted for this than the latter. Buffalo County farmers often sold dressed pork, at Winona, for two cents a pound, while many a farm woman and girl carried eggs or butter to the local markets trading it off for six or eight cents per.

Thus we raised wheat and more wheat until we finally harvested mostly straw. Of course, during the Civil War, when wheat still yielded fairly well, many who had help of their own and were longheaded enough, made a stake but others did not take advantage of this opportunity and then both taxes and things that we had to buy were abnormally high. The demand for meat, during that period, also absorbed most of the oxen on the farms, they being replaced by horses brought from Iowa, Illinois and the southern part of this state. With the advent of railroads in this and in Trempealeau County the marketing of livestock and dairy products became possible and as wheat farming was simply out of the question, we finally switched to diversified farming, although, owing to the low prices obtained, that

81

was not very profitable but something had to be done. About that time the much despised and bitterly criticized farmers' institutes came into vogue. Leaders like Dean Henry and W. D. Hoard, ably assisted by others, went about the state advocating diversified farming and the restoration and conservation of the fertility of the soil.

This movement was bitterly opposed, on the one hand, by near sighted grain buyers and implement dealers and on the other, by chronic knockers, who oppose all real progress and advancement with much noise and meaningless phrases, such as, "Them fellers can't learn me nothing". With patience and perseverance the leaders won out and dairying and live-stock farming were gradually introduced. Co-operative cheese factories and creameries were organized, clover and alfalfa were becoming more and more general, hillsides were converted into pastures and hayfields and erosion, where it had not already progressed too far, was checked. Purebred livestock, especially sires, was introduced, commodious barns were built and wheat growing was practically abandoned, hardly enough being grown to feed the ever increasing flocks of poultry.

Another factor that has done much toward the advancement of agriculture, is the work done by our County Agricultural Agents. Being continuously on the job and making contracts with individuals and individual problems, their work is even more useful and effective than was that of the institute conductor and in the proportion that his work is more important, is it being obstructed and belittled by the same element that objected to and fought the institutes. When I was a member of the legislature, there was a law allotting these agents to a certain number of counties and the quota was filled. I introduced a bill enlarging the quota and an agent was allotted our county and also to a number of others, who applied. I mention this not in a spirit of self-laudation but simply to inform those of my erudite fellow farmers, who criticised me for this, that I would do it again and again, should opportunity offer, for I know that it was a step in the right direction and every day our present county agent, as well as his predecessors, bear me out, for never has the county had more untiring and earnest workers in its employ than the county agents.

Systematically, conservatively, cautiously and steadily agriculture forged to the front until Buffalo County became one of the leading dairy sections of the state. Prices at first very low, grew better and real prosperity, if not affluence was noticeable on every hand, our farm buildings and equipment being second to none and our livestock ranking among the best.

Then we were plunged into that cursed war, accompanied and followed by that deceptive inflation and the boom. We all lost our heads, some more, some less, buying and spending beyond our means, not realizing that such conditions could not endure. This is not offered in a spirit of criticism for only a few of the ultraconservatives resisted the temptation and farmers were not the only ones to be caught in the whirl. It is not my province to locate the blame for let the one who is blameless cast the first stone. More, much more could be said on this subject but this article has grown too long already and taking it by and large this county is far better off than most sections, but without referring to the economic situation, allow me before closing, to utter a few words of well meant advice and with them a warning. I love the land from which we draw our sustenance, our very life-blood and as one who has grown old in the service of agriculture, pardon me for assuming this attitude. Long before I became an actual tiller of the soil I advocated, by word of mouth and pen, every movement that tended to the real advancement of agriculture and the betterment of conditions on the farm and that means the betterment of everyone no matter what be his or her vocation.

We farmers have been entrusted with a "Talent" which we are, in duty bound to not only conserve but, if possible to nurse, increase and multiply. True, we own a deed to our landed possessions but they too will ultimately dwindle to a space spanning but little more than six by three feet square. Let us therefore strive to so manage this trust – for in reality we are only tenants and our tenure is short – that we may pass it over to our followers, the coming generations, if not in better shape, at least in as good shape as it was when we took over. This is a sacred duty and it should be the first aim of every tiller of the soil. Much mischief has been done but much of it can be remedied. We may not grow rich by so doing but it should add to our peace of mind, for taking bread out of the mouths of unborn babes is a most unpardonable act. Let us therefore refrain from denuding our hillsides of growing timber, let us not crop the soil so as to deplete it but let us return to it all and more than we take from it. Let us cultivate crops that do not drain the fertility of the soil. Let us look to some of the countries in the Orient, where such practices have wrought dire disaster and then let us turn to some of the European countries, where conservation, practiced for centuries, has helped to retain the fertility of the soil aye to improve it. Let us so take care of this "Talent", intrusted to us that when the day of reckoning comes we may deserve, that highest of all praises, "Faithful servant, well done". I hope this may be received in the spirit in which it is tendered, "With malice toward none, with charity to all".

Being so earnestly interested in the conservation of the soil, I can not close this article, without adding, as a postscript, to it the introductory remarks used by an authoress, who some time ago treated the subject of soil conservation, in one of the leading women's magazines.

"The Land – mother of all of us, of every living thing. The first wealth and the last! For from it comes every essential of human life and almost every longed-for inessential. No miser ever covets gold with this deep primitive hunger of a man for a stretch of earth he can call his own and can treasure and enrich and finally give to his children when he dies. And now that certainty, that feeling of permanence, is giving way to a frightful conviction that it is not so. Land this most lasting of all things, is blowing away with the winds, is running away with the streams. How can a man, even with frantically willing hands, hold it back? And the answer is that no one man can, but that all men – and all women too – must work together in this greatest disaster our country has ever known. No farm is just a far-away farm to you now – it's the loaf of bread on your table. Maybe next year – or the next – that loaf of bread won't be there, unless you help".

How the Buffaloes Came Back to Buffalo County

Six miles south of Alma, Wisconsin, on State Trunk Highway No. 35, just as you reach the Pioneer Farm, now occupied by Nic Weinandy and family, but originally settled by those typical pioneers, Mr. and Mrs. J. P. Stein, a valley branches off to the left, and those

Albert Huber, in the days of his buffalo venture.

who follow the road leading to it will be surprised that just below Cochrane the valley again opens into the Mississippi valley, and the side road again joins Highway No. 35, which it left about three miles farther north at the Pioneer Farm. This valley, by its original Swiss settlers, was named Rose Valley (Rosenthal). Between Rose Valley and the main valley of the Mississippi there is a bluff that equals in height the other bluffs that face the Father of Waters in this vicinity. Over half a century ago Casper Huber, one of the founders of Buffalo City, settled on this bluff and opened a farm. Here he lived in 1888 with his wife and a large family of grown-up children, happy and contented in a comfortable home, for the Hubers were thrifty people. Some of the older children had already struck out for themselves, one

85

of them Gustav, living on a farm in the Red River Valley, near Warren, Minnesota.

To this place in the summer of 1888, two of the sons, Albert and Charles, went in quest of work in the harvest fields and to visit their brother. Here they heard something that interested them and they acted accordingly. In the wilderness on the Red Lake, some distance to the east, were two Buffalo calves offered for sale. This appealed to the boys. They were hardy, practical fellows, but who knows whether, subconsciously perhaps, they were not actuated by something sentimental, something romantic? Was not Buffalo County their birthplace? Was not their father one of the founders of Buffalo City? Why then should not they become the founders of a buffalo herd and thus aid in the perpetuation of this almost extinct monarch of the plains? I admit that perhaps they never stopped to ask themselves this question, but I like to speculate that it had something to do with their final decision to undertake this venture, and a venture it truly was.

Albert Huber Feeding The Buffaloes.

The buffalo calves were owned by Mrs. Ole Cathre, widow of an erstwhile cowboy. Ole, while employed on a ranch among or close to the Rockies, together with other venturesome cow punchers, conceived the idea of capturing some buffalo calves and by crossing them with native cattle, to produce a hardy breed of ranch cattle. They went to work and Ole's share of the booty was six calves. With these he started for his claim on Red Lake. When he reached home but two of the orphaned infants had survived the enforced separation from their mothers. They appeared to thrive in partial captivity, but poor Ole's fate was doomed, for shortly after his arrival, he succumbed to the dread disease, tuberculosis. This left his poor widow with a 'white elephant,' in the shape of two buffalo calves, on her hands.

The Hubers found the calves in a strong corral built of pine or tamarack logs, and it did not take them long to make a deal with Mrs. Cathre satisfactory to both parties of the transaction. During the winter the calves were kept at Gustav's farm and treated kindly, but attempts to tame them were only partially successful, for the call of the wild was still strong in their blood.

Charles Huber, part owner of Buffalo Herd.

The next question was how to get the calves to Buffalo County but the boys were equal to the occasion. A heavy wagon was so rebuilt that between the front and rear wheels there was a separate stall or pen for each of the buffaloes. This was covered with canvas. Boxes on both the front and rear of the wagon contained the necessary outfit and equipment for the trip.

Thus started the march for Buffalo County. At the towns en route, stops were made and the animals exhibited, a small admission fee being charged. In this manner the animals walked all the way in their stalls and tent. Finally the home farm was reached with the nucleus of a buffalo herd that was soon to be started there, for there was one of each sex. The animals were turned loose with the cattle on the farm and seemed to take kindly to their new environment, the long walk and constant contact with man having partially reconciled them to their lot.

Charles Huber went into the livestock business, buying cattle for shipment at Cochrane and then at Alma; thus caring for the buffaloes became Albert's job. Their aim was to raise not only purebred buffaloes, but crossbred cattle. Success, at first was slow. The first two years they had one cross bred calf to show for their trouble, although about a dozen cows had been bred to the buffalo bull.

87

About half of these died before calving, while the calves of the others did not live to grow up. Something was fundamentally wrong and correspondence with "Buffalo Jones," of Kansas, who was also raising buffaloes and cataloes (cross breds) did not shed much light on the subject, although some good hints were given. Albert had to work out the problem alone. He had bred some purebred and highgrade cows to the buffalo bull, some of them Galloways with black curly coats, but the experiment was a failure. He then tried scrub cows and success crowned his efforts. After starting along these lines the boys had very little trouble and, following the advice from "Buffalo Jones," they succeeded also in raising purebred buffaloes from the cow they had brought from Minnesota.

Another encouraging feature was the fact that their crossbred cows were not real hybrids or "mules," but would have calves when bred to a purebred buffalo. Thus, after many disappointments, they had a good start, their herd in 1897 numbering eight buffaloes, eleven three-quarter breds, and six half-blood cows.

The two original buffaloes were what is known as mountain buffaloes, being smaller and darker in color than the regular prairie buffaloes, their humps also being more pronounced.

In 1895 a trade was made with the Lincoln Park Commission of Chicago, whereby in exchange for one of their cows the Hubers secured a bull which they named Lincoln, and which from that time on, headed their herd. He was of the prairie buffalo type.

Things began to happen now. Huber's farm became to be known as "The Buffalo Farm." Visitors from far and near thronged the place, but Albert received them all very courteously and was ever ready to show them his pets. This was before the days of the automobile and the number of visitors was but a small fraction of what it would be today.

The herd increased apace, so that at one time it numbered thirty-eight animals, while in all fifty-one were born on the farm. The job of caring for the animals was, however, a most strenuous one and only a man with patience, perseverance, good judgment, and love for the work could have stayed on it and succeeded as Albert did. Before leaving for Wiener, Arkansas, where he had planned to make a home for himself and family, and where now successfully conducts a rice plantation, Mr. Huber disposed of the herd with the exception of one that went to his brother Charles and two that he took with him. Of the latter, one died and the other was sold.

The following disposal was made of the herd from time to time:

Frank Ostremba, Royalton, Minn., 2.

J. W. Knapp, Rockford, Ill., 2.

Burgess & Hanson, Luana, Iowa, 7.

Pawnee Bill, Austin, Minn., 1.

Frank Bostock, London, England, 1.

J. W. Washburn, Passaic, N. J., 3.

The twenty head that were for sale at the time the herd was dispersed, went to Pawnee Bill, Pawnee, Oklahoma. Five had been slaughtered; eight had died or been accidentally killed, two of them from rattlesnake bites.

This in brief, is the story of how buffaloes returned to Buffalo County; only, after a stay of about a quarter of a century, to be again returned to the prairie country, but not to rove over the broad expanse without restriction for all their trouble and work the Hubers may have reaped at least a reasonable compensation, and that they may prosper in their new home, where Albert and his family live. His brother Charles, who so ably assisted him in the enterprise, died at Cochrane, Wis., a number of years ago.

A BUFFALO STAMPEDE IN BUFFALO COUNTY
(from the Buffalo County Journal, August 26th, 1897.)

Only those having crossed the great plains twenty-five years or more ago, know what this means. The people of Buffalo County and especially those of the Town of Belvidere, would scarcely believe that such a dangerous stampede had occurred in their very neighborhood and no doubt, had it been known, that such a thrilling event was about to transpire, numerous spectators would have been on hand to witness the scene – of course from a safe distance.

The buffalo herd, owned by Charles and Albert Huber, recently broke out of the large pasture, in which they are kept, at a place where an old, decayed tree had fallen over the fence and started down the bluff into

Lincoln, Head of Herd

Rose Valley. It being a warm, pleasant day, Mr. Suhr and his family were enjoying the shade of a large tree in front of their house, when suddenly their attention was attracted by a low, rumbling noise, sounding like distant thunder, which as it came nearer, seemed to fairly shake the earth. Our friends gazed toward the west in a dazed manner, expecting to hear the blast of Gabriel's trumpet, as the noise seemed to increase, coming nearer and nearer. To their surprise they saw Mr. Suhr's five horses coming down into the valley at a mad pace while, at their heels, enveloped in a dense cloud of dust, followed a dark and compact looking mass of shaggy animals bellowing and snorting in a manner, to put fear into the most daring and courageous adventurer.

Mr. Suhr, with rare presence of mind, accomplished what even an old buffalo hunter might have shrunk from undertaking. He hurried to the barnyard toward which the stampede was rushing pell mell. (they were now close enough that the onrushing mass could be distinguished as a buffalo herd). Frantically waving his hat, he shouted at the top of his voice but the horses rushed through the gate almost trampling upon their master, in their rush for a haven of safety, while the gate closed upon their heels with a dull thud. The buffaloes, with the monster bulls, Tom and Lincoln, in the lead, instead of crashing the gate as might have been expected, came to a sudden halt, the whole herd staring at Mr. Suhr, who pale as a ghost stood before them. For a few seconds they tried to solve the riddle of this apparition, then shaking their shaggy heads, in disgust, they turned about and walked away starting to graze as quietly as if they had not been responsible for any undue excitement.

About this time the manager and part owner of the herd, Albert Huber, who with his family had spent the afternoon away from home, returned and noticing an unusual peace and quiet about the place, began to investigate and found that his charges had escaped, evidently in quest of scenes and pastures new. He followed their trail into Rose Valley and found them contentedly grazing, with Mr. Suhr and his three sons guarding them as unconcerned as if they were herding a flock of sheep. Turning out his native cattle, pastured close by in the valley and driving them among the buffaloes, he succeeded in getting the whole herd home, the would-be fugitives marching complacently in the rear, keeping time to the tinkling of old Bossy's bell. Thus ended the stampede of Buffalo County's buffalo herd. The herd, above alluded to consists of twenty-five head, among them four full blood bulls.

Few men would have the patience or would care to spend the time required in an attempt to domesticate and tame "the monarchs of the great plains", that Mr. Huber has shown in this enterprise. He has succeeded in an undertaking in which many have failed and that is the successful crossing of the buffalo with our domestic cattle. The cross, thus obtained, is a very hardy animal that can withstand the rigors of the most severe winters without shelter. Their fur is very much like that of the full blood buffalo, and their meat is superior in quality to that of the best range beef. The whole herd is fully domesticated and in a few years, is bound to increase very rapidly.

(From the Buffalo County Journal, May 24, 1900)

Hon. S. D. Hubbard was down from Mondovi Sunday and in company with Charley Huber, drove down to the Buffalo farm to see America's largest wild animal in captivity or rather in a domesticated state. Mr. Hubbard came in the interest of the State Agricultural Society and his object was to induce the boys to exhibit a carload of their buffaloes and cataloes, at the coming fair to be held at Milwaukee next fall. The boys now have about forty of the animals, comprising full-bloods, half-bloods, three quarter-bloods and seven eights.

Agricultural Development

From the log-cabin to the modernly equipped farm house, from the straw-shed to the up-to-date barn, from the scythe and cradle to the mower and selfbinder, from the flail to the steam thresher, from the ox-cart to the automobile, the tractor and the auto-truck, and from the message carried by the barefoot boy to the one transmitted from farmhouse to farmhouse by rural telephone, is a far cry, and yet all these changes have taken place within Buffalo County during the past sixty years and most of them during the last half century, or since the Civil war. It is true that although these changes came on gradually, the contrast to one who has lived through all of them is nevertheless so great as to seem almost marvelous, while those of the younger generation seem to take all these things which they enjoy, in a matter-of-fact way and seldom if ever stop to think how they were brought about and what were the strifes and struggles, the privations and hardships endured by their ancestors to bring about the conditions that exist today.

That they may be brought to more clearly realize all these things and better appreciate the many comforts and conveniences which they enjoy, the present generation may profitably spend a few minutes in reading about what their ancestors did, and therefore it seems not out of place in a work of this kind to devote some little space to conditions as the early settlers found them on coming here and the first attempts at developing the agricultural resources of this section. That they were necessarily crude and progressed slowly is due to many adverse circumstances, among them the scarcity of money and everything else necessary in carrying on the work.

The topography of Buffalo County, of course, had much to do in determining its adaptability to agriculture and although the broken nature of its surface, in some ways, detracted from the advantages offered along that line there were other compensating features which tended to bring to a realization the expectations of those who had faith in the agricultural possibilities of this region. The many streams which drain the surface, cut up the county into valleys which are separated by high hills, locally designated as bluffs, hence the tillable land is found in these valleys and on the ridges of these bluffs where they are not too narrow and rocky. Although there is some slight difference in climatic conditions between the valleys and uplands the products are practically the same.

Before the date of settlement "prairie fires," as they were commonly called, although they occurred in places that could not properly be designated as prairie, were of frequent occurrence and left a large part of the county, especially the wider valleys, free from trees and brush, while the shaded slopes and uplands or ridges of the bluffs were generally heavily timbered. This, of course, tended largely to induce the first settlers to make their homes in the valleys or in the open country, since clearing a piece of land from heavy timber was by no means an easy undertaking. Other features that favored settlement in the valleys, were the proximity of water and the fact that the market places along the Mississippi were more easily reached by following the creeks and rivers to their mouths. We therefore find the earliest settlements close to the Mississippi or near the mouths of its tributaries, where the soil was perhaps neither so fertile nor the land as level as farther inland and the determining factor was evidently proximity to market and ability to communicate with the outside world.

Although the so-called prairie lands, above referred to, yielded readily to cultivation, those who settled upon them, nevertheless, were confronted by many difficulties and had obstacles to overcome that to the present day farmer would appear insurmountable. In the first place they had no roads, for although they followed the watercourses, there were swamps and marshes, steep banks, fallen trees and ledges of rock, besides boulders, etc., to obstruct their passage and oftentimes they were forced to unhitch their oxen, unload their loads and not unfrequently to take apart their wagons in order to cross some of these obstructions. Railroads there were none within a hundred miles and without roads or bridges transportation was a serious problem indeed. However, this was but one of the difficulties that the pioneers met with. There were houses to be built and fences to be put up and all the material had to be brought some distance, as timber was scarce in the valleys and what there was, was unfit for building material.

As an illustration, a story which was related to me many years ago and some of the details of which I may have forgotten, may serve.

"A young man, who in Switzerland had followed the occupation of weaver, located near one of the principal streams in the county, considering the place well adapted to a prospective millsite. He came there practically empty-handed and without a cent of money. All he had was an axe and two augurs, one of them, I think, being a borrowed one. Thus equipped, he set about to build a house and manufacture his furniture. The walls of his cabin were of small logs, chinked and plastered with clay. The roof was of slabs and bark, thatched with pine boughs and grass, while the floor was of puncheons, hewn with the axe. The door had hinges made with the axe and the two augurs. Not a nail was used in making either the cabin nor any of its equipment. The table and chair were made by hewing a block on one side and by inserting stakes for legs on the under side, while the bed was a bunk of puncheons, built against the wall, covered with twigs of white pine, of which there was a grove surrounding the cabin. This, with a few wooden pegs driven into the wall, completed the equipment. Deer in large numbers disported themselves in the prairie across the creek and in the woods back of the cabin, prairie chickens and partridges were abundant, while wood pigeons by the million flew by, but all this tended only to make the young pioneer's mouth water, for he had neither gun nor ammunition, nor trap nor snare. In the waterfall below his home, were splendid trout in large schools, but as he had neither hook nor line they were safe from him, his knowledge of woodcraft being about equal to his resources for hunting and trapping – a minus quantity. He did not remain there very long and the spot where his cabin stood is today still a wilderness, for although the mill was built, it is located farther down the stream and was built by one more experienced and more blessed with this world's goods, our friend locating on some of the fertile lands in the valley where by frugality and industry he amassed a comfortable fortune which he is now enjoying in his old age, a retired gentleman-farmer."

Such were some of the conditions that confronted the pioneers and although not all of them started in this primitive way, the log cabin and the trusty axe played a major role in the history of every pioneer.

Coming as they did mostly from Europe, although in the northern part of the county the early settlers were from the East, they found things vastly different from conditions in their old homes. There they had fairly comfortable houses, good roads, cultivated fields, schools and churches, and their homes were in or near villages or hamlets. They were not used to improved farm machinery, hence they were in this respect, at least, not handicapped. Many of them were professional men, tradesmen and factory workers from the cities of Europe, but taking counsel of their more experienced neighbors, they soon adapted themselves to the new circumstances, for they had come here to make homes for themselves and their families. They exchanged work and clubbed together in various ways. A breaking plow was a fortune and its possessor was a man much esteemed and sought after, and a yoke of oxen often made the rounds of the neighborhood helping out here and there. Oftentimes two settlers who owned an ox apiece would work together. The grain was cut with the cradle bound by hand and often threshed with the flail or trampled out by cattle, several neighbors clubbing together for that purpose; but one of the first farm machines to make its appearance was the threshing machine. It was, of course, a primitive affair, driven by what is known as a horsepower, only that oxen were first used instead of horses, and a little later on it was often a mixture of both that yielded to the long whip of the driver.

J. P. Stein is said to have raised the first grain in Buffalo county. He broke some land in the summer of 1851, procured two bushels of wheat from Galena, Ill., sowed it in the spring of 1852, and raised a crop of seventy-four and a half bushels. The threshing was done with a flail. The first barley was also raised by Mr. Stein. He secured a gallon of seed from Wabasha and raised seven bushels. Mr. Stein resided between Alma and Fountain City and kept a stopping place for travelers.

Among pioneer threshers were Balthasar Carisch, Florian Schneller, the Meulis, the Ochsners, the Walds and others in different sections of the county. The machines were often kept a-going as long into winter as the deep snows would permit, and to lug an outfit from one valley to another on bobs was not less common than for a man to carry a borrowed breaking plow across the bluffs on his back. Mills were also among the early conveniences that the pioneers were blessed with, although some of the very early ones were forced to grind their grain by hand in a coffee mill. Flour was available only at river ports, being brought from Galena, Ill., by boat in summer and by teamsters who toted to Ft. Snelling, in the winter. This, however, could be procured for cash only and the price was about twelve dollars a barrel and "thereby hangs a tale," for few were the fortunate ones who had that sum in solid hard cash, as gold was the only currency acceptable among strangers. Wild-cat money, issued by irresponsible banks, there was an abundance of, but as it was little better than a promise to pay, given by a stranger in some far-off state, it was rather a handicap than a convenience, for no one would accept it for fear that it might become worthless over night, which was too often the case. Farmers paid their hands in goods or merchandise which they got in exchange for the grain they took to town and wages were as low as fifty cents a day for harvest hands, the price of grain being correspondingly low. But to return to the subject of mills, they were established at Holmes Landing, now Fountain City, at the Bear Creek, now Misha Mokwa, and on the Mill Creek, near Alma, at a very early date, while Gilmanton, Modena, Waumandee and Mondovi were thus blessed soon thereafter, for a mill was indeed a blessing to a community.

As before stated, in order to reach the market or mill, farmers followed the water courses, and in order to cross the bluffs, wended their way up one ravine and down another, but soon, as towns were organized, roads of some kind were built, and although they were of a primitive nature, they answered the purpose for a long time, being better than no roads at all, and although some good bridges were built and an occasional stretch of permanent roads was constructed, it was not until the coming of the automobile that the state and county took a hand in the business and a system of roads was planned, and although this is, at this time, in its infancy, it promises to become one of the most important steps in the advancement of both the agricultural and social interests of the county.

Shortly after the introduction of the threshing machine the reaper made its appearance – not the self-binder of today, but a machine that cut the grain which dropped onto the platform back of the sickle and was raked off in sheaves by a man who clung to a kind of seat fastened to the rear of the platform, a herculean task, indeed. This was soon superseded by the self-rake, a reaper with a raking attachment that deposited the sheaves, which were tied by hand. Harvesters which were equipped with a stand and elevator on which two men rode and bound the grain, were, in the seventies, equipped with wire binders, which, however, were not quite satisfactory, while the self-binder of today, which was invented a few years later, is as perfect a machine as man can make, doing the work of half a dozen men better than it was ever done by hand in the days of the reaper or the cradle. With the self-binder came a new era in the history of agriculture.

In the early days marsh or swale hay was considered the only hay, and those who lived on the bluffs and in the valleys where no marshes were near, drove for miles after that hay, which in reality was little better than hundreds of tons of straw and cornstalks which went to waste on their farms. Timothy as a cultivated hay crop was early introduced, and clover soon followed it, so that today they are the main forage crops, while marsh hay, which was usually cut with a scythe and raked up by hand, receives little consideration. Modern hay tools, such as the mower, the hay-rake, hay-loader and hay-mower, make it possible to harvest large crops with little expense and in a short time. Alfalfa has been cultivated to a limited extent, but owing to some difficulty in obtaining a stand, does not receive the attention which it perhaps merits. With the introduction of the reaper and threshing machine, horses became more common, and about the outbreak of the Civil War most farmers who had become fairly well located had at least one span of horses. Newcomers and beginners, of course, were still content to start with a yoke of cattle and thankful to have that. About this time many began to come from the older counties of this state or from the east, and most of them brought their horses with them, as did a few of the very early pioneers who came from the southern part of the state. Cows were kept in sufficient numbers to supply the home demand for milk, butter and cheese, as everyone in the villages had his own cow and there was no demand whatever for dairy products nor any way of shipping them. Thus the raising of small grain became the one and only thing left for our farmers to do, and with the Civil War and big prices those who had plenty of help and a large acreage under cultivation became quite prosperous and made many improvements in the way of new buildings, etc.

After the war, help was again more available, hence a greater acreage was tilled and some improvement being made on the roads, more grain was marketed. Another thing that tended to increased production was the fact that many of the returned soldiers took homesteads and began to farm for themselves. The more remote coulies and the uplands or bluffs were now being rapidly settled. This land was not open or prairie land, but much of it heavily timbered or covered with a growth of brush and necessitated much work in clearing before it was ready for the plow. Although all this had to be done by hand, stump-pullers and dynamite having not yet come into use for that purpose, there was hardly a field opened before all stumps had been dug up and removed, and a field of grain or hay with stumps left in it was a rare sight indeed. This was extremely hard work, but speaks volumes for the thoroughness with which the pioneers went about their work.

Thus wheat became the watchword, and to raise wheat and more wheat was every farmer's ambition. This went on for a number of years when nature began to rebel against this system of soil robbery. Rust, blight and chinch-bugs all took their toll of a crop that both in quality and quantity was far below what it had been but a few years before, and the thoughtful farmers who had had experience with fertilizers in Europe, began to see the handwriting on the wall and considered a change of methods, while many who had come from the east after going through this same experience there, began to make preparations to heed the advice of Horace Greeley and "Go west," where new opportunities and more virgin soil awaited them. Nor were the easterners the only ones who chose this easy way of solving a vexatious problem, for there were soil robbers in abundance among the immigrants, hence many a foreigner rather than return to methods of fertilization practiced in Europe, chose to drift with the current and also went west. This exodus made room for others, and many of the Norwegians now residing in the county came about that time.

The opening of vast areas in the West by the advancement of the Great Northern, Northern Pacific and other transcontinental lines of railways, made wheat raising with all its handicaps an unprofitable, if not a losing, proposition here. Thus the ones who persevered and held onto their farms here became indeed hard pressed, for without railroad facilities and with the prevailing low prices there was little encouragement to enter upon diversified farming. But all things come to him who waits, and finally the Burlington was built along the Mississippi, the Omaha came into Mondovi, and even before this markets on the Green Bay, in Trempealeau county, had become available to residents in the eastern part of this county. With only river transportation during part of the year, the shipping of livestock was an impossibility, and dairying and poultry raising were handicapped in a like manner. Some dressed beef and pork was marketed at Eau Claire and Chippewa Falls for use in lumber camps, but this was a very uncertain market, and to most of our farmers, very remote.

Conditions as above described applied to all sections of the country, soil robbery being by no means confined to our county alone. The federal and state governments therefore, by means of bulletins and farmers' institutes, proposed to correct this matter.

Although the people who are always ready with their little hammer to "knock" every innovation, were extremely busy, and these institutes were for some time rather unpopular as the farmer resents to have bookworms come and tell him what to do, better judgment finally prevailed, and now institutes, held in different parts of the county, are always liberally patronized, and together with the different agricultural schools have done much toward advancing the agricultural interests of the county. Thus diversified farming became introduced into Buffalo county partly by necessity and partly by education derived from bulletins, agricultural papers, farmers' institutes, schools, etc.

Wheat raising was out of the question, and the only remedy lay in turning to dairying and livestock raising; therefore the advent of the creamery, the cheese factory and the pure-bred or high-grade horse, cow, hog, sheep and chicken.

As above stated, dairying to the extent of supplying the home with butter and cheese was practiced by almost every housewife as a matter of course, just as she spun the yarn and knitted the socks and mitts in the early days, but as a business proposition little was done along this line before the advent of the railroads above mentioned. There were, however, a few attempts at cheese making in pioneer days that deserve notice.

Joseph L. Rohrer, one of the progressive pioneers who settled in Rose Valley in 1856, brought with him from a down-river point a number of cows, and coming from that part of Switzerland where the manufacture of cheese was the chief and only industry, he at once embarked in it and kept it up until he retired from the farm which he later owned near Cochrane. Jacob Baer, who lived near him; Fred Moser, of Gilman Valley; William Ulrich, of Waumandee; and John H. Johnson, of Mondovi, all entered upon the same venture later on, but before the establishment of regular cheese factories. There may have been others, but these were some of the pioneers, and when all the obstacles they met with in regard to marketing their product, etc., are considered, they certainly deserve honorable mention.

There were factories for the manufacture of American cheese in and near Mondovi and at Gilmanton before the factories now in operation were opened, but these have all been superseded by creameries. Of the factories now running, the ones in Mill Creek and Pine Creek valleys, in the town of Alma, were the first. The Mill Creek factory was first operated on the farm of the late Jacob Wald, and for many years he was the leading spirit in managing it and promoting its interests. Charles Maier was the first cheesemaker there and the product was Swiss and brick cheese. The factory in Pine Creek valley was organized by Michael Meisser, Paul Accola, Nic. Kindschi, Wieland Allemann and others, John Eberli being the first cheesemaker, and its products being the same as those of the Mill Creek factory, although both, together with a number of other factories in operation in that town, now make American cheese. In the vicinity of Alma cheese factories are very numerous, and during the summer months regular weekly shipments are made from that station. When the first factories were opened, milk was at times delivered for the price of about fifty cents per cwt., yet this was better than nothing, and the farmers who received it were perhaps as well satisfied as those who today get three dollars for the same quantity.

Attempts at establishing creameries were made here in the eighties, Arcadia, in Trempealeau county, having operated one for several years before and drawn some trade from the eastern part of this county. Among the first was one at Alma, but owing to lack of good roads, scarcity of cows in the vicinity, poor business management and other adverse circumstances, this proved a failure, and due to the establishment of cheese factories in the vicinity, the project was never resurrected.

With the establishment of co-operative creameries, this industry received an impetus in this county. There were, of course, different parties active in their establishment, but above all others there was one who made co-operative creameries his one and only work, and he talked and wrote on this subject whenever and wherever opportunity offered and when opportunity did not offer, he made it, for he went into communities and held meetings for the purpose of organizing creameries and was always enthusiastic in advocating this progressive step. He was a retired farmer and Civil War veteran, and as he could not be without work, he devoted himself to this task and gave counsel and advice without ever asking or expecting compensation. He acted as secretary and general manager of the Modena Co-operative Creamery for years at but a nominal salary. This man was the late John B. Meyer, of Modena, and when the roll of honor of Buffalo county agriculturists is made up, his name should appear well towards the top.

There are now in active operation in the county thriving creameries at Mondovi, Gilmanton, Modena, Burnside in the town of Nelson, at Nelson, Waumandee, Cochrane and Fountain City. All are prosperous and have done much towards advancing the interests of the respective communities in both a business and agricultural sense.

At an early day, in fact, immediately after the Civil War, attempts at introducing pure-bred livestock were made, but for several decades when prices were so low that a young beef, for instance, would not bring more than a hide brings now and a good cow not as much as a calf is worth now, interest in improved stock naturally flagged and was not revived until conditions improved in a business way.

H. N. Muzzy, of Modena, was among the first to make an attempt at introducing pure-bred cattle by shipping in a few Shorthorn bulls from the East. They were prime animals and were disposed of in different parts of the county and left their mark on the herds wherever they were placed. The late L. J. Claflin, of Gilmanton, shortly after the Civil War, went east, to Vermont, I think, and returned with a large flock of pure-bred Merino sheep of fine quality. This flock he kept on his farm for many years and it furnished the foundation stock for many a good flock in the county. The most important step in horse improvement was the purchase of the Percheron stallion "Horace Greeley" by a Mondovi stock company. This is "the horse that made Mondovi famous," for with him started the movement which has made Mondovi and, in fact, all of Buffalo county the home of the best farm horses in the state, that community having taken grand champion honors not only at state fairs, but also at the International.

In these days of rapid accumulation of wealth, financial success is often considered the only thing that counts or is worth while, and men who have been eminently successful in developing and introducing improved livestock are not considered successful breeders unless they pile up stacks of money, but although money is a very convenient commodity, it is not the only thing that spells success. Among those who have been prominent in the introduction of pure-bred livestock and active in the fostering and development of this important industry, Hon. W. L. Houser, of Mondovi, deserves special mention. As editor of a country newspaper, he found little opportunity to indulge in this hobby, but gradually he worked into it and became a pioneer in the introduction of some of the best horses and cattle ever brought to this county or state. He went into this work enthusiastically, for Mr. Houser is passionately fond of animals, and being a man who loves all the world and everything in it, he is specially fitted for having charge of animals that require extra care and kindly treatment. He has a statewide reputation as a successful breeder and has been at the head of the movements instituting the baby beef contests, sheep and hog contests and other activities along those lines in the state. He has done much for the advancement of agricultural interests in the county and state and for this should receive due credit.

Since the establishment of creameries and cheese factories and advanced prices for their products, the interest in pure-bred dairy cattle has been revived, and among the breeds represented are the Holstein-Friesians, the Jerseys, the Guernseys and a few Brown Swiss and perhaps some Ayrshires, there being, however, no pure-bred herds of the two last mentioned breeds, but only a few individuals.

Among the prominent Holstein breeders in the county are: Henry Knecht & Sons and Krause Bros., of Waumandee; Nic. Weinandy and John Stuber, of Belvidere; Kaste Bros., William

103

Herman, Alfred Haigh, Irvin Haigh, Emil Haigh and Marks Bros., of the town of Lincoln. The first purebred Holstein sire was brought to Buffalo county by William Ulrich, then of Waumandee, who, when he retired from the farm, had the nucleus for a fine herd. Another good herd was that of John Farner, of Waumandee, who took his cattle with him when he removed to Colfax, this state. Among those mentioned there are some exceptionally good herds, and besides these there are scores of high-grade herds with pure-bred sires at their head, especially in the cheese factory districts. Thomas Irvine, secretary of the M. R. L. Co., who, by the way, was also a breeder of purebred Jerseys and standard bred trotting horses, bought a fine herd of Holsteins in the state of New York and for a few years kept them on his farm at Beef Slough, but on removing to St. Paul, took them with him onto a farm near that city. A few animals from that herd were retained in the county and used as sires on grade herds and the results were very satisfactory.

The Jerseys were early introduced into the county, and among the best and largest herds first kept were the one of Thomas Irvine, above alluded to, and one owned by W. L. Houser, both of which were, however, dispersed. Buffalo county now has a Jersey breeders' association and in the northern part of the county there are some good herds of pure-breds, while herds headed by pure-bred sires are very common throughout the county. Among the prominent Jersey breeders are the following: James Dillon & Sons, Wm. Armour & Son, F. J. Seyforth, Earle Franzwa and Otto Witte, all in the vicinity of Mondovi. There may be a few purebred herds in other parts of the county and also in Pepin county, but the above are among those who take the most active interest in the breed. The Guernseys are less numerous than the Jerseys, although many grade herds, headed by pure-bred sires, are to be found in different parts of the county. Some of the pure-bred herds are those of C. W. Pace & Son, C. H. Adams and Mrs. George F. Krampeter, all of the town of Naples, while George B. Sankey, just across the line in Pepin county, also has a fine herd of pure-breds.

The dual-purpose breeds, like the Red Polled and Brown Swiss, are represented by grade herds in different parts of the county, but the writer has no knowledge of registered herds of those breeds. Some good herds of Red Polled cattle are owned by the Allemans, Christs and others in the town of Montana, while Otto Farner, of

Gilmanton, has a high-grade herd of that breed. Frank Kuehn and Charles Jahn at one time kept some Brown Swiss cattle in the town of Lincoln, but at present there are no registered herds of that breed in the county.

Of the beef breeds, the Shorthorns are the most numerous in the county, there being a Shorthorn breeders' association in existence. There are numerous herds headed by pure-bred sires and among the owners of registered herds are: Whelandale Farm, Mondovi; E. O. Klein, of the town of Cross; Ashton Bros. and Martin Bros., of Glencoe; John Carrothers & Son and J. P. Ward, of Canton; F. G. Theisen, of Montana; C. J. Rongholt, Anton Dworschak, Ole Aase, Louis Aase, Carl Aase, Hovey Bros. and Paulson Bros., of Dover; and Hitt Bros., John Risch and Paul Lanicca, of the town of Alma.

The Aberdeen Angus were first introduced into the county by W. L. Houser, of Mondovi, who bought his foundation stock from the champion herd of Mr. Martin and also some prize winners from Roesch & Gelbach, of Potosi, this state. From this herd, known as Ethelwold Herd, foundation stock was supplied to all of the herds now owned in the county, while sires have been furnished to a number of farmers who breed grades for marketing purposes. In 1914 Mr. Houser sold his entire herd to E. F. Ganz & Son, of Alma, and the herd is now known as Buena Vista Herd. James Allison & Sons, of the town of Maxville, and M. O. Quarberg, of Modena, also own registered herds of this champion beef breed, while S. A. DeMarce, of Arkansaw, Pepin county, who secured his foundation stock from Buena Vista Herd, has a herd numbering some twenty head and intends to embark in the business on a large scale. His herd, known as Forest Vale Herd, numbers among it some very promising individuals.

Many grade herds of Herefords in the county are headed by pure-bred sires, while Sam Glanzman & Son, of Gilmanton, own a number of pure breds.

The livestock industry, here as well as elsewhere, received a great impetus with the introduction of the silo, which enables its owners to keep a large number of cattle on a comparatively small acreage. Shredded cornstalks are also largely utilized as fodder. The first silo in the county was built in 1887 by William Ulrich, of Waumandee. W. L. Houser and M. M. Farr built theirs soon thereafter.

Scientific methods are coming more and more into vogue, a progressive step in the interest of agriculture being the adoption of a resolution by the 1918 county board for the engagement of a county agent.

The horse as a factor in the development of the agricultural resources of this county is entitled to a prominent place. Before the advent of the railroads and the automobile it afforded the only means of rapid transit known to our people, and in transporting various conveyances for business or pleasure his services were much in demand, and for that matter are yet, as well as for the cultivation and harvesting of crops. The first horses brought here were of the general purpose type and rather small in size. It was claimed for some that they had Morgan blood, but however that may have been, they were certainly tough and wiry for their size and rendered valuable service both as drafters and drivers.

The first attempts at improving the breed were made by importing grades from Illinois, Iowa and other sections, but soon there was a demand for pure-bred sires, and one of the first Percherons to be imported was the horse "Horace Greeley," owned by a Mondovi stock company. He proved to be a remarkable horse and laid the foundation for the large number of excellent horses that have been produced in and around Mondovi. Encouraged by the success of this venture, others were induced to buy pure-bred horses, mostly of the Percheron breed, and it was not many years before good-sized drafters were not an uncommon sight.

One of the first to go into the breeding of pure-breds on a large scale was W. L. Houser, of Mondovi, who has made a state-wide reputation for Ethelwold Farms on his Percherons, Clydesdales and standard breds. Although Ethelwold has produced some grand champions of the Percheron breed, Clydesdales are Mr. Houser's favorites, and his achievements with animals of that breed at the International are a source of pride not only to himself but to all lovers of horse flesh in the county. Among other Percheron breeders are: James Dillon, Whelandale Farms; and Will Hurtley, of Mondovi; Frank E. Rockwell, Modena; Louis Haunschild, Gilmanton; Herman Luther, Nelson; and Emil Loesel, of Lincoln. Others who did good work in advancing this breed by bringing pure-bred sires into the county are: August Schreiner, Antone Quarberg and G. C. Parish, of Mondovi; Jacob Wald, of Alma; Wm. Schaub, of Lincoln; George

106

Kindschy and John and Florian Flury, of Montana; and Otto Hohmann, of Arcadia. A large number of Percheron stallions were also owned by stock companies organized among the farmers, and in most instances good results were obtained. Clydesdale stallions were owned by Andrew Florin and Conrad Christ, of Montana, and Jacob Beck, of Fountain City, while Henry Eikamp and Gustav Kurtzweg, of Lincoln, specialize in Belgians. Outside of Mr. Houser's trotting stock not many were kept for breeding purposes in this county, and although stallions were kept at different times and places, our farmers stuck to the raising of drafters, and in this they have succeeded well. Taken on the whole, our farmers own a high class of working horses and thousands of good horses have been exported from the county, among them some for the army, and there are many left that would have withstood the rigid test required by the government buyers. Horse breeding has received more care than any other line of animal husbandry in this county and much credit for this is due those mentioned and others in their line of business for providing our farmers with good breeding stock.

When the county was first settled, many bare hillsides offered a fine opportunity for sheep pasture, but with onward march of cultivation prairie fires were materially checked, or at least confined to limited areas, so that almost all the uncultivated land is overgrown with trees and brush and no longer fit for sheep ranging. The number of sheep kept in the county is therefore not near what it was in the early days, or some forty or fifty years ago. Other causes that have discouraged the sheep industry are marauding dogs, wolves and unfriendly legislation. The great war, even before we got into it, again greatly stimulated sheep raising, as the price of both wool and mutton went out of sight. The sheep business was put on a paying basis, but the scarcity of breeding ewes, their high price and the prevailing inexperience along this line acted as a damper, so that not so many sheep were bought as might have been the case otherwise. Through the activity of Messrs. Dillon and Houser, of Mondovi, several hundred lambs were sold to the boys and girls of the county, and as the youngsters took a great interest in this work, as well as in the calf and pig clubs started by the same gentlemen, this small beginning may be the nucleus of many a future herd. Of the 10,519 sheep in the county, the towns of Glencoe, Mondovi, Nelson, Naples, Canton and Maxville have the largest number.

While some fine graded herds are owned in the county, it is rather difficult to ascertain who are the owners of pure-breds, but most of those who have the grade herds use pure-bred sires, mostly Shropshires. James Dillon & Son and Whelandale Farms, of Mondovi, have pure-bred herds of Shropshires.

Of the Merinos, which were introduced at an early day by the late L. J. Claflin, very few are left, most of them having been discarded during the nineties when the price of wool had sunk to a level that made sheep-raising a nonpaying business.

In the early days when spinning and knitting were among the regular household duties, a small flock of sheep was a common thing, and if an estimate of the amount of wool worked up in that manner could be made, it would surprise many of the readers of this work. Now that almost all of this work is done in factories and the farmers are able to pay for the finished product, the spinning wheels of our grandmothers have been relegated to oblivion or are kept as honored relics of the past and the family sheep has either disappeared or been superseded by the commercial herd.

Although hogs were kept by the very earliest settlers, hog-raising on a large scale or for commercial purposes began with the coming of the railroads, which made possible the shipping of live hogs. During the Civil War pork was very high and some hogs were raised and sold dressed, being shipped from Winona or Eau Claire in the winter. Some were also sold to lumbermen for use in their camps in the pineries, but all this was not enough to make the hog a commercial factor in the county's farming operations.

In connection with dairying, with skim-milk as a by-product, the hog industry has become one of the most important branches of farming in the county and the proverbial mortgage lifter has performed that function on many a farm. The breeds most common in the county are the Poland-Chinas, the Berkshires, the Chester Whites and the Duroc-Jerseys. Most farmers keep grades of either of these breeds and some also keep crossbreeds, but pure-bred sires are becoming rather the rule than the exception. Among those who at an early day began to introduce pure-bred swine are: the late L. J. Claflin, the late Thomas Dillon, and others in different parts of the county, the Chester Whites and Poland-Chinas being the breeds first introduced. Now there are many pure-bred herds in the county and without taking a census it is impossible to mention all the owners of pure-bred swine as well as those of horses, cattle and sheep, hence reference to a few must suffice. Among Poland-China breeders are: John Sutter & Son, Fountain City; W. H. Armour & Son, F. J. Seyforth & Son, and Stewart Saxe, Mondovi; L. Kennedy & Son and H. O. Tiffany, Nelson; L. J. Rosenow, Waumandee; and Oscar Hitt, Alma. Leading Chester-White breeders are: Geo. A. Stamm, Modena; J. F. Gobar and Fred Grob, Alma; and Geo. Muehleisen, Cochrane. Some of the pure-bred Duroc-Jersey breeders are: F. J. Seyforth & Son and A. R. Pierce, Mondovi; C. F. Reinhardt and Theodore Roemer, Nelson; Nic. Weinandy, Cochrane; and E. F. Ganz & Son, Alma; while James Dillon & Son, of Mondovi, are breeding pure-bred Berkshires.

A man who has taken a leading part in advancing the county's agricultural interests and who has been more specially interested in promoting sheep and swine husbandry, is James Dillon, of Mondovi. Mr. Dillon has had charge of these departments at the state and county fairs, and during the past year as a member of the County Council of Defense, has been active in the promotion of calf, lamb and pig clubs, and in conjunction with Mr. Houser, has aided the young people of this county in making a most excellent showing at the state fair and at the International.

More and more the production of poultry is becoming an important branch of agriculture. From the humble biddie that arrived in a prairie schooner to the flocks numbering hundreds is about as big a step as that from 6 cents a dozen for eggs to 50 cents. Flocks of poultry are now found on every farm and pure bloods are very common, all breeds being represented. The ones most common are the Leghorns, Plymouth Rocks, and Rhode Island Reds. Turkeys, geese and ducks are also raised in large numbers. One hundred thousand dollars a year is a low estimate of the value of eggs and poultry shipped from this county, although that figure may be a surprise to many.

When, shortly after the Civil War, the price of hops went soaring skyward, and farmers in some of the older counties made fortunes in a year, some of our farmers embarked in that enterprise, but overproduction sent prices to a level that discouraged this industry, so that hop-raising has been entirely abandoned for many years. Grapes have been cultivated spasmodically, but never in large tracts, the only one who embarked in this and made a success of it, being the late Conrad Ulrich, who went into this first on his farm in the town of

Waumandee and later for commercial purposes at Fountain City. His success was largely due to his experience in Switzerland and to his untiring efforts and perseverance. Others have successfully conducted small vineyards for home use. Apples can be successfully grown here and with proper care and cultivation, do well, but as this is lacking in most instances, orchards are not as numerous nor as profitable as they should be. Orchards are found on many farms, especially on the bluffs along the Mississippi river. One of the leading apple producers is J. F. Gobar, of Alma, who has a fine orchard of several hundred trees and has demonstrated that the apple may be successfully grown in this county, and it is to be hoped that this practice will become more general and that in the not distant future every farm may have its orchard of apples, plums and cherries, all of which thrive with proper care, as do raspberries, strawberries and other small fruits. Sorghum has been cultivated off and on in small patches, but cheapness of sugar and syrup and increasing prosperity consigned this industry to oblivion until the scarcity of sugar, caused by the war, revived it. Raising cucumbers for neighboring pickle factories has been practiced to a limited extent, also the cultivation of sugar beets, but the prevailing scarcity of labor has put a stop to this. At Mondovi there is a canning factory, and much truck is raised there to supply it, while truck and vegetables for home use are abundantly produced on our farms as well as in the gardens in town, and to a much larger extent since the war started than before. The cultivation of tobacco has also been experimented with, but the acreage was small, lack of experience and shortage of labor being among the drawbacks which prevented the growth of this industry. Honey, although not strictly a farm product, deserves to be mentioned here, and apiaries are found on a number of farms. Among the county's successful pioneer apiarists, the late Jacob Wald, of Alma Town, and the Butlers, of Nelson, deserve special mention. Potatoes have been cultivated mostly for home use, but the past two years saw a great increase in the production of tubers, and many carloads have been shipped from the county. Wheat-raising, which had been practically abandoned, was resumed in response to the call by the Government, and lo and behold, it produced so abundantly that it may again become a staple crop. The test cure has done wonders for our soil, and the plagues that drove wheat away seem to have disappeared for the time being, at least.

In conclusion, let me state that the farmers of Buffalo county, although somewhat conservative, are a thrifty, thriving lot, and that for improved and modernized farm buildings this county holds its own with any community, and it will not be many years before it will take a place in the front ranks with older communities as regards improvement in livestock, seed grain, highways and other things that spell progress and prosperity.

When the settlers first came to Buffalo county, the United States Land Office for this region was located at Mineral Point, in Iowa county, this state, and the entering of land therefore entailed a long and tedious trip. On July 30, 1852, a United States Land Office was opened at La Crosse, a much nearer and more convenient place. Few entries were made before 1854, and practically none before that time were made for agricultural purposes.

The first surveys of land in Buffalo county were made in 1848 by D. A. Spaulding. At that time there were small settlements at Holmes' Landing, now Fountain City, and at Twelve Mile Bluff, now Alma. There was also at least one settler in Nelson. Mr. Spaulding in that year surveyed township 20, ranges 10, 11, 12 and 13; township 19, ranges 10, 11 and 12; and township 18, range 11. He started to survey township 18, range 10, that year, but did not complete it until 1849. S.W. Durham then took up the work. In 1849 he surveyed township 24, range 13; township 23, range 13, and started township 24, range 14, completing it the following year, 1850, in which he also surveyed township 23, range 14, and township 22, range 14. John Ball started work in 1851, surveyed township 23, ranges 11 and 12, and township 22, ranges 12 and 13, and started township 21, range 13, completing it in 1852, in which year he also surveyed township 21, ranges 10, 11 and 12; township 22, ranges 10 and 11; township 23, range 10; and township 24, ranges 10, 11 and 12.

The first land in the county was open to pre-emption and sale in 1849. June 18 of that year township 18, ranges 10 and 11; township 19, ranges 10, 11 and 12; and township 20, ranges 10, 11, 12 and 13, were placed on the market. On Aug. 18, 1851, the land opened included township 22, range 14; township 23, ranges 13 and 14; and township 24, ranges 13 and 14. Township 21, range 11, was opened Oct. 17, 1852, and on Nov. 15 of that year township 22, range 12; township 23, ranges 11 and 12; and township 24, range 12. The rest of the county was opened in 1853. On July 15 of that year were opened township 21, range 10; township 22, range 10; township 23, range 10; and township 24, range 10. The next day township 24, range 11, was opened. Oct. 17 of the same year, 1853, township 21, range 13; township 22, range 11; and township 22, range 13, were opened. On Nov. 15, 1853, township 21, range 12. June 13, 1856, the land was withdrawn in order that a route might be selected for a proposed railroad. In that year Congress had made a grant of land to be held in trust by the state of Wisconsin for the purpose of constructing a railroad from Portage City to the Mississippi river at La Crosse, with a branch from Tomah to some point on the St. Croix river. The grant was conferred on the Milwaukee & La Crosse Railroad Co. and the head of which was Byron Kilbourn. In 1857 the Tomah-St. Croix branch was chartered as the Western Wisconsin Railroad Co. One of the routes chosen for its line was through the northern part of Buffalo county. The grant specified that the railroad was to receive all the odd numbered sections in a strip twelve miles wide, six miles on each side of its line. All the remaining land in a strip thirty miles wide, fifteen miles each side of the line, was to be open to pre-emption at double rates, that is, at $2.50 an acre.

The Buffalo County Agricultural Society was organized June 10, 1872, with Robert Henry as president, John Hunner, Jr., as secretary, and J. W. DeGroff as treasurer. The first annual fair was held Oct. 9, 10 and 11, on section 12, township 21, range 12, in Lincoln township, near what is now Cream, the grounds being southwest of the bridge crossing Little Waumandee creek in front of what was then the Lincoln House. Lincoln township paid a bonus and was guaranteed the fair for five years. The first three fairs met with success, but then the interest declined. The grounds were in a central location, but the nature of the soil was such that the slightest rain turned the place into a pool of mud. Then, too, there was but one tavern within six or eight miles. It was therefore decided to seek another site. The people of Buffalo city offered a gift of eight square acres of land and a bonus of $200, the people of that city to bear the expense of moving the buildings, fences, railings, posts and the like to the new location. The people of Alma offered to furnish grounds free for ten years, to fence the grounds, to dig a well and to erect necessary buildings, including a hall 24 by 60 feet, horse and cattle stalls, sheep and pig pens and a fenced half-mile race track. The Alma offer was accepted, and the grounds prepared about a mile below the center of the village on the road to Fountain City. These grounds likewise proved damp, and various unfavorable circumstances prevented the success that had been hoped. The fair was kept alive by contributions from the village of Alma and from private citizens. In 1880 and 1881 the interest in the fair was at its lowest ebb and the grounds were seriously damaged by the high water. But in 1882 a most successful fair was held and things looked bright for the future. Two interesting features of the 1882 fair, still remembered, were the walking race and the ladies' horse race. The winner in the walking contest had walked fifty times around the half-mile track when the contest was ended. A small fair was held in 1883. Then the construction of the railroad through the grounds rendered it impossible to hold further exhibitions there. Therefore, it was decided to remove the fair to Mondovi, that city agreeing to furnish suitable grounds free for ten years, to construct the necessary buildings and a race track, and to keep the place in repair. The offer was accepted, and beginning with 1884 the fair has been held at that place. Suitable buildings have been erected and the fair takes high place among the agricultural exhibits of Wisconsin, having won excellent recognition in many departments.

Agricultural Reconstruction Period in Buffalo County and Exodus to the West: And Other Articles

When "Ule" and I Helped Build the Northern Pacific

Some of you may consider this quite a statement to make but remember I do not say "built" but "helped build" and if it is true that every little helps, then we certainly helped build The Northern Pacific. This article, however is not to deal solely and entirely with that experience of ours but is intended to give a brief insight into a period that, in a way, spells a revolution in the affairs of not only Buffalo County but more or less, of every community of the Middle West, or at least that part of it east of the Mississippi.

At the time, in 1881, this county had been settled for over thirty years and fairly well populated for over twenty. People had come here from the southern and eastern parts of this state, from the eastern states and from Europe. Conditions as they found them here were vastly different from what they were in their old homes. They beheld the deep rich soil, covered with luxuriant vegetation and to decide that this must be inexhaustible was easy, when the abundant crops produced were contemplated. Those coming from Europe, of course, were accustomed to intensive farming but this was so different from anything they had ever experienced that the delusion appears natural, while many of those coming from the east were natural drifters, who whenever the soil gave out moved on. Then there were many who had

115

never before farmed and readily took the opinions of their neighbors for granted. Thus they lived on from year to year, trusting to their good luck in having found this region of inexhaustible soil. All the people with whom, as a boy I came in contact, were immigrants from Europe and had never had any experience with virgin soil and often when a load of fertilizer was hauled away from our barn, I heard the remark, "In the old country this would be worth money" and I, knowing that it was hauled away only because it was in the way, wondered how so it could be worth money. Another motive for hauling it may have been force of habit, for in Europe fertilizer had to be hoarded. More surprising may it be to you that some farmers, who built basement barns, remarked that they were handy because the manure could be pushed over the bank. This, to you, may seem an exaggeration but since the grain was always badly lodged in places where the fertilizer was spread, it was not so much in favor and considered unnecessary. This was true in the beginning, especially since wheat was the main, in fact, almost the only crop.

This practice led to a fallacious notion, namely that when grain was lodged the soil was too "fat", meaning rich and you would be surprised to learn how recently I have heard that opinion expressed. That certain elements which went into the making of the plant and gave stamina to the straw had been taken from the soil, occurred to very few for no information along these lines was being disseminated among the farmers. Then you must remember, as mentioned, in previous articles, there was absolutely no market except for grain and therefore very little corn and not much hay was grown, diversification of crops being a matter of little if any serious consideration.

Thus crop after crop of grain was being harvested and year after year the result became more discouraging. True, the grain grew tall and rank, especially so in wet seasons but before it could be garnered some calamity was usually visited upon it. Instead of the golden fields of grain, of yesteryear, before the heads were filled they would die off and the straw would crinkle down and become so brittle that it was nigh impossible to find any that was fit for a band to tie a bundle with. Black rust and blight took their toll. Grain being the only source of income many farmers could not hold out, in fact, none but those who were well established were able to weather the storm. Renters and farmers who had become involved through the purchase of land and equipment, were hard pressed and little hope for redemption was held out to them. Add to all these troubles the fact that wheat was often around fifty cents a bushel, cattle around a cent a pound and dressed hogs about two cents, while cream often brought not more than ten cents and sometimes less, for a pound of butterfat, with other produce in proportion. Wages of harvest hands, owing to the scarcity at that season, remained high until the coming of the selfbinder and the price of that machine was three hundred dollars or more. The rate of interest was still from seven to ten per cent, largely owing to the fact, that some of the notes and mortgages dated many years back, retained the old rate of interest.

With their backs to the wall, many of these farmers became desperate and resolved to get out of this dilemma as well as they could. Like the survivors of Napoleon's disorganized hordes, after the battle of Waterloo, they exclaimed in desperation "Save himself who can". Their only hope lay in the establishment of a new home in the far West.

The Northern Pacific had penetrated as far west as Bismarck, Dakota. James J. Hill had built the St. Paul, Minneapolis and Manitoba up the Red River Valley and on to Winnipeg, in Canada, while a branch of the Northwestern had been built through the southern part of Dakota Territory. North and South Dakota having not yet been divided. Stragglers had gone into the Red River valley in Minnesota and Dakota, others into the James River valley, in Dakota, while still others located on the Cheyenne and near the Missouri in that state. Years before this period many had gone to Western Minnesota but invading hordes of grasshoppers drove them from a district that now embraces some of the best farms to be found anywhere. Then like a distant trumpet call, came a faint cry from the far West, announcing that far up the Columbia river in Washington Territory, lay a region that fairly teemed, if not with milk and honey, with crops of wheat that were unequalled, by even those raised in this county in pioneer days. Up in the Palouse and Big Bend country beckoned a region that would grow wheat and more wheat. To go thither overland, was almost out of the question as the nearest direct approach, by rail was on the Northern Pacific, now completed to the Montana line. The most feasible route to go there was, by rail to San Francisco, thence by boat to the mouth of the Columbia and up that river to the promised land. This cost money and many could not go but you would be surprised with how little some started out, got there and made good. These conditions of course, confronted only the very early pioneers of that region, access to which was made easy by the completion of two great trans-continental railways into that fertile region.

Without the admonition of the venerable Horace Greeley to, "Go west young man, go west", there was sufficient incentive in prevailing conditions to stimulate that ambition, not only in the hearts of the young but also of the middle aged and oftentimes of those farther advanced in years. Is it surprising then that a general exodus took place. From country and town, from the Waumandee valleys, the Beef River, in fact from all parts of the county, whole families but especially the young, flocked to these beckoning wheat fields of the near and far west, for indeed wheat was still king.

Some of the conservative old timers, however, could not see it that way. They had come here to stay and hoped that some day conditions would re-arrange themselves. They believed in the good black soil and the rich chocolate covered sub-soil, the hills and valleys and the stately white, black and red oaks. Land was cheap and they figured that as an asset, worth an investment by anyone. I remember one time when "Ule's" father remarked to us; "Boys I think the Albertson farm could be bought for eight hundred dollars." This announcement met with less enthusiasm than derision and I am afraid that I was foremost among those to turn down a proposition to invest in a neglected, hilly farm when the "Golden Northwest" was beckoning. The old gentleman knew of our rosy plans and although he never said a word to dissuade us, evidently put out that proposition as a feeler and when it met with such a cool reception never mentioned it again. I may remark here that a number of years later, "Ule" bought that same farm but paid a lot more than eight hundred dollars for it and later sold it for five times that amount. Of course it was then in far better condition, having been operated as a dairy farm, in the interim.

This gives you a picture of the condition that farming was in, during the late seventies and early eighties, the latter period registering the beginning of the turning point, when thanks to the Experiment Station, the Farmers Institutes, Extension Work and other much abused agencies, the farmers of our county and state were made to see the error of their ways and turned from soil robbery to conservative farming, such as their ancestors in the British Isles, in Germany, in Switzerland, in Austria, in Norway and in parts of the East had been forced to practice for centuries past. The chronic knocker was, of course then as now, ever present and as the County Agricultural Agent and his work are assailed now, these activities were by him, assailed then. His assertion that "Them fellows can't learn me nothing", was shouted as loudly then as it is now and it was as true then as it now for "Where ignorance is bliss 'tis folly to be wise".

I suppose that all of you, who knew him, have guessed who "Ule" was and to those who have not guessed it I will only say that he was the mail carrier who, years ago, used to speed down Main Street behind "The Black Prince", in an attempt to beat Train No. 52, to the postoffice and generally succeeded, for both that driver and that horse hated to be beaten. He was also, for about two decades, janitor at the County Normal and there made many friends. It is therefore needless to state that I refer to the late Ulrich Wald, who was always known to all of us as "Ule".

At that time, I was teaching in Mill Creek valley, his home, thus it happened that we planned on this undertaking jointly. There were, of course, incentives and inducements, besides those already mentioned. The Railroads were sending out circulars with glowing accounts of riches awaiting those who would heed the call of "The Golden Northwest". Then we had friends who had emigrated to the Red River valley and other Eldoradoes but we felt that we had to venture farther west still. All that winter and especially toward spring we talked this project over and finally decided to go.

We did not get much encouragement from home but there was not much opposition made manifest, for our folks were conservative and while they did not believe in ventures, seemed to think it might not hurt us to try. Oh yes, by the way, we had one fellow conspirator, who kept advising and encouraging us and he was neither young nor inexperienced. This was none other than the elder John Brethauer, who at an early day had come to Alma and established himself as a cobbler. By dint of industry and frugality he saved some money and bought what was known as the upper saw mill. This he traded to August Grams for the mill, in Mill Creek Valley. Mr. Grams had built up the business of his mill, so that it was rather a valuable piece of property. He was not a practical miller, himself and therefore always hired a good and experienced man to do that work and thus the mill enjoyed a good patronage. Mr. Brethauer, although physically handicapped was so ambitious that he never seemed to even notice that

119

defect but worked at any job alongside of an able bodied man and furthermore his ego was so abnormally developed that he not only thought but he knew that there was nothing that he could not do as well as any other man if not better. He took the mill over and almost immediately undertook to run it alone and unassisted. The result was that, after a few years it was in such shape that the flour that was turned out could not be used for bread. In those days the grain was crushed between two huge stones, one turning above the other. The faces of these stones had grooves cut into them which had to be re-cut or dressed from time to time. After witnessing this process a few times the new miller undertook it himself and finally he lost the mill but not for this reason alone for I really believe that he could have made it pay with what little custom he had grinding feed for the farmers. He however, had other troubles and leaving the mill to his family, he decided to go west and start in fresh. This he did and some years later returned to spend his reclining years here, having by dint of hard work acquired a competency which enabled him to do this.

I make mention of this for two reasons. First to show that we had a powerful ally, in this old and decrepit man, who did not fear to venture into what we were about to undertake and last but not least, to show what one with courage and determination can achieve, despite the handicaps of old age and decrepitude, by dint of will power, industry and frugality. Mr. Brethauer, who like myself, had a profusion of glowing literature, relating to our Eldorado, was eloquent on the subject and after disposing of some of his effects, netting him less than five hundred dollars, departed for the Twin Cities, preparatory to striking out for the West, in the spring, working in the mean time as flunkey, in a cheap hotel. No wonder he made money.

After my school closed in the spring – the term was six months only – I went home and made ready to go out west. I made a trip to Winona, where, among other things, I bough a revolver and an all leather bag, the latter being quite a luxury, carpet bags being still in vogue, while the former was considered a necessity by an adventurer into the Wild West, whether he knew what to do with it or not.

I took the stage to Fountain City, in the afternoon, leaving for Winona, per Steamer Robert Harris, next morning. On this "eventful" trip I had for a traveling companion, Sigmund Kammerer, of the Fountain City mill, formerly miller at Ochsner's in the Waumandee Mill. There was a very large crowd at the levee and on inquiry my friend informed me that the pastor of the local church and his family were leaving and their friends were seeing them off. I farther noticed among our fellow travelers, a young fellow who was very despondent, almost heartbroken and I wondered what might be his destination. This I did not learn until some months later. A trip from Waumandee to Winona meant more in those days than it does now or I might not have remembered all these trifles. Of course I had been away from home and even to Winona before. I had to stop there all night, on my three days' trip to Platteville, where I attended the Normal, one winter. So you see I was not quite as green as I might have been. Yet I recite this to call your attention to what was, at least, an event in those days. It not only gives you an idea of the extent of the travels of the average farmer boy but also of the time required to get from place to place. With a good team the trip from Waumandee to Winona and back could have been made in one day but the way I traveled it took part of three days. Now some do it in an hour.

Thus armed and equipped, I was ready to aid in the conquest of "The Wild and Woolly West". So one morning in early spring my brother, Casper, undertook to take me to Mill Creek. It was really not early spring but the frost was just about out of the ground, it being one of those retarded seasons. Our regular route to Alma would have been via Anchorage, Cream and Herold but that was not to be thought of, for a considerable stretch of the road immediately below Cream, was practically bottomless, while across the Belvidere Bluff, the stiff, red clay made progress almost impossible. We therefore drove past the Anchorage school, turning at the little brick church, just below, into Jaeger's valley across the bluff into Rose Valley and thence by the regular road to Alma and Mill Creek. This was by no means a holiday excursion for the horses but at least we got through, thanks to a good team and a good driver. Thus we traveled in those days.

Twelve Mile Bluff was always an object of interest to me and as we approached it that day, I told Casper that the saying was that the steeple-like formation that jutted out from the main rock, shook in the wind. Casper watched it and remarked "By gosh, it does". There was a strong east wind blowing and the rock appeared to be swaying back and forth but I tried to explain this away, laying it to an optical illusion, caused by a clump of birches, that grew on the rock, swaying in the wind.

121

Galileo said, "The World do Move" and Casper said, that rock does move. It did and how? Few, very few of those who read this, will remember that steeple or pinnacle, on the face of Twelve Mile Bluff, for within an hour after we had driven beneath it, it did come down.

Thousands upon thousands of tons of limestone came thundering down the hillside and only the heavy growth of timber saved Laue's mill from utter destruction. Quite a number of men were then employed in the mill but the landslide or rock slide occurred during the noon hour, while the men were to dinner, otherwise some of them might have been injured or killed, since at least one big boulder stopped right above the mill. Most of them, however still cling to the hillside having become imbedded alongside of the trees that held them. It would be worth while for the Boy Scouts and others, on one of their hikes, to look over this scene of the rock slide, of 1881 and at the same time consult some of the few who remember how Twelve Mile Bluff looked before that tower slid away from it. It would farther prove profitable to learn more about this bluff, for Twelve Mile Bluff is a historic land mark. Ule and I went to town the next day and on getting here were informed of what had happened and went to view the result of this debacle. Some of the trees were broken and all of them barked and bent to the ground, while huge boulders strewed the entire hillside. It was a veritable scene of devastation and yet, to the casual observer, hardly a trace of it remains today. Young trees have grown up and shrubbery partly hides the boulders. Twelve Mile Bluff is still there, as well as the face of Count von Bismarck, plainly visible as you approach the bluff, coming north on Highway No. 35, but the tower, which was so close to the main rock, that venturesome young swains would exhibit their prowess to the gay lassies accompanying them, by jumping across the dividing chasm; is gone and no trace of it remains, but the huge boulders clinging to the hillside.

After having spent a few days in Mill Creek valley, during which time I remember, Ulrich and I practiced some target shooting with our revolvers, we left for Alma, where we were to board the Steamer Lion, for Wabasha whence we took the Milwaukee train for St. Paul. The boat left in the afternoon and there was neither crowd to see us off, nor excitement at our departure. There is however one little incident connected with our departure, which I consider worth mentioning. Before we left, John Bruegger came to the levee and taking Ulrich to one side, handed him something, with explanations. Ulrich told me, after the boat had pulled out, that what "Johnnie", as he was familiarly known, had handed him was ten dollars, not as a parting gift but for business reasons. Ulrich had bought something from Johnnie, who was clerking in Tester's store and in payment handed him a gold coin – in those days it was not considered a crime for common people to handle gold coins – Johnnie made change but on going to the till, later on, found that what both had taken for a ten dollar piece was a double eagle or twenty dollar piece and to square things, he hastened to the levee to make the correction. This may not have been a remarkable thing to do, in fact, almost every business man would do it but not all of them. At any rate Johnnie Bruegger rated high with both Ulrich and me, ever after.

A story of this exodus to the far West would, however not be complete without brief mention of Johnnie Bruegger. He had come from Watertown, this state and was staying at the Massasoit House, the landlord, Emil Leonhardy, being the husband of his sister. He secured employment in Tester's store, where he soon became popular with the patrons of the place as well as with others in town and the surrounding country. He was of a rather quiet and unassuming disposition but friendly, in a modest way. He was a master turner and became a prominent and useful member of the local Turnverein. Some of the younger readers may have but a vague understanding of what a Turnverein is and I take the liberty to suggest that it would be worth their while to find out by consulting some of their elders, who may know, for turning and "Turnvereine" were worthwhile indeed and it is a pity that they have become obsolete.

John Bruegger did not go West during this mad rush, in fact, he remained here until the Great Northern Railway had been built well into or through North Dakota, when he located at Williston, in that state. Here he went into business and with wonderful foresight and business acumen forged to the front, expanding on every hand and soon becoming identified with every civic and commercial move in that town. In fact, the words Williston and Bruegger got to be almost synonyms. He gathered about him almost all, if not all, the members of the Bruegger family, including the Emil Leonhardy family, of Alma. Co-operating and co-laboring, they were leaders in building up the place and always Johnnie was in the van and the master mind.

That part of North Dakota is deeply and everlastingly indebted to this enterprising pioneer.

He was no plunger but his activities to help in the up-building of the community, were extended to the surrounding small towns and the farming country and that meant extension of a vast volume of credit and when successive crop failures and resulting money stringency befell that region, he was caught with enormous sums on his books and sustained heavy losses, as was the case with others who were public spirited and open-handed. During his career, he was induced to become a candidate for the Democratic nomination to the office of United States senator, although popular and deserving, he was no politician. He did not know the ropes and had he known them, I doubt whether he would have cared to pull them. At any rate he lost out in the primary. North Dakota, being strongly Republican, the Democratic nominee who had won out over Bruegger was defeated in the election but received balm for his wounds by being appointed Comptroller of Currency, by President Wilson. Nothing of the kind happened to John Bruegger, as might have been expected, for as later developments have shown, a fellow who returned a gold coin, although paid him by mistake, could hardly be considered fit (?) for political recognition. Yet many, very many, besides the two farmer boys herein referred to, unite in saying "Hats off to John Bruegger" and I am glad that on the occasion of a short stay in that state, during the campaign, I asked my friends and others whom I met, to vote for him and I could not, at this time refrain from paying a well deserved tribute to one of the real pathfinders of the Great West.

After a stop at Beef Slough, The Lion wended her way between logs and booms and through the "Cut-off" back into the main channel of the Father of Waters and finally landed at Wabasha. Here we had supper in Baumgartner's Hotel and while eating, I heard from the kitchen, the clarion voice of Mrs. Casparis. She was the wife of one of my former teachers and for five years, of my school days, had lived in the teacherage above our school room but owing partly to my inborn bashfulness and partly to the fact that my mind was engrossed with the big things to come, I did not have the temerity to seek an interview with this old friend. After supper we shouldered our satchels and wended our way to the Milwaukee depot back on the prairie. It was back on the prairie, owing to a policy pursued by that road, of passing up every town that failed to come across with a bonus, required by its magnates, even La Crosse being given the same treatment, much to the chagrin of said magnates, who later spent large sums of money on stubs giving them access to erstwhile spurned marts of trade, verifying again the old saying that, when the mountain refuses to come to Mohamed, Mohamed must go to the mountain. In the waiting room of the depot we sat and lay until after midnight, when a mixed train came along, taking us to the getaway of the Great Northwest, where we arrived next morning.

St. Paul, although far from being what it is today, was the first larger city that we had ever seen or entered and we passed through the Union Depot, then nearing completion, wide-eyed and open-mouthed. In and out, vast throngs were hustling and bustling and compared to the peace and quiet prevailing in the palatial present day structure this old landmark, whose destruction by fire, some years ago was hailed with acclaim and rejoicing, by the crazy mobs and even by the press, was indeed a busy mart. This unseemly demonstration in favor of a new structure, to me, always appeared an outrage and the "White Elephant" that replaces the erstwhile busy mart seems almost to be just a retribution to that unworthy outburst of joy, in the face of a calamity, for a destructive fire is always a calamity. Be this as it may, we entered St. Paul through the old depot, when it was not quite completed and then as well as often thereafter when I elbowed my way through the crowds. I considered it a wonderful structure.

Coming out of the depot, we climbed a sand hill and got into town and what a wonderful place it was. There were some four story buildings and the second story of one of them occupied by a fur trader, was decorated with a real stuffed buffalo. That was an inspiration, especially to Ulrich who, I always suspected was induced to go west more by a desire to hunt buffaloes than to take up land. At any rate the first thing we did, after finding a hotel, was to buy two repeating Winchester rifles and about a hundred rounds of 45-60 cartridges apiece. Thus fully armed we were prepared to help in the killing of the monarch of the plains. I must confess that this enthused me but little but with my partner it was different again, for he was a real hunter, while I had never even shot a rabbit. Our next job was to look up Mr. Brethauer for although we knew that he was not bound for the same destination as we, he was going west and we desired to farther consult with him. Finding him neither at the Green Tree House nor at the Wild Hunter, where he had previously been, we returned to our quarters at the American House for dinner. Mr. Brethauer had found even more remunerative quartered than he had occupied before, as we later learned from him.

The spring of 1881 was one of great floods, in the Northwest and "Old Man River: was at his peak on the day we reached St. Paul. From the brow of the hill, somewhere near where the Roberts Street bridge now crosses the river, we watched the floods inundating West St. Paul. The entire town was under water and ever and anon some barn, shed or other outbuilding began to wobble and float down river and we said to each other, "That town is doomed for good". Fancy our amazement, when coming back to town, we were greeted on every hand with placards offering for sale choice real estate in West St. Paul. We remarked if we went back to Alma we might get some of it cheap when it floated by. That by raising the townsite above the high water level it might become valuable, did not occur to us. Yet, the bargains offered that day were no doubt, real bargains but we were not interested in anything on this side of the Mississippi and had we been, we could not have financed it. Thus the only interest we had in that flood was sympathy for the people in the stricken town, little dreaming that it would rise from this disaster, greater and better for the experience, for there was no loss of life. Often, on crossing the Roberts Street bridge have I looked down upon that town and tried to visualize it as it was in the spring of 1881.

Since we were not interested in buying any of those floating lots in West St. Paul, for reasons already stated, we started for the depot, after supper, lugging our Winchesters and satchels. Here we sat, awaiting the departure of our train and watching the well ordered coming and going of the crowds and listening to the stentorian announcements of departing trains by the train dispatcher and when he finally sang out, "The Northern Pacific; all aboard for St. Cloud, Great Falls, Moorehead, Fargo, Valley City, Jamestown and Bismarck, all aboard", we got up and boarded the west bound train for Bismarck. Soon after boarding the train, we went to sleep and daybreak found us in the Red River valley, approaching Moorehead and Fargo. Passing through Mapleton, we came to Dalrymple and got a glimpse of gigantic operations on the great Dalrymple farm, where seeding was already in progress. As far as eye could reach, stretched the coal black fields, level as a floor. Here dozens upon dozens of seeders passed down the fields side by side, followed by harrows, every one of them drawn by four horses. This was a new sight for us, since at home all implements were drawn by one team only. It was a great sight but as we passed on, this was soon overshadowed by another, more spectacular. To the right of us and to the left of us the fields were literally covered with wild geese. You can imagine how this sight impressed a hunter like my friend, Ulrich, who was fairly itching at a chance to try out his new Winchester. This was, of course, out of the question and did not much bother me. This continued for hour after hour, whenever we passed a field that was being seeded. The geese were as numerous as the wood pigeons, at home, only they were not quite so nimble and I trust not so destructive to the seed grain.

For miles there would be neither fields nor geese but ever and anon we could pass a siding, or proposed station, where someone attempted to ape the great Dalrymple, in trying out farming on a big scale but often, as I learned later, with little success. The siding were numbered in rotation, the naming of them awaiting the establishment of a town. Of course, places like Valley City, Tower City, Jamestown and other had been started and named. Others were known simply as fifth, seventh or tenth siding as the case might be. Small lakes or large ponds were visible on every hand and these too were literally covered with wild geese that made my friend's trigger finger itch and I did not blame him for never then or thereafter did he get a chance at this noble game, while here he actually saw and had to pass up millions.

Late that afternoon our train pulled into Bismarck and we had arrived, for here was "Where the West began". The depot was connected with a big hotel, a huge frame building with the imposing name of Sheridan House. This was too big for us or rather for our pocketbooks and we walked into the town looking for a hostelry that was more to our liking or rather that better fitted our circumstances. On entering the business section we saw, in front of a store, a dapper young fellow eyeing us and stroking his mustache. Looking from him to me, Ulrich exclaimed, "Isn't that Albert Utzinger?" I was about to make the same remark and was quite sure that it was but first we were intent on getting located, then to go back and look him up. Arriving at the hotel we were required to register and on the pages of the hotel register the name of A. W. Utzinger, Crookston, Minn., stared us in the face. Now we were doubly sure for some years previous our friend, Albert, had left Alma for Crookston. While here he was the leader of the famous brass band of which P. E. Ibach, Ottmar Probst, the Furrer

127

boys, Jacob Weinandy and others, whose names I do not now recall, were members. He was a master musician, music teacher and bandmaster and withal a hale fellow well met. We knew him well, especially I, since his uncle Henry Utzinger who lived near Bangor, was married to my mother's sister. We re-traced our steps at once, to look him up and found him still there. He grinned at us saying "It's a wonder you fellows wouldn't speak to a fellow". We retorted that the boot was on the other foot and he being an established resident in the burg, was in duty bound to extend its hospitality to us, which he of course would have done had he been as cock sure, at first, as he now pretended to have been. Were we glad though to meet him? Here, in a strange land, we met up with a friend and one who was not a tenderfoot but a seasoned sourdough. He worked for a baker, who had a grocery store in connection and it was his duty to attend to the latter. This store, owned by a Swiss, named John Jegen (He had become Americanized and spelled it Yegen) became our headquarters while in Bismarck.

The railroad which had been built as far as Bismarck by the Jay Cooke interests, came to a standstill there when Jay Cooke went under, in the early seventies, on that eventful day known as "Black Friday". Financiers, connected with the railroad company had made it a point to secure possession of all prospective townsites, before locating a station. In the case of Bismarck, which was expected to become a railroad center and a more or less important town, a band of squatters had planned to beat the capitalists to it and the result was a fight to the finish. To deceive the squatters, the road was surveyed to a point, in the river bottoms about two miles below the present site of the town and building in that direction was in progress, in fact, the road was practically completed and the squatters had possession of the proposed townsite, when under the cover of night, the company started with a big crew, laying a temporary track to the present site. The squatters, however, were not caught napping but broke camp and squatted on the present site before the track reached it. This in fact, was the only feasible site, for the very spring when we got there the fake town, which was in the river bottoms, would have been under from twenty to thirty feet of water, while Bismarck was high and dry. To be thus outwitted by the plebes roused the ire of the land company and to spite these sooners, the company built its shops and round-house, in the bottoms across the river and called the town Mandan. Both towns grew and prospered, in a way but between them there was bitter rivalry. The Bismarck paper never printed the name, Mandan but instead persistently referred to the place as Fifteenth Siding, while the Mandan paper retributed by referring to Bismarck, as Fourteenth Siding. That feeling was general with everyone in both towns. The railroad company especially fought Bismarck to the bitter end but as is generally the case in a matter of spite work, they finally concluded that to cut off their nose to spite their own face was neither pleasant nor profitable and were forced to eat humble pie.

As above stated, the Cooke interests had built the road as far as Bismarck and there had to let go. Some years later a newspaperman, of German descent named Henry Villard (I was told that the name had been Americanized by changing it from Hilgert to Hilliard and then to Villard) took hold of the company and succeeded in raising sufficient capital to complete the road. At that time he had to continue it from Mandan to the Montana line but there was no bridge across the Missouri. Thus the company had its shops and roundhouse on one side of the river and its road on the other. Trains were taken across on a huge ferry, consisting of tracks laid between two side-wheel steamers. This was a means to the end but only a makeshift. Bismarck, farthermore, had the edge on Mandan, owing to the fact that it had a first class steamboat landing while Mandan was about two miles distant from the river and all the freight for the forts and trading posts on the upper Missouri and Yellowstone had to be transferred at Bismarck. This left the rival town high and dry, as we might say but that was not literally the case for in the spring of 1881, before our arrival, the Missouri had gone on a rampage. It rose to such proportions as to almost reach the depot at Bismarck and Mandan was practically inundated. Stacks of drift ice were piled house-high in the streets and all the buildings besides being flooded, were filled with "Missouri mud" when the flood receded and no one who has never seen it can have any idea of what Missouri mud is. The boat landing, which had been close to Bismarck was now a couple of miles from the depot and new docks and warehouses had to be built but the railroad company lost no time in getting ready for the up-river trade.

Work on the N. P. extension had not begun and being forced to stay in Bismarck, we went to work assisting to raise a barge which had become imbedded in the silt during the freshet and here I learned what Missouri mud was. Two of us were carrying a railroad tie, when the leader fell and I was pulled over forward but being up to my boot-tops in the slimy silt could only crouch forward. Either I had to leave my boots behind or be extricated by my companions and the latter was done. This was Missouri mud. It is soft, smooth and sticky as glue. To get to this job we had to cross the river, and two men, who had sailed on the Great Lakes, rowed us back and forth. On landing us one day at noon, they positively refused to row us back, the whitecaps being high and with a dozen men in each boat, they considered it hazardous. In case of a spill the best swimmer would have been helpless for the water was so saturated with fine silt that it would have soaked into our clothes and weighted us down. When a pail of water was drawn from the river there would be so much sediment in it that more than a fourth of it would be mud, in the bottom of the pail.

We continued, for a few days, in the attempt to raise that scow out of the mud, by means of telegraph poles for levers and ties for fulcrums and as a foundation, but as soon as the ties were pushed under they sank into the slimy Missouri mud. One day, on our way home, Ulrich complained of being dog-tired and I remarked that he worked too hard. He bitterly retorted that the trouble was that just because some of us shirked, the rest had to do more than their share. I understood the implied meaning of this remark but made no reply. My partner had worked one winter in the pineries and before the season was over had come home, all played out, while I had spent all my winters either in going to school or teaching and therefore was rather soft and not fit to do two men's work like my over-ambitious friend. My summers had always been spent doing routine work on the farm while he had performed such arduous work as grubbing. For instance, on one occasion, on a job of clearing second growth timber. This, I think, he did in company with Rudy Mueller and Chris. Bardill and all of it by hand with the grub-hoe and shovel and their pay was twelve dollars an acre. No wonder I could not stand up alongside of a fellow who had made money under such circumstances for those boys had indeed done two men's work and today it would puzzle half a dozen fellows to do it. Those were real workmen and they never thought of going on strike but considered themselves lucky to have such a job and were justly proud of having accomplished it.

We abandoned that job about where it had been begun and I know not nor do I care whether it was ever accomplished but I suppose that my partner always had a faint suspicion that with enough he-men at it, that job could have been done, Missouri mud or no Missouri mud, but he did not have his grubbing partners with him to help him do it.

Our evenings and off days were mostly spent in Yegen's store and both the proprietor and our friend, his clerk, were intent on persuading us to desist from going farther west and locating on lands near Bismarck. Mr. Yegen especially, was very insistent, showing us over his own homestead, near town and enlarging on future possibilities, going so far even as to remark, "There is no reason why those hills should not eventually be converted into vineyards like the hillsides of Switzerland". This remark was induced by the fact that there were wild grapes growing in the Missouri bottoms. But neither the Missouri bottoms nor Missouri mud had any fascination for us. My partner was intent on shooting buffaloes and I wanted to locate in the "Golden Northwest". One day while we loafed in the store, a lanky, haggard man, a veteran of the Civil War, (they were then not yet old men) entered the store stating that he had returned from the Yellowstone valley. On hearing this, Albert immediately asked him what he thought of the Yellowstone country, for our information of course. The prompt reply was, "She's an ante-deluvian hell-roaring devil". This retort, of course, pleased both him and his boss and was greeted by both with peals of laughter. However, it neither phased nor discouraged the buffalo hunter nor the homeseeker.

Mr. Yegen employed, as a helper in his bakery, another Swiss, a Bernese, who had been all over the west and spun all kinds of yarns for us. This store was the Mecca of the few Swiss, in the town and here we met two chums and Bernese cronies of the baker afore mentioned. They had been (Senns) cheese and buttermakers in their home among the Alps and thence had been transferred to Norway where they were to practice this art and instruct others in it. There they had spent many years and one of them had married a "Norske Jente" and had a large family. They had come to Bismarck from upper Canada where they had learned a smattering of English and thus acquired a jargon that was amazing. They talked but one language and whether it was intended to be Swiss, Norwegian or English, it was always the same, a mixture of all three, much to the amusement and confusion of Ulrich, who understood well, about two thirds of what they said, while the rest was guesswork and he considered them a couple of funny old chaps. I was not so considerate and generally reminded them to try and confine themselves to one or the other of these languages but with little success. They however gave us much information on conditions prevailing in the Land of the Midnight Sun.

Two younger brothers and a sister of John Yegen also lived at Bismarck. They were new arrivals from Switzerland and their brother tried his utmost to locate them on some of the hills around Bismarck. This did not appeal to them and their stubborness, as he called it, aroused the displeasure of Alderman Yegen. One of them, Chris., with whom I became well acquainted, told me that he did not see why there should not be as much of an opportunity for them in a new town, as there was for John at Bismarck. The prosperous business man resented this attitude and did not approve of what he called their high faluting notions. Why should those greenhorns aspire to undertake, at once, what it took him years to accomplish. It did not occur to him that they were not as green as he imagined and that even in the Praettigaeu valley, their old home, things had changed since he left. He insisted and they refused. This irritated him to such an extent that he, at times, referred to them, not only as greenhorns but as "Schwyzerchueh", I wondered whether this compliment was not partially intended for two other fellows, from Alma, who could no less, than his brothers, see possibilities that awaited them among the hills around Bismarck.

Allow me to digress and give a brief account of the part that these so-called "Schwyzer-chueh" took in developing the West. Tired of this constant nagging and bossing of their prosperous brother, the boys finally decided to give him a rest and go west to try their luck. Alderman Yegen really meant well by the boys but went at it in the wrong way, forgetting that his younger brothers could be as independent as he. With a team they started west and I understand, stopped temporarily at railway workers' camps, supplying them with bakery products which they produced on a primitive outfit, carried with them. Be this as it may, they finally arrived at Billings, Montana, when that town was in its swaddling clothes and considering this an opportunity such as had been offered their brother, John, when he arrived at Bismarck, they went into business. I had not heard of them for years, in fact not until I had been in business, at Alma, for some time when, one day, my friend, Chris. Allemann, of the town of Montana, entered my office, accompanied by a stranger. Addressing me in his abrupt, frank manner, he said; "Edwin, this is my friend, Branger, of Lewistown, Montana, and since I have to go up to the courthouse, to serve on the jury and do not want to bore him with the routine proceedings of court, I want to leave him with someone who can entertain him intelligently and by whom he may perhaps be entertained in the same manner." Flattered by being thus distinguished, I assured him that I would be pleased to oblige both him and his friend.

How much Mr. Branger got out of this visit, I know not but if he got half as much out of it as I did, it was a most profitable and enjoyable occasion. In a roundabout way, I think from my friend, George Miller, I had learned that the Yegens, were established in that part of Montana and that the brother of Chris. had been in the Judith basin. On inquiring about the Yegens, of Mr. Branger, he replied by saying that he knew them indeed, since he and Chris. Yegen's brother were married to sisters. Their father-in-law, a Graubuendner "Landsman" of theirs had in early day squatted in the "Basin" and become a prosperous ranchman and extensive land owner and together with his sons and sons-in-law, had established a regular little baronetzy, in a little Switzerland among the fertile valleys of the rockies. The Yegens, he said, were the first word in Billings, where they had valuable holdings of real estate and were the leading bankers. Chris. Yegen was the mayor of that city and in that capacity had put the "Lid" on. In other words, he had put a stop to gambling and other orgies prevalent in frontier towns. In fact what the Brueggers had become at Williston, the Yegens had become at Billings only more so. Besides their interests at Billings they owned extensive horse ranches in charge of the brother, with whom, by the way, I had not become so well acquainted as with Chris. On this I got more definite information, from Martin Allemann, who, I understand, was for years in charge of a ranch, where their pure bred draft stallions were kept. This shed some light on a matter that puzzled me, when on scanning a map I had seen a station named Yegen and had wondered whether Alderman Yegen's "greenhorn" brothers might perhaps be, in some way, connected with this and it was, I learned, indeed their shipping point. I last heard of the Yegens, in 1927, when Mrs. Ganz and I, on our trip to the coast, met Miss Brandt former principal of our county normal, in the St. Paul depot. She informed us that she was state inspector of high schools for the eastern district of Montana. My first question, of course, was; "Do you know the Yegens?" The reply was; "Who, in Montana does not know the Yegens?" This was followed by an extensive account of

133

their business activities, in short she spoke of them as leaders in every laudable enterprise and as men of unquestioned integrity and ability. Being interested in a network of banks and extensive commercial enterprises, the depression, of course, must have had its effect on their business and although I have no details, I hope and trust that they may have weathered the storm, for you can not keep good men down.

This may not be helping to build the Northern Pacific but it is part of the history of the development of the Great Northwest and it may interest some of their Graubuendner countrymen, as well as others, to learn of the part that men like the Brueggers, the Yegens and that old pioneer of the Judith Basin have had in it.

The time arrived when we bid good-bye to Alderman Yegen, to Albert Utzinger and the rest of our friends as well as to the old scow, still peacefully resting in the Missouri mud and for all the worry that I had on that score it may still be resting there, although my partner may have felt some compunctions at leaving an unfinished job behind. That was not his way of doing things. Grading crews were getting ready to pull out of Mandan, going by train as far as Track's End and thence on foot and by team. To join one of these we crossed, on the Transfer, to Mandan and found that one Lamey, of Wabasha, was getting a number of cars ready to be transported to the end of the road thence to drive to where his grading job awaited him. He had a full crew but took on as many as desired to go that way, as blind baggage. There was no objection to going that way, least of all from the railroad company, since the only thing for us to do after getting there was to go to work for them and the fare back was five cents a mile.

We climbed into a car towards evening and found dozens of others, mostly Lamey's employees there. There were not many settlers nor stations west of Mandan and as it was night we would not have seen anything anyway and when day broke we were west of Dickinson and the first thing to interest us, was a dog-town or prairie-dog village. This covered hundreds of acres and thousands of the little fellows were gamboling about in the early sunlight. Soon we entered the Bad Lands and the sight, offered us, was indeed most interesting. Round hills both peaked and with flat tops, rose like little islands from the prairie and some of them showed layers of both red and black on their sides. Then there were endless tracts of petrified forests that looked for all the world like dry windfalls. These have long disappeared the material having been shipped east to be manufactured into fancy table tops and other ornamental articles. These things were absolutely new to us for although we had heard of the Bad Lands we had not expected anything like this. When we reached the Little Missouri the road passed through a cut that looked as if its sides had been built up from broken crocks or tiling and we were told that this was scoria and that it made first class ballast for the roadbed. We heard much theorizing among those in the car, how these little hills were of volcanic origin as well as the scoria. The fact is, the red and black strata exposed on the sides of the hillocks, were alternate layers of bituminous coal and burnt clay or scoria. This was caused by the coal having been set on fire from prairie fires or some other cause and the resultant heat having burnt the clay into material that looked like tile or pottery. Some portions where the fire, for some cause or other went out, were left standing and by erosion those buttes were shaped. This theory, at least, looks more plausible than the volcano story.

Here the banks of the river were high and steep, forming low bluffs not sloping like our bluffs but sheer and almost perpendicular and, of course, utterly devoid of vegetation of any kind. On seeing these steep banks we realized where some of the Missouri mud came from and we learned later that the Yellowstone was an equally liberal contributor. On the banks of this river, I suppose about where Medora is located now, was Fort Little Missouri, an outpost occupied by a couple of companies of infantry. Their quarters were mere barracks or log cabins built of cottonwood timber, cut in the river bottoms. Of fortifications, of any kind there was not a sign, unless the fact that the bark had not been removed from the logs, when the cabins were built, might be figured as fortification. The steep river banks, above referred to, were also lined with black streaks, strata of lignite coal and by the way, I read some time ago, an article in the American Magazine, stating that the coal, in this region alone, notably on Sand Creek a tributary of the Little Missouri, was sufficient to avert a shortage of fuel, in this country, for centuries to come. I hope that those who made this calculation were better mathematicians than the lumberjack, who some fifty years ago indignantly told me that the pineries of northern Wisconsin could not be exhausted in a million years.

Our train wobbled on over the rough new track and finally arrived at Sentinel Butte, which was in the main, merely a canvas town. Track's End or the base of supply from which the material for laying track was forwarded by a special train, serving that purpose, was some distance farther on, I think somewhat farther than where Beach is now situated. Here we got off and started to walk toward the scene of operations. We had practically abandoned the plan of joining a grading crew, perhaps because it was hard to get my partner past a place where work was to be had. Rifles and satchels on our shoulders we trudged across the prairie and after some time, to me it felt like a day's march, we came to where a pair of majestic elk's antlers was nailed to a telegraph pole and I remarked to Ulrich. "We are now entering the Territory of Montana", or something to that effect. Toward evening we arrived on the scene of operations and were assigned to a bunk in one of the cars fitted for that purpose. This bunk was devoid of either blankets or anything else along that line. We had a blanket apiece and with the shafts of our boots for pillows, went to sleep. Pretty tough for a couple of fellows used to feather beds. Next day we bought two more blankets and foraged some empty gunny sacks that the teamsters had discarded and filled them with hay that the horses had left over. This made better pillows than our boots yet the latter had amply served our purpose and are really not so bad provided you know how to arrange them. In case you wish to try it out I will be glad to show you how to do it. We evidently slept well for it was not until we awoke next morning, that we noticed the snow that had blown in on us during the night, the ventilation slides having been left open.

The next day was the eventful one when "Ule and I started to help building the North Pacific". The workmen, numbering a couple of hundred, were a motley crowd, most of them "dead broke". Some had been taking a winter's vacation while others who had worked in the woods, were strapped during the period of waiting for the spring work on the N. P., to open and almost all the tokens used in poker games, were navy beans furnished by the cooks. Ever and anon one of the old timers would size up a greenhorn, remaking "That fellow is going to work for me this summer". This meant that we would be the victims in future games after coming into money on pay-day. This of course, was one of their standing jokes.

The track-laying contract was held by Winston Bros., of Minneapolis, and while Phil. Winston, on horse back and clad in over-alls and duck coat, supervised the work, his brother Will; headed the office force.

There was, of course, a boss over every section or division of work and they must have sized us up right when they gave us our jobs.

Ulrich was sent to the very front and given a pick, with which to drag or pull ties up onto the dump, while I was given a job to hold up the ties while the spikes were being driven. I do not remember what the technical name of my job was but I had to use a crowbar with a block of wood attached as a fulcrum and bear down on the end of it. There were four in Ulrich's crew in the start but he told me that some of them did not amount to much and almost every day one or two quit and moved on while two of them, Ulrich and a deaf and dumb he-man (if not giant) held out and seeing that they liked their job, the boss soon neglected to fill the occasional vacancies and the two did alone what had been considered too much for four. This they did, of course, at the same pay that they drew before. They not only did the work but occasionally we would come to a crosstie on which quite a conversation had been scribbled, between those two gentlemen of leisure, the deaf-mute, being able to read and write.

I will now attempt, as well as I can remember to re-construct a tale of life in a construction camp and the mode of track-laying, as practiced half a century ago. To one who is familiar with present-day railroad building, this will appear primitive indeed. Although I was never employed at grading, I know that most of it was done with scrapers, wheel scrapers having just been introduced but most of it being done with the old kind. Then there was station work. This was a one man's job with shovel and wheel-barrow and years later I saw traces of it in the Trempealeau and Chippewa bottoms along the Burlington. The ditches from which the ground was removed were equilaterally cut from the sod and the yardage from which the workmen's pay was derived was obtained by measuring these excavations, which was the reason for making them so accurately. Yes, even in the days of constructing the Burlington such primitive methods were employed. One scorching, hot July day when I took passage from Alma to La Crosse, on one of the first Burlington locals, in charge of Conductor Sullivan, I think, I saw on the prairie between Alma and Fountain City, a gang of men shoveling dirt onto a flat car and among the crew I recognized a grey headed, old friend of mine who was performing this menial labor to raise money to pay a debt incurred by signing a note for another who would have been far better able to do this work than my old friend. On many a morning, on our way to school, had we met his bent form coming up the road on his way to mass, with his hands folded on his back and well do I remember his cheery "Good marnin children, Good marnin". The facts in this case were revealed to me, when years later, he came to the schoolhouse where I taught, to exhibit to me the papers in the case and again when I called on him as census enumerator. I only hope that he may now be reaping the reward that he so fervently and hopefully looked forward to, for he certainly deserved it. But now back to my story of railway construction and I trust that my readers will pardon me for this digression.

The real "Bulls" of our gang were the fellows who handled the rails, for although the rails were not steel but iron and only part the size of present day rails, this was a grueling job. The rails were brought from Track's End on a flat car and the gang had to transfer them onto a lorry by hand. This lorry was a huge pushcar with iron rollers on the ends. This car was pulled by a horse hitched to a long rope. This horse was, by a rider, galloped to the required place where the rails were needed, when the brake was applied and the men took hold of the ends and when the boss sang out something like, "Whoap Down" the iron dropped not with a dull thud but with a metallic ring and woe to the toes that were not in their proper place when it landed. In fact, one fellow did have his foot in the wrong place once. He was sent to the hospital but soon came back on crutches and hobbled around the camp. There was no such thing as workman's compensation, in those days.

After the rail was dropped the straps (without flanges) were bolted on and the end and center spikes driven home when the lorry rolled on until the last rail was unloaded and back the horse galloped for another load while the rest of the spikes were driven home. The track was then temporarily lined up and the tampers followed with their shovels to work the ground under the ties. The road was now ready for travel by the construction train. The ties, mostly seasoned cotton-wood and elm and green tamarack were hauled up by team and distributed along the track. It was on the surface of the smooth tamarack ties that the deaf-mute and his partner scribbled their occasional conversations, above referred to. When they found time for this no one but they themselves knew.

For our accommodation, as stated, there were huge box car kitchen and dining rooms with bunk rooms upstairs. Our bill of fare was simple but substantial. No fresh meat and no vegetables, not even potatoes, for they were four dollars a bushel, at Mandan. Cured ham

(Pork you know, was two cents a pound) with navy beans was the staple. Then there was good bread and biscuits, puddings and custards, pies, etc. and of course, tea and coffee, with sugar but no milk. Then we always had stewed, dried blackberries. These came without any lining and had been picked and dried by Indians. They were superficially washed but were always more or less grimy. We were given to understand that they were made part of the menu to counteract the effects of the alkali water, which we drank. One morning the cookee varied his usual call to breakfast by singing out, "Roll out, tumble out, any way to get out" by adding "Eggs for breakfast this morning". Did they roll out and tumble out and did they eat eggs? I took more than I usually eat but although they were not spoiled they tasted stale and I could not get enthused over them. Some fellows boasted that they had eaten a dozen or more. They were packed in salt barrels with chopped straw, for keeping them from being broken.

We could have stood the "grub" all right but the water was something else again, especially with Ulrich, used to that sparkling spring water, gushing out between rocks or bubbling up from the sand. The water was dipped up from pools on the prairie and had the color of strong tea and where it had receded the grass was covered with alkali crystals, for all the world like hoar frost and this is no exaggeration.

A "water-monkey" carrying two pails suspended and a dipper in each pail made the rounds, starting in front and going down the line until he reached Ulrich and his partner. To counteract the alkali a pound or two of oatmeal was put into the bottom of each pail and whenever the supply ran out the pails were refilled and the watering taken up where it had been left off. Often when the end was reached, the dipper had to be pressed down into the slop to produce something to drink and Ulrich remarked to me that it was just like slopping the hogs, at home and I might have truthfully added, only worse. One night we stopped at a place where a grading camp had been and there was a square hole with cool water in it. The next evening Ulrich proposed that we go back there to get a drink. On returning to camp he said he was about as thirsty as when we started out for the water hole, which after all contained nothing but alkali water but Ulrich said it was at least not luke-warm. Every day we laid out a mile or more of track thus we never camped in the same place more than one night.

139

Our water-carrier was a meek little German, from Milwaukee, who was not used to such environments but no one bothered him for it was beneath the rough-necks in the crowd to condescend to bother with a tenderfoot and we were all left severely alone. There was another German from Milwaukee, a husky, up-standing fellow. He was the water carrier's brother-in-law and by trade a cook and baker but had to do common work here, as the jobs in his line were filled. We got quite chummy with those two.

When we left Bismarck there was not a green leaf to be seen anywhere and since coming out onto the prairie there was not even a tree, to say nothing of a green one, thus one afternoon when I espied ahead of us something that looked like green current bushes, I could hardly wait for six o'clock so that I might investigate. Supper was dispatched with celerity and off I rushed for my green bushes. They were the tops of box-elder bushes, growing along a creek. It was a sizeable creek of clear, cold water and after drinking my fill, off came my rags and with one bound I was in the clean, cold water. That was a real treat but on returning to the camp, Ulrich said, "Your boss was looking for you to help unload a car of ties, on over-time pay". Well that was that. I probably had incurred the displeasure of a grouchy boss but I had a drink of clear water and a good swim. Next day (Sunday forenoon) we laid the side-track for a station near Beaver Creek.

It was, I think, during the following week that measles broke out in the camp and Ulrich had never had the measles. Crowded into the bunk car and with about half a dozen drinks daily, of slop out of dipper that everybody from the iron gang down had used before it reached him, what chance did the poor fellow have? In the mean time, I had developed a beautiful case of quinsy and was confined to the bunk-car. I was not surprised when one evening my friend came in all flushed and remarked, "I guess I have the measles". There were some more remarks about keeping children away from the blanked stuff when there would be an opportunity to take care of them at home, only to cause them to be exposed to it in some wild, isolated place. Well, he was a very sick boy, who had kept at work as long as he could wiggle, of course. Everyone was solicitous, in a way, and the cooks furnished me with tin after tin of hot ginger tea, which I carried to him as hot as I could bear it but he always shook his head and remarked "It might be all right if it were warm". This alarmed me for it was not only warm but hot. My quinsy was, for the time being forgotten.

Next Sunday morning one of the crew who wore buckskins but had, for some reason, neither gun nor ammunition begged me to let him have Ulrich's rifle and to go hunting with him. Ulrich said it was all right, provided I went along. I dragged myself away from camp but soon lost sight of the professional hunter, who fairly skimmed over the ground. I lay down in the sun, all in, when I heard a shout from some fellows, who had started out after us and on looking up I beheld, within close range, a beautiful black-tail buck standing in front of me. I was a fairly good marksman but besides being weak and shaky, I could not look into those velvety, brown eyes and shoot that beautiful animal and I have never felt real sorry since. I dragged myself back to camp, where an account of my valor had preceded me and I was duly razzed, for my inefficiency. The hunter, with Ulrich's gun also returned, in due time, but had no such opportunity as I.

After dinner, it was noised about that in a gully, close by, some bootleggers had a couple of barrels of whiskey and the unanimous verdict, in which our Milwaukee friends joined, was that this was just the medicine that my patient needed. I therefore set out for the bootlegger's camp and purchased a good sized bottle of the stuff, which after having received the O. K. of our Milwaukee friend, I presented to my patient. He took a liberal draught of the "medicine", and remarked that he needed some of that tea for a wash. On returning, imagine my dismay when he whispered, "I can't talk loud anymore". My first thought was, "His vocal chords are paralyzed". Here I was with a boy on my hands whom his mother could justly accuse me of having enticed into this wilderness only to become thus afflicted. Now I did really forget my quinsy.

The consensus of opinion now was that the patient had to be taken to a hospital and the nearest one was at Fort Abraham Lincoln, on top of a bluff, near Mandan. Our Milwaukee friend whose name I never learned also advised this. Names were no object in our gang and Ulrich was known as Frog (Frenchman) while I went by the name of Turk (Swede) our complexions determining our nationality. How wise it was to keep one's own counsel, I learned early in the game. One night when we were in our bunks, a discussion arose as to whether Dakota and Montana were states or territories. The consensus of opinion was that while Dakota was a state Montana was a territory.

Attempting to act as umpire, I was about to pipe up when I got a nudge with an elbow in my ribs (they were already much in evidence) and heard a hiss in my ear, something like "Halt's Muul" meaning "Shut up" in good English and shut up it was. Thus much for intimacies in that gang.

My Milwaukee friend offered to buy my Winchester for which he paid me, in cash, what it had cost me. To me it was good riddance and to him, I hope it proved a bargain. I went to headquarters and succeeded in wheedling out of them sick-passes to Mandan, although they intimated that I was really not very sick, although, as far as being able-bodied was concerned, I was really the worst off of the two, for Ulrich had recovered from the measles all but his throat trouble. I could talk loud enough but my weight had dwindled to a little over one hundred sixty pounds, from a normal of two hundred.

Before speaking of our return trip I must mention the fact that every day grading crews passed our camp and one day, my old school mate, Albert Binder, on passing waved at me and shouted "Hello Edwin". At another time I saw a form limping toward camp and at once, made it out to be John Brethauer, on his way to Miles City, per stage coach. The stage fare hurt but the poor fellow could positively not make it on foot. Ulrich also met him after dinner. Then I must mention another thing which especially distressed my partner. Wherever we were out on the prairie, the landscape was dotted with white spots, one of them covering an acre or more and lo and behold these spots were made up of scores of buffalo skeletons bleeching in the sun. Thus at times hundreds, aye thousands of these skeletons were in sight. Some of them had been killed only a year or two before and here was a passionate hunter, with a first class gun, only a year or two too late.

Some years later, I read an account in a magazine about two Boston lads, who were in this very territory and used their heads. They bought an old team and wagon and picking up these bones, shipped them east by the car load, to say nothing of the horns which were all perfectly preserved and within s few years brought fancy prices. So there would have been a chance that would have suited me, had I only thought of it but I fear it would have been poor consolation for my friend who had come out west too late. One morning we therefore climbed onto a flat car, part of the construction train, that was to take us to Sentinel Butte. Here we had to stay until in the afternoon of the next day. Having a lot of time on my hands, I wandered out upon the prairie and just out of town happened upon a pair of elk's antlers, which I raised up by the tips and standing between them they reached up to my shoulders yet they had been left lying by the one who had butchered the animal and by me also. After this exercise the swelling in my throat broke and I was rid of the quinsy. We had to stop all night but could not get a room so we were assigned the wash room for sleeping quarters. It was close quarters but better than out of doors. In the morning my bed partner happened to touch the floor with his hand and whispered "Is this where I have been sleeping all night?" I told him that although the floor was soaked from a leaky sink and we had to furnish our own blankets and our own boots for pillows, our night's lodging had cost us only fifty cents apiece.

After traveling all next night we reached Mandan early in the morning and I proposed to go and make inquiries as to ways and means of getting to Fort Lincoln and the hospital. My patient replied you may go if you feel like it but I do not see any need of doing so on my part. That ended my plans and as I had for myself never needed any hospital care I agreed to go with him back to Bismarck. We got onto the Transfer and after landing climbed up the bank and trudged on toward the old town, that we had left not many weeks before.

We walked but a few blocks before we again espied Albert Utzinger, not in front of the bakery but in front of a saloon, where he served as part-time bar tender, leading an orchestra in a vaudeville show in the evening and also conducting a brass band. Glad again, we stepped in a three handed game of "jass". Soon we heard a voce behind us, asking "What in the duce are you fellows playing"? and on receiving the reply "jass" the onlooker said "I'll be blamed if you are not all three from Alma, Wisconsin, for that is the only place where that game is played." He had worked on the Beef Slough Rafting works and knew what he was talking about.

To show how small a world this is let me relate another case in point not connected with this story but an incident concerning Easterners in the West and especially the game of jass. Conrad Wald, Ulrich's cousin, was sitting in a card room, at Aspen, Colorado with his prospecting partner, when the latter nudged him, saying, "Say Con. Did you ever hear of a game where they say, nell, boor, stack, three cards sack and meld?" Con's reply was "Did I? Boy, I was raised on that. Almost every evening I went to my uncle's house and although I was never taken into the game, I sat and watched four old cronies play it. That's jass, but where in the world did you hear of it?"

"In a little town, called Waumandee, back in Wisconsin".

"Why that's just a few miles from my old home and one of my cousins is married to a Waumandee boy."

"What's his name?"

"Ganz".

"Pshaw, I was to his sister's weddin'. I came up there from Illinois with a young fellow, named Jake Angst, who took over his Dad's farm and Sundays I used to go to the little town and play that game with a bunch of Swiss farmers".

Those two boys had known each other for years and worked side by side, prospecting and mining but never had it occurred to either of them to ask the other where he was from. That was the western code and still is among miners and cowboys. They had nothing to hide from anyone but lived up to the code until this slip revealed a glimpse into their past. This miner's name was Charley Hurlburt but inquiry from my old Waumandee friends revealed little but that they vaguely remembered such a man until I asked Pulaski Johnson, that star reminiscenser, who brightened up at once and remarked "Of course, do I remember Charley."

Some time after Con. had quit mining he met Charley in town and with a shout of joy the latter approached him, saying "I've made a strike of fifty thousand dollars and am going right back to Wisconsin to buy the best ranch in Waumandee Valley." Poor Charley, never again saw old Waumandee but I am glad to say that later on, he again struck it and this time for seventy-five thousand dollars, which he forthwith turned into a trust fund, placing it with the Pythian Lodge, to which he belonged. This insured him a safe income for life, the residue going to the order. Thus, at least one prospector finally came to his senses and both his Wisconsin and his Colorado friend, assured me that, at heart, Charley was a prince of a fellow.

Speaking of jass, I could not well omit this story which gives another close-up view of life in the "Wild and woolly West of by-gone days." But now back to our game, at Bismarck. I lost the first one and got a horse laugh from my adversaries and it was audible on the part of both of them. Was I glad? Willingly would I have lost a dozen games to hear that rollicking laugh of my friend, who had again regained control of his vocal organs. Two more games were played with the

144

same result and every time and at intervals during the games rang out that ringing laugh. When we left the place to look for a hotel, Ulrich remarked "Heck, you didn't lose all those games. Albert jiggled the chips, taking some from your pile and placing them onto mine etc." My reply was, "What the deuce do I care where the chips went to or came from, as long as you got your laugh and your voice back." This was the second and perhaps the last game for me in a saloon but it was immensely gratifying and satisfactory to me and all I had to say was "Halt's Muul," and he did, outside of peal after peal of laughter. We stayed at the hotel that day but the next afternoon found us shoveling sand onto a wagon, for the road commissioner of Bismarck, who had picked us up, strolling on the streets. Half a day of this, in the sweltering sun, was enough and we again went to work for the N. P. R. R. Co.

Ulrich got a job helping to build that "S" curve approach to the N. P. R. R. bridge across the Missouri. It was handling a wheel scraper and the implement being a new invention and yet very crude it was hard to handle but that did not phase him. I got a job as section hand in the yards, which included the tracks near the depot as well as those near the levee.

Here we again met our Swiss-Norwegian friends, one of them working with me and one with Ulrich. The one who had a family, commiserately informed us that during our absence, his oldest "Jente" had become enamored of a young German and our chances had therefore gone aglimmering. As a consolation, he continued that there was another younger one still to be had and one day when we worked on the outskirts of town he remarked, "There comes my other Jente". What I saw, was a little girl pushing a baby carriage and mischievously I asked, "The one inside or the one outside of the carriage." He replied that he meant the big one of course and that next year she would be fourteen. I told him that I was not interested in cradle robbery and that the only Jente that I was interested in had been fourteen a number of years ago. Yet Ulrich and I always referred to him as "Schwiegervater", even though we were not interested in his Jentes.

Day after day the boats came down the river and all were loaded with buffalo hides to within a few feet of the tops of the smokestacks. All the boats were Nigger-boats and on every arrival the Niggers went on strike and their wages had to be raised before they

145

started to unload. This they did by dragging the hides, which were stiff as boards, by holding them by the tail over their shoulder. They were then handed to an expert (?) stacker who stood on top of a pile, about the size of a big straw stack. While performing this work, the stacker always kept the top layer looking like a plate or dish, pitching the hides leisurely outward and upward. On watching them, one evening, I remarked to Ulrich, "Do you think it would pay the owners of those hides to hire us at the rate of ten dollars a day to do the stacking for them?" His reply was, I don't know, but he did know and I soon found out.

In order to lay a side-track, which was needed on the levee, we had to pull out the corner of one of these stacks and lo and behold, when we reached the second tier the hair came off the hides in big blotches and thousands of big, fat maggots wriggled all over them. The work was stopped then and there and next day a crew from Minneapolis was at work taking the stack apart and sprinkling the hides with a solution of Paris Green. When I asked the foreman, what they were going to do about it, he said they would patch them up with calf hides. To the question of how many hides were in the stack he replied, "Oh about fourteen thousand". How much do you think they could have saved by paying us ten dollars a day for doing this job in a workmanlike manner, which good grain stackers could have easily done?

There were other stacks like this on the levee. I do not remember how many but there must have been more than a hundred thousand hides at a time. We learned that a single hunting party had killed 28,000 buffaloes up on the Yellowstone the preceeding winter. They would surround them, shoot them all down and then move on. Another gang would follow up and perhaps cut out the tongues and with the aid of a pony jerk off the hides and leave the rest to the wolves and coyotes and the skeletons to bleach in the sun. The hides, the man from Minneapolis told me, cost them about $1.50 a-piece, including calf hides. This was not hunting. It was slaughter and I know that a hunter like Ulrich would not have gotten a kick out of it. Thus he really did not miss so much.

Another big event, during our second stay at Bismarck, was when the Steamer General Sherman docked at the levee, not with a cargo of buffalo hides but of Indians. The General Sherman was not a Niggerboat but a Government boat. She came in one Saturday night

146

and had aboard Sitting Bull's band of Indians, captured in Canada. Among others with the "Big Chief", as I remember them were Crazy Horse, Low Dog and Crow Dog, with their squaws. Their captors offered to take them up town on the stub train that ran from the levee to the depot but the chiefs solemnly and defiantly shook their heads, refusing to ride behind a fire and smoke spitting "Devil-wagon". A requisition was sent to Fort Abraham Lincoln for canopy top, three seated spring wagons, each drawn by the regulation four mule team and in them the notables proudly rode up to the ball-room of the Sheridan House. Here they sat smiling and grinning along the walls, while the curious crowds inspected them. The "Bull" was a rather fat, unimpressive looking Indian and did not appear the killer that he was reputed to be. In those days bosom shirts, buttoned behind and with a stiff tortoise-like bosom, in front, were in style. Sitting Bull wore one of these but it was buttoned in front with the bosom behind, looking for all the world like the shell of a turtle, on his back. To cap the climax, the shirt, originally white was now dirty and of an ashen gray color. All of the Indians wore correspondingly unique uniforms, none appearing clad in blankets. They all had their hair very neatly done up and braided. Sitting Bull's coiffure being especially neat. It was so nicely parted that the hairs seemed to have been counted and where his braid had been gathered there was left a circle so perfect that it might have been designed by a pair of compasses. All parts of his scalp exposed by the parting of the hair were dyed a brilliant red. Outside of this decoration none of the Indians wore any paint.

They enjoyed being in the limelight and seemed to have a good time. Sitting Bull, who could scrawl his name soon began to commercialize this as well as his popularity or notoriety. He signed autographs at a quarter per, while his numerous pipes etc. brought all the way from a quarter up. They spent the afternoon on the boat, which was laid up for Sunday, going down river after midnight. The rest is history.

One day it was announced that President Villard's special would pass through Bismarck and it did about 6 p. m. Landlord Bly of the Sheridan House, prepared for a grand reception. Albert Utzinger was hired with his band and the depot and hotel were decorated but it was a case of, "Smarty had a party", for although somebody came he paid no attention to either the blacklisted City of Bismarck, the band or Landlord Bly; remaining decorously and quietly in his private car

147

during the half hour's stay. What kind of an ovation he got at Mandan, his own fifteenth siding, I do not know.

On the third of July, while working on the section, we heard a bass drum up town sounding like the tolling of a bell. An Irish friend of mine, in the crew, told me that they were tolling for General Garfield who had been shot. He meant the president, of course.

Next day there was a big celebration and a ball game between a mine from Fort Lincoln and some local players. Mandan probably had a ball team too but a game between such rivals was out of the question. I had for company my schoolmate, Albert Binder, who had returned from his grading work out West. When we came to where the free ice-cream was being dispensed, it had melted and I thus missed my first taste of that delicacy. There were fireworks in the evening and Albert dramatized the affair, by attributing every pyrotechnic display to "Old Moeckel", who seems to have been at the head of such affairs in Albert's boyhood days, at Fountain City. Thus we celebrated the Fourth at Bismarck and I have never seen Albert since.

Soon after the Fourth, I left the section, for with the thermometer registering 110 above, at times, it got too hot for me. Albert Utzinger, who was a harness maker, now worked for two brothers, who came from Watertown, Wis., and of course, were friends of our own Johnny Bruegger. One of the brothers had a farm about four miles out of town and offered me a job. This was more to my liking and I bid the Northern Pacific good bye, for good. I got along very well without them and I know that no one missed me, for as a railroader I was short of being a howling success. My new boss, who was rather odd in some ways, put me to work breaking the prairie, which would have suited me fine had it not been for the abundance of "niggerheads", which dulled my plow so that it had to be hammered and filed, at least once for every round that I made. My boss, who had spent much time in Western Kansas and claimed that he could smell water, then put me to work at pulling ground up from a well he was digging. One day toward noon, he told me that he could smell water. I got a gallon tin pail and letting it down to him shouted, "Prove it". He dug extra deep in one corner of the hole and sent up a pail of muddy water. After leaving it to settle, I got my first drink of good water, since coming out West. It was free from alkali, while up to then we got our supply from pools in a marsh. We now curbed the well, up to the top of the water level and from then on, lived high.

One day we drove five or six miles farther out into the hills, (John Yegen's prospective vineyard) where another harnessmaker from Watertown, who worked in the shop for my boss, had a homestead. Here we were to make hay and lo and behold, before supper, my "watersmelling" boss dug about three or four feet down to a ledge of rock and here too, we had a spring of good, fresh water. After making a stack of hay we returned to the home farm and one day, while we were nooning in the shade, my boss remarked, that the southwest wind which had been blowing for some days past, ought to soon produce some grass hoppers. He had, of course, seen them before but delighted in being mysterious. Pointing up in the air he remarked, "can't you see them?" On receiving a negative reply, he told me to close one eye and cup the other with my hand. I replied that it could hardly be snowing with the thermometer at over a hundred in the shade. He replied, what looks like snow, is the hoppers, you greenhorn. I had guessed as much but would not rob him the pleasure of enlightening a greenhorn. When I asked, what now? He calmly replied that if the air was still full of them when the wind went down they would settle right here and they did.

On Sunday morning, July 31st, on my way to Bismarck, where I figured on taking a train for the harvest fields in the Red River valley, I passed his field of oats, still green and it was literally covered with the pests. Thus I saw vanish the oats that I had allotted to the four horse team I had been driving but I was not badly worried for I knew that my boss made enough in the harness shop to buy oats for his horses and meet other expenses on the farm. His oats were rather mediocre anyway. On the flat occupied by Bismarck there were however some fine, ripe crops of grain. One field of waving, golden wheat covering a section, owned by ex-President Hayes was exceptionally fine as was a large field of oats, running right up to the city limits. Here too, as I walked along, I saw these marauders at work and the heavy kernels of oats dropped to the ground, as one by one they were severed from the stems. That beautiful field had always been to me what in the popular vernacular is known as, "A sight for sore eyes" and now it too was doomed to destruction.

I got to town and there Albert Utzinger informed me that my partner had left for Crookston the night before. This puzzled me as we had agreed to leave on that Sunday. Arriving at Yegen's store, I was given another surprise when the alderman held out a copy of the

Pioneer Press to me, remarking "See here what one of our countrymen has been doing down your way." Down our way it was indeed, for the paper contained a detailed account of the Held tragedy in Eagle Valley. Mr. Held and family had come from Praettigaed, in the Canton of Graubuenden, Switzerland and on the advice of one of his countrymen, he bought a farm in this valley, a veritable colony of his own country folks. He located on the place and made plans to operate the farm, when things began to happen. The broad fields of tall, waving grain began to turn white and gray instead of golden yellow, black rust and blight having taken their usual toll and to cap the climax, the draft with which he was to pay for the farm, due to arrive from Switzerland, failed to come. All this so worried him that he became insane but showed no sign of it, outside of being despondent, until he committed the rash act, related in the daily handed me. The previous Sunday, it stated, on his way to church, the neighbor who had advised Held to buy the farm, noticed the deathly quiet prevailing at the Held homestead and on investigating was met by a sight which so impressed him that he was never again the same man. In the yard lay the dead body of Mrs. Held with an ugly gash in her forehead, while other members of the family were found dead and dying all over the premises, Held with a bullet in his brain. Two boys had slept in the hay barn and while dragging herself to look after them, Mrs. Held had fallen dead in the yard. It was a ghastly tale ameliorated only by a recital of the heroic efforts made by Doctor Hidershide, of Arcadia, to save the lives of some of the wounded children.

Day and night without cessation he remained on duty and succeeded in saving the lives, of, I think, three of the children. At this I was not surprised, for had I not heard of his heroic work during a diphtheria epidemic, when for several weeks, he was on the road day and night catching snatches of sleep, while his driver took him from house to house where the scourge raged. This doctor may have been neither an eminent physician nor surgeon but he certainly was a true type of "The Country Doctor". At the very time that this rash act was committed that draft had arrived and was lying in the postoffice at Fountain City. Later on, I met two of the Held children and my friends, with whom they were visiting, told me that they said that the white scars above their temples were made by a stranger, who one night came to their home and killed their parents and sisters and brothers. They were fine children and may they never have learned

150

the truth. I, much later, also learned that Mr. Yegen had real cause for being so agitated, since he and Held had been schoolmates, in the old home. This he did not tell me but at any rate, they came from the same village.

Tragic as this story was, it was not all the calamitous news that this copy of the "Press" contained, from down my way. There was more. A span of horses had been stolen from my friend, Fritz Thuemmel, near Fountain City. He and his son-in-law, Mr. Clausen, who was a deputy sheriff, went in pursuit but the horses had been turned loose, owing to the fact that they were so heavy with foal that a rapid escape was impossible. The thieves, who were hidden near where the horses were found, however, forced the deputy sheriff to take them to the northern part of the county, in his two seated spring wagon, keeping him and Mr. Thuemmel well covered with their guns. The trip was made during the night, of course. In some out of the way place between Mondovi and Durand they made him swear to not reveal their whereabouts and went toward Durand, on foot. Mr. Clausen, evidently and justifiably, did not consider an oath exacted in this manner as binding. At any rate when the horse thieves entered Durand, Sheriff Coleman and his brother, who was his deputy, lay in waiting for them, with their Winchesters but alas, the desperadoes were too quick at the trigger for them and both officers fell mortally wounded. The murderers fled and for weeks, were hiding in the Chippewa bottoms, all efforts of desperate posses, to capture them proving vain, although I think, one of them had been wounded. Traces where a skiff had been pulled up on shore, were found also the left-overs of a steer that had been killed. I do not remember whether or not one of them was finally captured, then and there or whether he was brought back from Nebraska, on requisition papers but I do know that he never killed a sheriff or anybody else.

When he was brought into the Durand courthouse, for preliminary examination, a rope was unceremoniously slipped around his neck and he was dragged down the stairs and hanged to a tree in the yard, the enraged populace never stopping to tie the rope to the limb over which it had been slung but doing the job by hand. No questions were asked and to this day nobody seems to know or care who had a hold of that rope. I have forgotten the details of the other fellow's fate but do know that he too, soon came to a bad end. The story in the "Press", of course, dealt only with the murder of the

Colemans, the rest of it, I learned as it developed and at that I may not have all the details but the story is substantially correct. The murderers went by the aliasses of Williams and Maxwell but the latter was perhaps their right name. The Colemans were former Buffalo County boys, having resided on Maxville prairie and whenever I drive past that farm with that lane of jackpines, running from the house to the road, it must needs remind me of the tragic end of the two courageous officers who lost their lives, in the performance of their duty.

I spent until train time with my friend Albert Utzinger, reminiscing about by-gone days and getting firsthand information about affairs, in and around Crookston. He advised me to look up his brother, Conrad, who kept a hotel at Crookston. I have not seen this genial friend since but learned that he later on left for Astoria, Oregon, where his musical talent found recognition and where he has been employed as director and leader of orchestras and bands continuously. It was but a year or two ago that I learned he was still thus employed, although over eighty years of age.

When the train entered the Red River valley, the jet black fields that we had seen in the spring were now golden yellow and on the Dalrymple farms, instead of seeders, binders were now marching down the fields in files of dozens and scores.

At Glyndon, I had to change to the Manitoba road for Crookston. The land here, as well as all the way to Crookston, was level as a floor and mile after mile there was nothing but virgin prairie covered by knee-high, luscious grass. Ada was a familiar name since many Buffalo County people had located in that neighborhood, along the Wild Rice River. Here the country was well settled but farther on there were again those vast tracts of wild prairie and I could not see why such land was not being cultivated.

Arriving at Crookston, I forthwith went to Utzinger's hotel and the landlord greeted me like a relative although we had met but once or twice before. I had never met his wife but she was a fine, motherly woman and made me at home, at once. After dinner I drove, with John Moser, out to a farm which Utzinger was operating, his brother Henry, being in charge. As far as we drove the crops were exceptionally good and I remarked to Mr. Moser, whom I had known quite well in Alma, on the fact that so much of that fine land up the line was not being cultivated. At first he was rather evasive but when I could not understand, he told me it was too flat and would be hard to drain. I was surprised for I knew from the vegetation that it must be perfectly dry and not marshy. With one of his characteristic winks, my mentor replied, "You should have seen those flats about seeding time and you would have used a boat instead of a plow." This surprised me but I took Mr. Moser's word, for not only was he well qualified to render a decision but he was so loyal to the Red River valley that this admission was made with reluctance only but I really suspect that it was his way of saying, "Look twice before you jump." I was so used to shunning hills that I fancied that all level land was desirable, but now know better.

On getting back to town I looked around for my lost partner going from one to the other of our Alma acquaintances but no one had seen him or heard of him. With some of our Buffalo County friends, I then went out to their farm but worked a few days only, the effects of alkali water, getting the best of me. Coming back to town on Saturday, Mr. Utzinger told me to hang around until Sunday, when some friends of his would come and take me out to their farm, where a stacker was needed. Sunday brought Father and Mother Wiedenhoefer and with them their son, Karl, or as I learned later the old folks came with Karl but that was something that the old gentleman would never admit and Karl humored him, although on the farm he was boss but told me that I should let "Father" have his way and do things as I knew best. Father had stacked the barley but it had rained and the barley was "sweating" after that hard rain and Karl wanted a stacker who could build stacks that would not "sweat" after it rained, so I went home with them in the evening, to their farm, near Fisher.

Fisher was a small town on a branch of the Manitoba, connecting Crookston and Grand Forks. Every forenoon the train would go west and every afternoon it would return. The track from Fisher eastward was perfectly straight and when the train came toward you the front of the locomotive would loom up before you and when it was past, all you could see was the rear of the last coach. A strange sight for one, who as the saying goes, was used to tracks with curves, on rounding which the engineer shakes hands with the rear brakey. This piece of road, I think, formed the nucleus of the Great Northern of today. Between Crookston and Fisher this road was never far from the Red Lake River and between its track and the river lay a stretch of farm land as good as any out of doors.

From a point a few miles west of Crookston to within a mile of Fisher, all this rich land was owned by thrifty Germans. A group of these had come from Manitowoc County, Wis., having arrived there a generation or two too late to be able to take advantage of the homestead act but they had struck it here. All these families were related and had originally come from Northern Germany (Schwaben) as were several other families, relatives of theirs. So I had struck a veritable German colony, out on the prairies of the Red River valley and in order to reveal to you something of the busy, happy life led by them, I am going to deal, at some length on my stay among these good people. This will also show you the difference, in the pioneering practiced by them from the experiences of Buffalo County pioneers two or three decades earlier. All these farms extended into the river bottoms and therefore everybody had an abundance of fire wood and most of then lived in log cabins although the price of lumber in the big saw mill, at Crookston, was reasonable and some of those farmers had good sized frame barns.

Besides the members of the Wiedenhoefer family, already mentioned, there was a younger brother, Jacob, who worked for Karl and called him "Boss" and as boss I will also speak of him. They also had a sister, Marie. On Monday morning the boss told me that his father and I were to take one of their ox-teams and start stacking wheat. The rest of the force was to cut wheat with the horses and binder. Deliberately the old gentleman drove the oxen into a grand field of wheat shocks near the house, remarking that God's blessing rested upon that field and that it always yielded at least thirty-five bushels to the acre and I knew it would yield at least that. When I got down to pitch bundles to him he told me that when I had pitched six hundred bundles onto the load, he would tell me and we would start to unload. We finally accomplished this but not before I had been told that I did not know how to drive oxen. This I readily admitted, for although I knew the meaning of gee and haw, I knew nothing about swinging the whip, having never driven oxen before. We unloaded that load and when we had on another quota of exactly six hundred bundles, the old gentleman unhitched the oxen and wending our way homeward, we went to lunch but not before baiting the "Oexli" with a forkful of prime hay. In the house we sat down to what looked like a regular meal and when I finally hinted that we ought to get back to work, I was told that when there was not time for meals anymore, it was about time to quit work. After unloading the load awaiting us and one other, our stack was finished and would you believe it, when the stack was threshed it yielded about a hundred bushels. Thus it appears we had done a fair half day's work, in spite of the elaborate lunch. After dinner it started to rain just enough to stop work and the boss suggested that I accompany him to "The Landing". This meant Fisher, that station, in the days of the flatboat, having borne the name of Fisher's Landing and to the boss, who had himself helped propel flatboats, it was still, "The Landing".

William Wiedenhoefer, a brother of the boss, in company with an uncle, kept the Northern Tier Hotel, at Fisher. This was our destination the boss having an assortment of choice vegetables to deliver there. These were the product of their father's garden which was a model of its kind. Here we met August Wenzel, a neighbor and one of the group that had come from Manitowoc. He was a stately man, outstanding in appearance and demeanor. He was an accepted leader in the community, although few if any were conscious of the fact. He was diplomatic rather than domineering and had a way of getting things to go as he wanted them to go by leading his followers to believe that he was taking orders from them. Whenever he could not make them see things his way he submitted cheerfully. Thus he was easily the leader in civic, church and social affairs.

The boss and this neighbor visited until the train came in from Grand Forks. As it stopped, a young fellow got off and entering the hotel jumped upon the rail in front of the bar and reached across for the dice box. The two farmers stepped up beside him and without further ado, a game was in full fling and lasted until we got ready to go home half an hour or so later. Next day, just before dinner, the landlord – the uncle of the boss – drove into the yard and with him was this congenial, young man. This intrigued me and I asked Jake, who that young fellow was and the reply was, "That is our pastor." When I replied that on Saturday afternoon he had played at billiards in Utzinger's saloon and on Monday had shaken dice, at the Northern Tier, Jake simply said, "What of it, hasn't he as much right to shake dice as you have"? When I admitted that he undoubtedly had Jake continued by saying that if I still disbelieved him, I could go to the neighbor's next Sunday and hear him preach. I told him that I would, indeed and I did. I met him repeatedly thereafter and found him to be a fine fellow. He even helped out with threshing, in a pinch, when I sacked barley with a half bushel measure and he held the sacks for me. This was before the days of the automatic sacker. He adapted himself to his environment and some years later, when I returned to that community, Jake informed me that our mutual friend had given up some of his sportive habits, because some of the people did not approve.

After attending church services at the neighbor's, Jake announced that there would be a dance in the granary at the same place in the afternoon and we went. The jolly swains and buxom lassies of the community were present without exception and dancing started without any preliminaries. Imagine my surprise when during the dancing I heard the shout; "Hurrah for Fountain City". This apprised me of the fact that I was not the only one from down our way in that crowd and on looking about carefully I espied my fellow passenger on the Robert Harris, who last spring had been so downcast and despondent on leaving his home town. I asked him "What do you know about Fountain City?" and he replied, "She is the best little town it gives." When I farther inquired why he had been so sad on leaving home he replied, "You'd a'cried too if your mother was on the levee crying and your girl was waving at you from a window". When I replied that memories of his girl did not now seem to bother him very much he said, "There are others here" and indeed there were.

Cutting the grain was soon completed and stacking was then continued by the full force and there were no more six hundred bundle loads hauled although the oxen were sometimes used and Jake taught me how to drive them. Father Wiedenhoefer was busy in the garden and gave me no more advice on how to stack, in fact, his parting shot was fired on that first day, when he remarked that really the bundles that I laid slanted too much toward the outside. I did not tell him that this was done to prevent sweating after a rain, for he was a grand, old scout and I would not have made him feel bad for anything. Even if he did not know how to build a stack, he could do many things that I could not, among them being the successful cultivation of garden "sass" especially among giant cabbage heads. He supplied most of the Germans at Crookston and among them my Alma friends, with sauerkraut and fresh vegetables.

When we had almost finished stacking and I had taught my friend Jake how to do it, the boss in his brusque way, remarked, "When you are through here, you will have to go and do the stacking for the shoe man in town, who has a farm a couple of miles west and when he asks you what you have been getting, tell him $2.75 a day. I went there and the hired man and I had to do the stacking, with the aid of a couple of neighbors, the boss being in town to look after his business. Everything was all right but I missed Mother Wiedenhoefer's cooking.

When I came to town, on Saturday, the blacksmith asked me to do his stacking but as I used no fork and had worn no gloves, my hands were quite sore and I demurred but the smith said he would give me $3.25 a day and that would buy me gloves. I went and bought the gloves.

Monday morning September 25th, we started for the farm about ten miles north of town. We had the first frost of the season and it was a severe one and when the sun rose the wind began to blow almost a gale from the northwest. We walked behind the wagon the greater part of the way, to keep warm.

When we got there the hired man and I put on a small load and started a stack. When the other team did not come he looked up and calmly remarked, "They are mired." This I could not understand since the field appeared neither wet nor soft. Then I got an explanation. On the fourth of June all crops thereabouts were totally hailed out. The fertile soil aided by favorable weather produced another crop and that had ripened in September. However about the time it was being cut, it began to rain and some of it could never be cut. We kept our coats on while we worked and were cold at that. A neighbor was cutting wheat and while riding the binder, wore a buffalo coat and fur mitts. When I remarked on the peculiarity of the situation the hired man told me that the neighbor had no other overcoat and had to wear his fur coat to keep warm. I wondered what the folks at home would say when I told them that I saw a man wearing a buffalo coat while seated on a binder cutting wheat but when you are cold you must wear what you have.

It was really a remarkable feat for that wheat to sprout again from the roots after the entire plant, above ground, had been destroyed but fertile soil and favorable weather will work wonders. Farthermore the fact that the first frost was delayed until the twenty-fifth of September was another factor to be considered for it has happened that they had frost during almost any month, in that region. The quality of the wheat was good but the yield was around ten bushels to the acre.

Wheat was over $1.25 a bushel, hence the crop was worth cutting although you had to wear a buffalo coat to do it.

One afternoon a strapping young fellow came riding up to the stack that I was building and after conversation with the hired man, asked me to come over and stack his grain. He looked good to me and told me that he was up against it, for both he and his cousin had come from Ontario, where all the grain was put into the barn after it was cut, hence they knew nothing of stacking. I told him I would come and on the day I got through at the blacksmith's I started toward the east. I was about started when it got dark for twilight is short lived on the prairies. I walked along a road on the section line, in fact it was nothing but a wheel track, when suddenly I found myself wading in water almost up to my knees but there was nothing to do but go on and I finally came to the claim shacks of the Lee boys and in one of them which for the time being, they occupied jointly, there was a light and I walked in and was made welcome to the shack and the solitary bunk which the three of us occupied. When we went to work I found that most of their wheat had been cut with the reaper and not bound or tied. I stacked this loose stuff and topped it off with the few bundles that they had from a small field on which they had been able to use a binder. The boys were nice fellows and both named Jim Lee and they told me much about the primitive way of farming among the giant stumps of upper Canada, where no machines could be used and all grain had to be cut by hand and where Canada thistles grew as thick as hemp around the stumps. No wonder they were elated with this prairie country, in spite of hail and lack of drainage. One day, while up on a stack, I saw in a neighboring field a reaper, mired up to the axles and all around it acre upon acre of sheaves of wheat that had been cut but not tied, some of them floating on the water that had gathered on the low places. On inquiry, I was told that the field belonged to Charley Sweet and when I later related this story to Jake Wiedenhoefer, he told me that the man's name was not Charley Sweet but Melchoir Schwy but the fellows up here called him Charley Sweet, so without knowing it, I had been near the farm of Buffalo County's champion deer slayer.

Owing to another heavy rain, stacking was retarded and the Jim who hired me took me to town next afternoon. When I arrived at the Northern Tier hotel, Landlord Bill asked me to carry brick and mortar to a mason who was working on a chimney for him. On descending from the roof by means of an inner stairway, I saw hanging in the window, a newspaper with the columns turned and remembering that on the death of President Lincoln newspapers had such black columns, I concluded that President Garfield had lost out in his fight against the abdominal wound inflicted by an assassin more than two months before and when my Irish friend told me that the bass drum we heard on the third of July, was being tolled in honor of General Garfield, he was not far wrong. I was a great admirer of President Garfield and the first vote that I cast was for his electors and I not only voted that way but worked that way all day long. In the evening the boss and his brother Jake came to town and the former told me to come home with them since there was no use hanging around the hotel. Jake told me then that there were others up there on the prairie besides Melchoir Schwy, whom perhaps I knew. Yes, somewhere on that prairie lived John Ristow, Fred Michaels, Toby Valaer, John Obrecht, Behlmer, Grosskreuz and others from Buffalo County but I met none of them during that summer. There were, of course, others whom I did not know or whom I may not recall just now. In Crookston there were quite a few Alma people also.

Next day was Sunday and August Wenzel came over and asked me to do his stacking since he had to pull out his threshing rig the next day. He had a way of making me feel as if I were conferring a favor on him, in spite of the fact that he offered me the same wages that I had been paid when working among the bachelors, while at his place I was taken into the home and accorded the same hospitable treatment as at Wiedenhoefers. With the hired man I stacked all his wheat and we did it as well and as quickly as we knew how although the boss was away threshing. That is what happens when your boss is a leader and not a driver, for every evening when he came home he was pleasant and satisfied and Mrs. Wenzel was always that way. What a difference that was from raising scows out of the Missouri mud.

You may, by this time be wondering what had become of Ulrich, well so was I. When he did not show up at Crookston, I wrote to his sister at home, to find out whether they knew anything about him there. I might have written to one of his brothers but for some reason, of my own, I wrote to his sister. They must have heard from him soon after that for I got a letter giving me a few bare facts but from reading between the lines, I was able to piece out the following story. Arriving at the division point, Glyndon, Saturday night, he was obliged to stay over until Monday to get the train for Crookston, (the very one that I came on). On Sunday a German farmer came in looking for a harvest hand and would Ulrich pass up a job, even though it up-set all his plans? At any rate he went out into the country to work for this farmer but did not inform either me nor the folks at home for some time. Here he shocked all the grain single handed although it was customary to have two men to do this work. He also remained to help with the stacking where he pitched every bundle onto the stack from bottom to top single handed although, as he told me later, the fellow built nothing but big stacks. On one occasion, when part of a stack slid out for him, the fellow deliberately went to work laying bundles over the stack that much bigger. This got the pitcher's goat and he sent the bundles up with that much more force, not particular as to where they landed and when one hit the stacker's head he would simply say, (Nicht so scharf, Heinrich, nicht so scharf) and "Heinrich" as the boss always called him, got a lot of satisfaction out of it, for was he not doing two men's work? However he told his sister not to send any mail to that address as he was not liable to stay but stay he did not only through stacking but also through threshing, although he often had to sleep in the straw pile and he never again wrote to either his folks at home nor to me and we knew nothing of his whereabouts until he returned home in November. He did not like his job but he would not be a quitter and hated to explain after writing that he was apt to quit. So while where I was, he might have been in clover, he continued to be a drudge, just because he would not quit. His boss told him that over toward Barnesville there was a big settlement of Germans coming from a place in Buffalo County, named Waumandee. He never took time to go there and when I told him that I knew those people and he should have gone there, he smiled wistfully, saying he had meant to go there but there did not seem to be time. I supposed that when he had time he was too tired. That was the way he always was, "Business before pleasure".

When, in the following year we again went west to work in the harvest fields, he and his brothers again took the first job that offered and fared, if anything, worse. When one Sunday they came to call on me and partook of one of Mother Wiedenhoefer's dinners, Ulrich remarked, "Gosh you live like a prince". I told him that a man got what he went after and on returning home they told their boss that they either had to be served a square meal or they would quit. He did not want them to quit so he hired a "Norske Jente", for cook and gave her carte blanche and when we again met, Ulrich agreed with me that a man got what he went after and that it did not pay to let anyone ride you and yet I think that it was one of the others that put that ultimatum up to the boss. I knew however that they had a good cook, for she cooked for us the previous year when I did the stacking for the Fisher shoe merchant.

After doing Mr. Wenzel's stacking I followed his threshing rig but all the work I did was among those Germans and I always slept in a bed and always had good meals and plenty of it. Many amusing incidents happened among the threshing crew but to recount them would become too tedious and I will only mention that my job was sacking grain with a half bushel measure, which job I had accepted temporarily at the request of the Wenzels, three of whom owned the machine and at their request I kept it, for you always did what they asked you to do, just because they knew how to go about it.

The weather, during the few weeks that I helped with the threshing, was ideal and I enjoyed it. The machine was now nearer Crookston and we were out of the German settlement and therefore among strangers and the homelike atmosphere was a thing of the past and when a breakdown of the engine, necessitated a two day's layoff for repairs to arrive from Minneapolis, I decided to get ready to come home. I went back to Wiedenhoefer's and the boss told me that next day he had to take a load of "Kraut" to Crookston for his father and I could go along. During the evening Jake and I discussed another neighbor whom I had dubbed, "The Flying Ducthman" and the Flying Dutchman, he remained in that group. The nick-name came to being bestowed in this manner. Jake and I rode home from town with him one night, when on passing our cross road he whipped his team into a gallop and I asked him whether this was the train they called The Flying Dutchman and he replied, "I'll show you smart Alecks". There was then on the Milwaukee road a train by that name. It was fast but compared with today's Hiawatha described a snail's pace. Well, we got off by giving the end board of the wagon a hard push while we jumped. The fellow had worked on the flat boats with our boss and then as now seemed to have a domineering influence over him and this was resented by his brother Jake. He was a hard worker and fairly successful farmer and tried to be the big man in the community. He was a bachelor, not exactly by choice, for the girls did not like his domineering ways nor did anyone else. He was not one of the

Manitowoc group nor one of the Suavians (Schwaben) and while he was tolerated, he failed to become a boss. He was a driver and what August Wenzel accomplished without any perceptible effort he failed to achieve with all his zeal. This illustrates the difference between a driver and a leader, not only here but everywhere.

In Crookston, I settled up with the boss and when he paid me $2.75 per day, I reminded him that we had agreed on $2.50. His reply was, "Did I not tell Olson, the shoemaker, that I was paying you $2.75?" I took the hint and did never again say anything to question his veracity. Those people sure had been good to me and before I left, the old gentleman asked me to come out again and help them garner their next crop and I did.

I stayed at Utzinger's hotel, off and on, helping with the threshing and with the chores, since they would not accept anything for board. The helper around the hotel and part time on the farm was a Hoch boy from Wabasha and on returning from a trip to Wisconsin, Utzinger told him that things looked tough down his way, the Mississippi being on a rampage and everything being under water. After the ideal weather, we had been having, this was a surprise to me, as well as to him.

My objective, on coming west, had been to secure a homestead and our forced departure from "Track's End" frustrated my plans in that direction while around Bismarck the good farms, near the river had been taken and the stony hills did not appeal to me, although Alderman Yegen spent an afternoon, showing me the country. The railroad land, granted the Northern Pacific could have been bought very cheaply but where we were it had not been surveyed and we had not looked around. It could have been bought for a few dollars an acre, payable in common stock of the Railroad, which stood at about seventeen cents on the dollar, meaning a fraction of a dollar an acre. Years later I bought some of this land but the price had advanced considerably.

I spent a day seeing the sights of Crookston, especially the modern saw mill. This was quite a sight on the open prairie but the logs were floated down the Red Lake river from the pineries to the east and of course, there was a good market for the lumber here.

There was land to be had to the east, so I was told, for Alderman Utzinger was as much a booster for the Red River valley as Alderman Yegen was for the Missouri valley. So I got ready to go to

Red Lake Falls, then an inland town without a railroad. Early one morning I went to the hotel from which the stage coach started for the promised land and was told that Mr. Church would be ready to start at eight o'clock sharp. With eight o'clock appeared Mr. Church and on a three seated spring wagon, drawn by two sturdy horses we started out. The driver directed me to occupy the front seat with him, while the two rear seats were occupied by six Cannucks, or Canadian Frenchmen, three to a seat. It was a raw day, the wind blowing from the northwest. Soon after leaving Crookston the country became rough and hilly stones cropping out here and there, reminding me of Yegen's prospective vineyards, near Bismarck. It was a tiresome drive but Mr. Church was not bad company, while those in the rear seats parley voued in great shape. By noon we arrived at a small hamlet named Gentilly and the world seemed changed. My Mr. Church was greeted as Messieur La Chapelle and the English language appeared to be non-existent. The "Frogs" on the back seats, jumped off and entered a door and when we followed them in, we found them lined up against the bar, consuming canned sea food, lobster, sardines and frog's legs, with something on the side to wash it down or to stimulate the appetite. M. La Chappelle motioned to me to follow him and on stepping into a back room we washed and sat down to the table with the family where we were served hot soup with boiled beef and vegetables, a good substantial meal on a cold day and all for a quarter, not half as much as the "Frogs" spent on their mixed repast.

This country did not appeal to me and as I later learned was inhabited solely by French Canadians who eked out a precarious existence. But before proceeding on our trip to Red Lake Falls, I can not refrain from recounting an article, which I some years ago read in a magazine, with reference to this very region.

The community had built a church at Gentilly and to them was sent a young priest, direct from the vineclad hills of sunny France. No doubt there was enough work for him to do both in a spiritual and in a material way but among these desolate environments the poor fellow became homesick and I do not blame him for had it not been for Mr. Church, I myself would have suffered a severe attack of nostalgia, during the brief hour that I was forced to stay there. I certainly could put myself in his place, when I read that article. The poor fellow did what all other mortals do when in that plight. He wrote home and I suppose, there was a mother. At any rate, to ease his pains, they sent him a liberal portion of Gruyere cheese (or was it Roquefort, I do not exactly remember) and that was the salvation of not only the young priest but of Gentilly, as well. He was evidently a practical, young fellow, who asked himself, "Why should it be necessary to send to France or Switzerland for something that we could produce right here and why should the people waste their time and energy (they had no money to waste) trying to produce what the people on the fertile lands in the valley were producing, when here was an ideal dairy section going to waste?" He no longer had time for being homesick. He went about among the farmers talking cows, milk and cheese. He wrote home for explicit directions for making, curing and handling this cheese which was a sure cure for nostalgia. His efforts met with little response, in the start for the poor farmers wondered where the money for the cows was to come from but the man at the head overcame even this obstacle by personally securing the credit on the strength of the future output of Gruyere. He even established markets in advance so that when the cheese was being made there would be a sale for it. He made contacts in the Twin Cities to furnish this delicacy to epicures at a fancy price. In fact he did everything possible with such sagacity and foresight, as might have awakened the envy of a captain of industry. As is always the case when both brains and brawn are behind a movement, this venture proved a success in every respect.

The farmers got some returns for their efforts and in order to keep up with the program they had to be alert and doing, thus they were benefited not only materially and economically but their mental attitude was influenced to an extent that changed the character of the community. No longer was shiftlessness and irresponsibility the watchword for the people had had a taste of prosperity and progress and they liked it. They were no longer content to be called or to be Frogeaters for they were respectable, selfsupporting Americans and felt that way.

When I read that article and gazed upon the picture of the church with rows of automobiles lined up in front of it, I felt mighty good and had a strong desire for a chance to shake that young priest by the hand and whisper into his ear "Blest be Nostalgia". Equally impressive was the picture of the factory and the trucks lined up before it. If he, who makes two blades of grass grow where one grew before is blest, then this young man was certainly doubly blest. He aided his community in a material way and thus established in their minds higher ideals, encouraging them to strive after those higher things that are worth while. He may not have done much preaching on the subject but even in advancing Christianity this was one of the instances where acts spoke louder than words. I have never been back to Gentilly and before I read that article, never had a desire to be back and yet should I ever get back to Crookston, I would be sorely tempted to again make that trip even though I would not be privileged to occupy the seat of honor on Mr. Church's stagecoach. I would like to see that new church and the new factory and above all things I would like to see that priest provided he should still be there. Also would I like to witness the changes wrought in the country side, which at the time looked simply hopeless.

But back to M. La Chapelle and my trip to Red Lake Falls. The horses fed and dinner over, we again climbed into our seats on the primitive stage coach. The "Frogs" on the back seats were considerably heartened by their noon-day meal and had become rather hilarious but neither M. La Chapelle nor I paid much attention to them although they had provided themselves with a couple of large bottles that might have contained Seltzer but didn't. As we drove along, the hilarity increased in the same ration that the contents of the bottles decreased and finally developed into a row. This ended by the fellows on the rear-most seat coming to blows. It was not a fight to the finish for the combatants were done for before they began. Almost all of the blows went wild not on account of dexterous dodging but owing to faulty aim yet a few landed and caused bloody noses. Without a word in either English or French, M. La Chapelle handed me the reins and unbuckling the halters which had been fastened to the dash board walked to the rear end of the rig. Buckling a halter to each seat, he drew the strap across the front and thus fastened his passengers down securely, without a word from either him or them. It seemed to be all in the day's work and perhaps it was. In this improvised ambulance we proceeded toward our destination. Before descending the hill into Red Lake Falls, I cast a furtive glance backward and the sight that met my eyes mocks description. Their blood smeared faces a ghastly palor, the bodies of the victims of that carousal hung out of the rig supported by the halter straps that held them onto the seats. The poor fools had probably earned some money by working on a threshing crew back in the settlement and were now bent on getting rid of part of it, before going back into the pineries for the winter.

Red Lake Falls was a typical frontier hamlet. A German merchant of Crookston, named Kretschmar, had established a branch store, which supplied the scattered settlement with the necessaries of life and I think there was a mill, a hotel of a kind and a few straggling dwellings. This was the place, which it took us a long day to reach but today the trip could be made in about an hour, even in an old fashioned flivver. Here I was "A Stranger in a strange land", indeed. During the entire evening I heard not a word of English and the French that was spoken, was a veritable jargon of Cannuck patois of which I could not make out even a word. I was seized with an attack of nostalgia, which I fear, could not have been dispelled by Gruyere or even real Swiss cheese. Luckily I was tired and went early to bed. Early the next forenoon a man came in, who I was informed lived across the river in a section where homesteads were still open to entry. His name, I learned, was Jeffords and he offered to show me about. I must say that my enthusiasm for becoming a member of that community had almost vanished but he spoke my language and I gladly accompanied him on his return. He was on foot for there was no bridge connecting the town with the other side of the river. By the way, the Red Lake River has a tributary near this town, which the maps designated as the Clearwater but of which the natives spoke as the Eau Claire, which of course, to use a homely expression, was the same only different. When we came to the Red Lake river there was a cable strung across it and we ferried ourselves across in a skiff which Jeffords guided by holding the crutch of a small tree across the cable. A rope went to each shore and by means of this the boat was available to passengers from both sides.

About mid-day we reached the home of a German settler who had the threshers at work. Here we had dinner and Jeffords had to stay and help his neighbor and I did likewise, feeling that I ought to pay for my dinner. The threshing rig was a primitive horse power affair, both horses and oxen being used in propelling it. Most of this farm was covered with young timber, poplar, cotton-wood and soft maple and the farmer warned me not to take any land of that kind since one who had to do grubbing was at a disadvantage in competing with the prairie farmers. Well, I hope he made a go of it for he appeared to be one who deserved it. Along in the afternoon, Jeffords sent his hired man to show me a certain quarter section near his own home. The land was fairly good but nothing like what my German friends near Fisher had.

Nevertheless I jotted down the description and was now armed to tackle the U. S. Land Office, at Crookston. During the evening, that I spent at the Jeffords home, I was given detailed directions of the road leading to Crookston on that side of the river.

Next morning, after paying my bill, I started for Crookston and since my hosts had mentioned the big and little Black Rivers, as streams that I would have to cross, I began to look for bridges of some kind. On descending into a rather deep ravine, I came to a gurgling brook, about the size of the south branch of Mill Creek. At the same time a team came toward me down the opposite hill and when I asked the driver whether this was the BIG Black River he asked me where I came from and when I answered, "From Wisconsin", his reply was, "That explains it. Your Black River is a little bigger and at that it is not known as BIG." I trudged on and crossing another divide soon came to another rill which I now knew must be the Little Black River. There was no bridge across either but I had no trouble in stepping across them.

After ascending another rise, I saw before me the Crookston courthouse which then stood alone out on the prairie. All forenoon, as I trudged along, this landmark was before me, whenever I reached higher ground and finally it never vanished from my sight yet it was two o'clock p. m. when I finally walked into town. When I presented the description of my prospective claim, at the land office, one of the employees remarked to another, "Why this is the quarter that young "Blank" has filed on?" He, to whom I refer as "BLANK", I learned was the son of register of the land office. That settled my homesteading and with little regret I departed from the office. To this day I do not know whether Mr. Jeffords had shown me a quarter section that had already been taken or whether the clerks at the landoffice put one over on me and I never seriously cared, for with the hills and dales of Buffalo county and the fertile section between Crookston and Fisher, in mind, that homestead had not greatly appealed to me as a future home. In fact, my plan had already been to proof up and pay for the claim after a year's ostensible residence, as many others did. A year or two later a railroad, coming from the east, cut through that section and the town of St. Hilaire is now located but a few miles from the quarter that I had intended to locate on but I never felt that I had missed much by losing out on that deal.

167

After partaking of a belated lunch at Utzingers, I visited with the people who had been so kind to me and whiled away the time with young Henry Utzinger and a cousin of both of us from Bangor, who was visiting there, thus missing the regular train for St. Paul. Fortunately I was able to take another train, which came an hour later. This necessitated a change at Barnesville and took me to St. Paul via Breckenridge instead of Fergus Falls, making my arrival at my destination a few hours later than by the first train. This did not bother me much for I was asleep almost all the time, in spite of the fact that the seat which I occupied in the smoking car was made of hardwood slats, something like the rear seats in a school room. It must be remembered that I had walked about thirty miles the day before and that ride to Red Lake Falls had not been a holiday excursion either, thus I was able to sleep without using my boots for a pillow, even.

On arriving at St. Paul, I espied among the throngs at the Union Depot, Professor Thayer, of the River Falls Normal but did not feel like butting in on him and figured on passing by un-noticed, since I felt a little the worse for wear after my night's rest (?). He had however espied me and accosted me with the remark "Say, you have been playing hooky". He was on his way home from Alma, where he had been conducting the annual Teachers' Institute. He gave me an account of the meeting and I was pleased to hear that he had missed me. This made me feel that my time could have been more profitably spent there than at land hunting, yet in a negative way the time thus spent was not entirely wasted for the experience may have been worth the effort.

It was still raining and misting and the sand on the street leading up from the depot was literally reduced to slush. I now saw what Mr. Utzinger meant when he told young Hoch and me that things looked terrible down our way. I had to go and call on the Swiss Consul, Mr. Utzinger having intrusted me with a message to him. He was very cordial and much interested in the Red River country. He showed me maps and blue prints, relating to a project for establishing a drainage system for the prairied north of Crookston in order to avert conditions such as prevailed there this season, to which I referred in writing of my experience, while at work stacking up that way. You will remember that I mentioned the fact that in some places machines, used to cut the grain had been mired. A canal with tributary ditches was built and it afforded some relief, as Mr. Schwy, who was

168

interested in the project as a member of the town board, informed me, years later when we discussed this matter, at Alma. I had to spend the rest of the day in the city and I again went to the brow of the hill overlooking West St. Paul and there it rested tranquilly on the west bank of the river, as if there had never been a flood peril such as I had witnessed but a few short months before.

Late in the afternoon the Milwaukee train pulled out and I was on my way to Wabasha arriving there late at night. It was a dark, damp night and almost all the lights were out when I got into town, after having tramped across the prairie, from the depot. I stopped in front of a hotel and pounded lustily at the door, when someone looked out of an up-stairs window and asked, in German, "Who is here?" I answered, "Never mind John, just open the door and get me to bed". As usual, the first man to run across when getting to Wabasha, was my friend, John Jost and as usual he took care of me, the funny part being that he put me to bed without even recognizing me, for next morning when he got up he wanted to know where I had come from and I told him that I came out of the bed that he had put me into.

Here it was Sunday and I was at Wabasha and next morning my school, at Mill Creek was to open. The Steamer Lion did not run on Sundays but John told me that there was a fellow who would take me to Alma in a skiff, in the afternoon. We loafed around. John showing me through the store where he worked and after dinner was about to make arrangements to have me transported to Alma, by skiff. Just about then came, floating through the mist, a sound that was sweet music to my ears. It was the whistle of a steamboat and when we went to the dock to investigate, there was The Robert Harris, of Fountain City. I lost no time in asking Engineer Heck whether he could take me to Alma and the reply was "You bet, we have to take on wheat for Paul Huefner there anyway". This suited me and I got on board at once. This was better than a skiff ride in a drizzling rain and fog.

In due time we got to Alma and I was now about to embark on the last lap of my journey. Leaving my satchel at a hotel I struck out for the bluff and the path to Mill Creek Valley, which started out from Olive street, between what is now Passow's house and garage. Thence it meandered up the hillside and past the present location of the beacon light and within a stone's throw of where I now live. Had on that Sunday afternoon, an apparition appeared out of the fog and said to me, "Young man, here is your homestead," I would certainly have replied by saying, "Dear ghost, thou art mistaken", or something to that effect. To my right and to my left, in front of me and behind me, loomed up in the fog the majestic boles of tall oaks. This was all right, in a way but I did not feel like starving while I grubbed those giants of the forest. Well, they were removed before I bought the place but by someone better qualified to do that kind of work than I was and thereby hangs a tale. The poor fellow who did it, did not earn his salt but that is another story again and I am here, all right.

This path was, in those days, a regular thoroughfare and hundreds of dozens of eggs and hundreds of pounds of butter were carried to town from Mill Creek, via this route, by women and girls and one of them lives right by the side of the old path, now. About eighty rods from where the beacon is, the path forked, one branch leading down the valley toward Laniccas and the other along the ridge toward Josts. When I got to where I thought the path would lead to Laniccas, I turned into the brush to the right, expecting to strike the path that led down the valley. Imagine my surprise when after going quite a stretch, I again found myself in the same old path and there I discerned footprints in the moist path. I formed a theory that while I had wandered in the woods, someone had walked from Mill Creek to Alma and that it was someone from town, for he wore rubbers and country people, at that time, wore stout boots that needed no additional protection from the mud. I considered myself quite a Sherlock Holmes until I found myself out on the point where the high line now reaches the top of the bluff and below me saw The Robert Harris steaming down the river. The fog in the valley had lifted while on the bluff I was surrounded by dense clouds. Thus I was disillusioned and to my sorrow, found that I was not much of a Sherlock Holmes after all, for the tracks in the path were my own and did not lead from Mill Creek to Alma but vice versa and humbly I retraced them and kept the path along the top of the ridge and finally heard some cow bells and then found a herd in a field. Knowing them to be Jost's cattle, I started them out, trusting them to lead the would-be Sherlock Holmes out of the wilderness. However I may explain that I had never traveled the path on top of the ridge before, hence my bewilderment.

The cows got home and so did I, in the eleventh hour for the opening of school was to be to-morrow. Mr. Jost, who was a member of the board, told me that the people were wondering whether school would start on time or not. Well, it did and the pupils were on hand, trusting that I would turn up in time. Remember that this was long before we had even heard of such a thing as a telephone. Among other things, Josts informed me that Ulrich had come home the day before and that pleased me immensely for I knew that I was being held responsible for his return although, it was no fault of mine that we had become separated and that he had not written home for months.

After supper I went over to Wald's place to see Ulrich and perhaps for another reason, which it is not necessary to mention, because it is not in any way connected with the building of the Northern Pacific, directly or indirectly. When Ulrich saw me he broke out into one of those hearty guffaws that some of you so well remember and I thought to myself, "If you think you fooled me, remember that you fooled yourself, for you certainly did not have as nice a place to work as you would have had where I was." We had much to tell each other and Ulrich's mother gently reminded me of the promise we had made to stay together and while I tried to explain matters, the guilty one took it for a good joke and laughed some more but I think that the main cause of his merriment was the fact that he was again at home, after the varied experiences that he had all around.

This is the end of our experience with railroad building and pioneering in "The Golden Northwest" and although some more things might have been said, while others might have been left unsaid my aim was to depict, to the best of my ability, conditions prevailing here as well as in the new Northwest, at that time. I trust also that the stories and anecdotes, interspersed in the article may not have tired you and after all many of them were illustrative, so that is that.

On two occasions I returned to the Red River Valley but only to help with the harvesting, as I had promised my friends. I liked the heavy sheaves laden with golden grain, I liked the rich, black virgin soil that produced them but above all I liked those kind and hospitable people that lived there. The golden wheat fields are a thing of the past being supplanted by rows of sugar beets. My German friends, with the exception of a few stragglers of the third and fourth generation are no longer there and their fertile fields are being worked by Mexican peons. I had always longed to, some day, return to that country but when my friend, Theodore Averbeck who visits there occasionally, informed me of all the changes that have taken place, I had no farther desire to go where I knew no one and where I might not even recognize my old stamping grounds.

There is, however, one incident which not only interested me but greatly surprised me, which occurred during my stay in the Red River valley, of which I forgot to speak before and mention it now because I consider it worth while.

One Sunday morning, on getting up and looking out of the upstairs window, a spectacle presented itself to me, such as I had read about but never dreamt of encountering here. No, it was not a herd of buffaloes nor a herd of antelopes, such as may have roamed over those prairies less than half a century before, but a mirage, yes a veritable mirage, such as we read of, in our schoolbooks, as occurring on deserts and this was certainly not a desert. I was sorely tempted to exclaim "Fata Morgana! Fata Morgana!" This is what my school books told me the orientals did on such occasions. Instead I shouted to my friend, Jake, to get up and come to view the wonderful phenomenon. He came to the window and complacently viewing the spectacle, asked "What about it? We see them almost every year." Excitedly I exclaimed "It is a Mirage! Eine Luftspiegelung!" The reply was, "That, I guess is so all right but those are all buildings, some of them ten and more miles north of us, and the one that looks like an elevator a hundred or more feet in height, is Toby's granary". When I asked what was the wonderful bridge in the back-ground, with hundreds of huge pillars, that spanned the entire northern horizon, he told me that those were the trees along the Snake River, some twenty or thirty miles to the north. Those trees grew in the river bottoms and were not ordinarily visible to anyone traveling across the prairie but now seemed elevated a hundred feet above that level. I was duly amazed at seeing the prairie covered with sky-scrapers, with a back-ground of a huge bridge, supported by hundreds of stately pillars but the natives seemed hardly impressed. I have since seen many wonders both natural and artificial but nothing has ever impressed me like that mirage, occurring in a place where I would never have expected it.

Yes, even now I would like to again live through those experiences tangible and intangible but all that is left, is a fond memory and recalling the Mirage, I again repeat with the Orientals, the word, "Fata Morgana".

A Vanishing Race

Some time ago appeared in the Journal an article on "The Forgotten Swiss" but the reason why they were forgotten was not explicitly stated and since I am cognizant of the main reason of this slight, I will before entering upon the subject in hand, briefly state it.

Switzerland was formed by a number of groups, who being sorely oppressed and mistreated, broke away from their parent countries and formed first a loose confederation, which later developed into the "Bund" and finally into the present day republic. These various groups that broke away from their mother countries, belonged to different nationalities and almost to different races, in a broad sense of that term. At any rate they spoke different languages and of all things cherished by a people, their language is perhaps the most important, aye sacred.

Thus the greater part of the inhabitants, former subjects of the Hapspart among the Vosgeses that had seceded from France, retained that language and in Tecino across the Alps, the Italian tongue still prevails, although to call one of that group a "Dago" or even an Italian, provokes a fight, no matter how big or strong the aggressor may be. Then there is another group, interspersed among the German speaking people of the Canton Grisons or Graubuenden, which although insignificant in numbers is about as clannish as any of the rest. I refer to the Romanic race who have a language and many mannerisms of their own and withal their language resembles the Latin much more than does even the Italian.

Although the German language largely predominates, it became necessary to recognize both the French and Italian as additional official languages. This fact of the different languages is the cause of the Swiss being sometimes classed with the nation whose language they speak and notably is this the case with the German speaking class. Theirs being but a dialect many of them after acquiring the real or "High" German in school, shirk the dialect and unlike their Italian compatriots like to be looked upon as Germans and not unfrequently have I heard one of them speak of himself as being "Cherman" or collectively as "We Chermans". Under such circumstances it is not surprising that a nation be forgotten.

To some Swiss people and to some of Swiss descent, it may have been surprising to read the list of names presented in the article referred to but by most of them the article is, by this time, perhaps forgotten yet I will to that list add, at least two names, of prominent Americans of Swiss descent. Admiral Farragut, was evidently a descendant of the Veraguths, of Graubuended, while ex-President Hoover, while traveling in Europe, made the statement that his ancestors lived on the shores of Lake Zurich and that their name was Huber. So much for the forgotten Swiss, who it seems are to a great extent themselves to blame for this obscurity that, in a measure surrounds their past but the subject of this sketch shall be that really forgotten race, the Romanics, who for centuries have striven and struggled to preserve their identity and have not given up the struggle yet.

This struggling handful of sturdy mountaineers are a most interesting group and I am only sorry that I have missed out on the many opportunities that I had of getting inside information on this remnant of a vanishing race. As above stated, the language they speak is closer to Latin than any other living language, even the Italian.

The theory is, and it is generally accepted, that when the hordes of Caesar, retreated from the Teutons under Arminius, some of the survivors failed to return to Rome but remained among the fastness of the Alps. Not all may have remained for the same reason or from the same cause. Some may have been cut off from the main body while others, tired of the glories and hardships of war, may, have intentionally deserted and sought refuge among the Alpine fastness of old Graubuenden. Be this as it may, here they are, here they have been for ages, partly in segregated groups in different valleys but often inhabiting a hamlet or village surrounded by German speaking neighbors but always they remained Romanic, clannish and aloof. They consider themselves the real "Graubuendners" and look upon their German speaking neighbors, who far outnumber them, as mere interlopers and when they raise their glass to the toast of "Viva la Grischa", the sentiment expressed includes no one of Teutonic or Normanic descent.

They are found in the Engadin, on the Hinter-Rhein and in other parts of the Canton but there was no group of them outside of the Canton of Graubuenden or as they call it Grisons.

Why should I want to speak or write of this group? For several reasons, the first and main one being, that among the early Swiss settlers of Buffalo County, this group took a prominent part in helping to make history. Second because they always appealed to me as a group apart, independent, proud and, to some extent clannish but always friendly and more refined than their associates and above all most of them were of a jovial disposition and on closer acquaintance became steadfast friends. Then two of my teachers were Romanic as well as, later on, several of my pupils. Thus I gained an insight into their mode of living but, as already stated, failed to gather more data.

How they struggled to maintain their integrity is proven by the fact that they maintained schools and even in the segregated hamlets and villages taught the Romanic language, using text books printed specially in that language. Looking at the practical side of the question, this was all a waste of time and energy but there is a sentimental side which can not be lost sight of and sentiment and romance loomed up big among those people. I understand that there was an attempt made to do away with this teaching of Romanic and in places it was tried out but recently, I learn, that there is a movement on foot to return to the old regime and revive old traditions and indeed they are many. They are great lovers of music especially the song both in their language and in German, some being masters along that line. Two of my intimate acquaintances, my teacher Anton Cajoeri and my old friend John Thomas Lanicca, that master basso-profundo, took part in quartets that participated in the program of the National Saengerfest, in the city of Bern. At this Fest are gathered the best singers of Switzerland and that means some of the best on the continent but these Romaners, easily held their own.

Of course there were authors among them, one of them, Nina Camenisch, having produced some rare literary gems. There were, of course, others but I neglected to get the information when I might have had it. I think, however, that the statesman and writer, Johann Gaudenz Salis von Seewis, was either Romanic or of Romanic

175

descent. Suffice it to say that Nina Camenisch was given due recognition, although a woman, which was quite out of the ordinary during the nineteenth century.

Yes there is another case where women received recognition. In one of these Alpine villages the women sit on the right hand side of the church, while in practically every other Swiss church that honor is reserved for the lords of creation, or at least that was the inflexible rule in the days of those from whom I have the following true story. "All the men were absent from that village (I have forgotten its name) fighting an invading army, when it was learned that an enemy detachment was nearing the village. To get there they had to pass through a narrow gorge. To prevent this the women gathered on both sides of this gorge and made ready, piles of heavy boulders, which when the enemy passed below them were released, thus crushing the invaders. Thus to this day, the women occupy the place of honor in the church of that village."

The isolated vales, long the abiding place of this sturdy race, are however, being invaded and neither courageous women nor heavy boulders suffice to keep out the invaders. They and their country have been discovered and tourists have taken possession of it coming and going all summer and all winter too. Modern hotels dot the hillsides, railroads follow the valleys and wintersports are the order of the day on the lakes and hillsides. The melting pot threatens to swallow up these primitive people. Contact with the outside world will make them forget their aloofness and finally they will become a part of the incessant maelstrom, that sweeps everything with it. Their manners, their customs are being changed. Their idiosyncracies, their provincialism, aye their simplicity are being swept away and subconsciously perhaps, they lose their identity and become more and more like the invaders of their long cherished privacy. The towering Alps, the yawning gorges no longer serve as sentinels. They have become a part of the outside world. Nothing but the traditions remains. Their horizon is widened, their contacts are greater, but will they be happier? I have my doubts. It is hard to trim an old tree to grow in a different direction or to assume a new shape and I fear that these innovations may be hard on this sturdy race, being forced from its rut.

Why should all this interest us? As I have already told you the early history of our community, our county, is closely interwoven with names of people of that clan. Among the early business and professional men, farmers and mechanics members of that race stood well in the front ranks. Permit me to mention but a few of them and pardon me for possible omissions due only to my failing memory. Among those I remember are the Polins, Tscharners, the Fimians and Rubens and the Carisches of Alma and Fountain City. Then there were the teachers, Anton and Florian Cajoeri and Paul Casparis, of Waumandee and Anton Marchion of Fountain City. Others were the Laniccas, Livers, Conrads, Castlebergs, Tavernas, DeCarisch, Durisch, Arpagaus, and others, in all walks of life, not to forget my old neighbor, Jacob Thoeny, the Waumandee blacksmith. Then some, not all, of the Ruedis and Leonhardys were wholly or partly of Romanic descent.

Here they too passed through the melting pot and among new environments acquired new manners and customs but most of them remained true to the traditions of the land of their birth. Their descendants of the second and third generation can not be expected to live up to traditions of which they know little or nothing, hence the title that I have placed at the head of this article.

When Crime Was Rampant in a Peaceful Vale

The narrative that I am about to relate, with the exception of some minor details, that I may fail to correctly remember or that I perhaps never got correctly, is essentially true but the names of the persons directly connected with it, are fictitious, while those of the innocent bystanders are given correctly. There is nothing incriminating about it but one hesitates to refer to facts that might embarrass our fellow-men and especially is this the case when most of the dramatis personae are dead and gone.

One morning, in the fall of the early seventies, my brother, Casper, happened onto the road that passed our house at a distance of some twenty or thirty rods, when he espied the constable of the town of Montana, come galloping down the highway. "Hi Pete, what's the hurry?" shouted Casper, as the dignified Constable sped by him. "Can't stop "Cap": can't stop; Criminal case, Criminal case", replied the speeding officer of the law. His curiosity aroused, Casper either asked his neighbor Philip Runkel or went up the road a little ways to Helwig's store, to get the necessary information to help solve this mystery, I do not now remember which but he came home with a tale which ran about as follows: --

Murder, bloody murder, had been committed up in Danuser Valley and what was more the body of the victim after having been foully done away with was consigned to a brush pile and incinerated. While diligent search revealed neither the bones nor any other charred remains, the fact that young Tony Schlenker, a lad of twelve years or so, was missing and no trace of him could be found remained. The Schlenkers, who had the reputation of being a rather coarse and quarrelsome outfit, had not lived in the community very long and I did not know them. It seems that the boy, who was himself not a saint,

179

caused them a lot of trouble and was often severely chastised. On one such occasion he was either driven from home or ran away, at any rate he arrived at the home of John Schindler, who lived near by and who was also a rather recent addition to the community. Here Tony was given sanctuary and a place to work and stay. This, of course, embittered the Schlenkers and although I do not know of any effort on their part to interfere, it is known that they resented the action of their neighbors. Then the rumor spread that Tony had disappeared and the Schlenkers, all at once, became very solicitous for the welfare of their child. Mrs. Schlenker, after exchanging some hot arguments with Mrs. Schindler, at the latter's home, was told that Tony had taken a ring, which Mrs. Schindler had left lying on a table and when this was discovered had been soundly whipped by Mr. Schindler, who told him that he ought to report him to the authorities. Her story farther ran that Tony went to bed and in the morning when they investigated they found the bed empty and the bird flown. To this Mrs. Schlenker hotly retorted that more likely, while flogging him, Schindler had killed her darling child and thrown his body into one of the brush piles that he had been burning. With this hypothesis established, in her mind at least, she went to the authorities with her version of the case.

Thus it happened that on that fateful morning, the constable of Montana had to see the justice of peace in the village of Waumandee. Both the constable and the Judge were ambitious young fellows, looking ahead to something better than their present official positions. The constable was a young farmer, who dressed a little better than the rest of the boys and withal had a good opinion of himself. The Judge, a married man, had come amongst us, some years previous and being a very good mechanic had successfully run a blacksmith shop and had his ambition been along that line he might have accomplished something worth while but with a bee buzzing under his hat, telling him that the office of sheriff would be a fine job, he neglected his work and spent much of his time in the neighboring saloons, although he was not a heavy drinker. It was company he liked and to swap stories with the boys to make himself popular. Both were good fellows at heart and we liked them both, in a way but that was the way they were and not the way they wanted to be.

Well, on the Monday after we had heard this startling news, I went to help our neighbor, Joe, with his threshing. He together with Matt and George, both of whom lived in Danuser Valley, owned a horsepower threshing machine. Joe, was married to Matt's sister and George had been married to another of Matt's sisters, who had however died some time before and now he was married to John Schindler's sister. When I came up to the machine, that morning, Matt and George were attaching a new rope to the machine for holding up the straw stacker. Winking at George, Matt remarked, "Do you think this rope would hold Schindler?" George who was a very mild mannered fellow replied, "I do not know, but I would not mind to help pulling at the end of it." This, coming from George, impressed me rather strongly but on the other hand, I reasoned that George was somewhat of a wag, anyway.

During the noon hour the mystery was discussed, at length but somewhat guardedly, for on that day the "Criminal case" was being tried, in the village but a mile away. During the afternoon, while George was "feeding" the machine, up came Robert Schindler, John's brother and stepping up on the feeder board, started to talk to George. George kept on feeding, wearing all the time, his little, crooked smile but when Robert finally put his arm over George's shoulders and spoke pleadingly, the latter gave Matt the signal to relieve him and stepping off the board went with Robert in his buggy, to attend court. The idea of pulling as the end of that rope had left him, in fact, he had never meant what he said.

Court was in session with full pomp and dignity, in a hall, adjoining a saloon across the road from the judge's blacksmith shop and a not overly large crowd, considering the serious aspect of the case, was present but then it was threshing time and in those days, it was business before pleasure. The trial was conducted, sans prosecuting attorney, sans attorneys for the defense and sans any officer but the Judge and constable, aforesaid. There was, however, a jury duly impannelled and the court did all the work that usually falls to the lot of attorneys in the case. Whether or not the jury was supposed to have final jurisdiction, I know not and I suppose no one else, connected with the case knew. The prosecution presented its case, the star witnesses being the Schlenkers and the constable, who testified that having diligently searched, he could find no evidence of human remains in the ash piles of the burnt brush, while the testimony of the bereaved parents consisted mainly in abuse of the defendant and the calling down of imprecations upon his guilty head. Whether there were any objections made to these procedures, deponent sayeth not.

The story of the defense was given by the defendant and his wife about as heretofore stated. The walloping had been administered by a belt which he wore in court and exhibited to the jury, stating that the buckle was always in his hand and never touched the boy. So that was that. An incident worth mentioning and told me by one of the jurors, can not well be omitted. Before the case went to the jury, the priest of the local church who happened to be present, felt it incumbent upon himself to make a few remarks. He admonished the jury to seriously weigh the fact that a man's life and liberty were matters not to be trifled with and that unless there was ample evidence of guilt no one should be convicted, especially in a murder case where the corpus delicti or body of the victim was not in evidence. The jury then, I presume in compliance with instructions from the court, bound the defendant over to the next term of court and the judge fixed the bail bond at Five Hundred Dollars. To sign that bond George was called away from that threshing machine and George did it, with a smile. So the case was disposed of, for the present and everybody went about his every day business, awaiting farther developments at the next turn of court.

Now accompany me to another part of the county, in fact, in those days it was a day's journey to get there. Let us go to Bohri's Valley where Gottlieb Bohri kept a country store, tavern, and dance hall. Although "far from the maddening throngs ignoble strife", this hostelry was a most excellent place to stop for rest and food, as I myself experienced. Besides these functions already mentioned, Mr. Bohri was postmaster at Bohri and also carried the mail from Fountain City to that place, the contract for that work being, of course, held by someone else but as Mr. Bohri had to go after supplies three times a week anyway, he also carried the mail and neither Uncle Sam nor anyone else was any the wiser for it, nor did it matter. Well, on the regular mail day Mr. Bohri, as usual, drove to Fountain City and there he read in the "Republikaner" an account of this crime and besides there was little else talked of, on the streets. Mr. Bohri being impressed with the enormity of the crime, on arriving at home related every detail of it at the supper table, never dreaming that he was solving a mystery. After supper he went into the part of the building, serving as store and saloon, to dispose of the merchandise he had brought home with him. After a little while he was followed by the boy whom he had hired a few days previous and on looking up, saw that the lad wanted to talk to him.

"Well Tom, what is it?"

"I gotta go home", replied the boy.

"Why, what's the matter with you. You are doing good work at digging the potatoes, husking corn and doing the chores, so why go home?"

The boy persisted that he had to go home and after being hard pressed, blurted out, "I am Tony Schlenker and gotta go home".

"Who is Tony Schlenker?" asked Mr. Bohri.

"Why the boy that was killed and burnt up, what you was telling about, at supper".

"Well what do you want to do at home?"

"Oh heck, I ain't goin home but I mean to go up to Waumandee, to tell them not to hang John Schindler, 'cause he never killed me nor never burned me up, nor even pounded me half as hard as they pound me at home, with a hickory stick. That's what I want to do".

"Better wait till morning and get a ride to town and from there out to Waumandee, Schindler is safe until court convenes."

"But I don't want them to hang him. The old folks sure will try to get them to do it".

"Well wait until tomorrow and I will give you a couple of dollars, so you will get to Waumandee, all right, in time to save Schindler's neck. But you are certainly a case and fooled a lot of people, including myself".

So "Tom", again became Tony and the murder mystery was solved and the great "Criminal case", was soon forgotten. I, later on, became fairly acquainted with him whom I have chosen to call John Schindler and found him to be one of those easy going, inoffensive fellows who would not hurt even a cat. Often in reviewing this case, have I pondered what might have happened under different circumstances. Supposing that instead of ultra-conservative, level headed people, the members of that community had been hot headed, impulsive fellows and supposing farther they had been addicted to the excessive use of liquor and incited by some fire eater, had taken the law in their own hands. What then? I would then hardly have been induced to tell this story in a rather humorous vein. It must be farther remembered that about then, stories of the Vigilantes were fresh in everybody's mind and that the notion that an organized body could take the law into its own hands, prevailed very generally. Under such conditions it is a credit to the community that no excesses were committed. Credit is also due to that priest, who although he may not have been posted on proceedings in court, spoke words of wisdom and they bore weight. Because he was respected not only by his congregation but by outsiders, as well.

Early Education

Written Especially for Local History Study in the Buffalo County, Wisconsin Schools, by E. F. Ganz.

In recounting one's experiences much of the material used is, of necessity, of a personal nature and the ego assumes a more prominent position and the first personal pronoun is more freely used than one would desire, were it not necessary as a means to an end. My readers will therefore bear the above in mind and pardon what, on the surface, may appear egotistic but in the presentation of facts becomes necessary.

Like everything else, in the pioneer days, education was, at first, of the most primitive kind but kept pace with the progress made in other lines, due largely to the fact that many, in fact, most of the pioneers came either from countries in Europe or from the Eastern states, where schools, public or private, had made fair progress and where higher institutions of learning had been well established. In Europe and especially in England and Germany prominent seats of learning had long been maintained but were patronized largely by the nobility and others of more than ordinary means, while in the East and South, of our own country, had sprung up academies, colleges and universities, to which all classes were admitted, and while they were not conducted on as grand a scale as their old world contemporaries, they reached more people and fired the ambition of even those who were denied the privilege of attending them. Reference to these schools is made to show the influence of such environments upon many of the early settlers of Buffalo County.

185

People deprived of all the commodities and many of the necessities of life, were in no position to establish an elaborate public school system and had to be content with what they could afford, and to be content with what they had, was one of the sustaining virtues of these pathfinders of civilization.

Every home was a log cabin and good old homes they were at that, hence every school was, at first either kept in one of these homes or in a like structure erected for that purpose, both material and labor being donated by members of the community, in a majority of cases. The furnishings and equipment were as primitive as the school house itself. Plain pine benches, often without a desk or table, a wood burner stove and perhaps a pail and dipper constituted, in almost every instance, the sum total of the equipment. You may think that I forgot some things, perhaps the teacher's chair, but since there were no chairs but only benches in the homes, such a luxury was, for some years, unknown in the school room. Of course there was a broom but that, very often was a home made affair, of birch twigs.

Black-boards, made of matched boards and painted black, were later introduced as were combination desks and seats, made of pine lumber by the local carpenter, these latter being long or wide enough to seat from four to five pupils and as one end would warp one way and one the other, they soon became a sort of improvised rockers. This was not so convenient for practicing penmanship or other exercises necessitating written work. Although the school which I attended, during all but one year of my school days, was housed in a two story frame building, with rooms for a teacherage upstairs, the blackboards and seats, above described, were the only ones I was ever privileged to use and that, in spite of the fact that almost all of our work had to be committed to writing, on slates of course, the only paper used being our copy books and the composition books which were used for home work only, but I am getting ahead of my story and must again return to the little log school house, of pre-war days, or rather built in those days, since some of them were still in use in the early seventies.

Since one of the urgent necessities of life is drinking water, all these buildings, as well as the dwellings of the pioneers, were erected near running water, if possible near a spring or a creek and thus in many cases the ground was rather damp and often soggy but as school was mostly kept in winter only, this was inconvenient at the opening and close of the term only. Not all farm houses nor all schoolhouses, could be built near running water and in such cases the water was often carried half a mile or more, however farmers thus located dug wells, curbed with stones or planks, as soon as possible and the water supply of the school was then procured from some neighboring well and later on a well was generally dug near the school house. These wells, shallow as they were, often proved unsanitary affairs and not until the advent of deep, drilled wells, did either farms or schools, so located, have a supply of pure water. Although nothing was cheaper than land, in those days, school grounds were, as a rule limited and in many cases the school house was built on a bushy hillside or, as already stated, on a low, soggy spot, but there were exceptions, even in those early days, where an acre or two was allotted for a school yard or play grounds.

So much for buildings, equipment and playgrounds, now for the most important factor, the teacher. Licensing of professional men and women, in those days, was not taken very seriously. A man who had the advantage of a college education, in the old country, as Europe was always referred to, with little special preparation chose the profession that best suited him or for which there seemed to be a demand, thus after a cursory examination a man was admitted to the bar and on payment of a small fee a physician's diploma was secured, while almost anyone, who was so inclined, took up teaching. It may therefore be readily seen that during the early stages, Buffalo County's teaching force was somewhat of a motley array, ranging from college graduates with but a smattering of English, to girls just out of school, with but a rudimentary knowledge of the three Rs. This is, by no means an exaggeration but a true statement of conditions as they existed, in the very beginning of things. I have personal knowledge of a man who studied for the priesthood, serving his community, first as teacher and later as doctor and most faithful service did he render, although his kindly disposition may have been a greater asset, in the last named profession, than his efficiency. At any rate he tried his best to serve his fellowmen.

Conditions, such as these, could exist only where the authority of licensing the teacher and supervising his work was, with very few exceptions, in the hands of men absolutely incompetent and unfit for the job. Every spring, at the annual town meeting in every town in the state, a man was elected town superintendent of schools and as his compensation was either nominal or nil, the office went begging and was often filled by persons who were almost and in some instances, entirely illiterate and it was their duty to pass on the ability, educational and otherwise, of the teachers to be employed in the town. Far be it from me to offer criticism on the individuals, for the few of them with whom I was personally acquainted, were men of integrity and evidently tried their best to do the right thing, but the system was such a failure that some years before I became of school age, it became obsolete and the office of county superintendent of schools was established. This was the most drastic step taken for the advancement of education in the early history of the state and marks a radical turning point in educational affairs and the progress of our public schools. The office has always been in the hands of competent men and women and although I have been personally acquainted with almost every one of them and their work, I do not consider it proper, nor do I feel qualified to pass judgement on them or their work, therefore suffice it to say, that our schools have fared well under their direction and supervision. However, as this article deals with the early history of education, I cannot refrain from mentioning the names of two men who, as county superintendents, did real pioneer work in advancing the educational interests of Buffalo County. Any old Buffalo County teacher will readily guess that I refer to Robert Lees and Lawrence Kessinger. Both were eminently qualified for the position and both performed their work efficiently and faithfully. Physically the work was little less than heroic, for from bucking snowdrifts in winter to wallowing in almost bottomless roads in the spring and fall, their task was by no means an easy one but their work must be done and done it was. The encouragement and kindly criticism, offered the teachers by these men, did much toward placing our schools where they are and in many ways, these pioneers smoothed the paths of those who were to follow in their footsteps. Therefore I trust that none of the last named may feel slighted when I say a few kind words for these two pioneer educators, who long ago have passed on to their reward but whose good work lives on and on.

Locally the responsibility has always rested with the school officers, a body of three persons known as the school board. No two school boards were ever alike, although in a general way, their duties were almost identical. Among school boards there have always been two extremes; the ones who left the school to the lowest bidder and the ones for whom the best was none too good, and I fear that only too few people realize that the last named were real public benefactors, provided of course, that their judgment was sound. There were always boards who belonged to neither of these classes but followed the line of least resistence, biding their time and trying to combine economy with efficiency and thus abiding by the law of averages they have generally secured average teachers. School boards are elected by the people and while in some instances the voters show a deep interest in their selection there are cases where the choice is left to go by default and often to the detriment of the children in the district. Before county school board conventions were held, there was no organized effort nor united action and there is not any doubt in my mind that these meetings have furnished the school boards with a lot of valuable information which, in turn, has born good fruit.

Among the early day organized efforts to aid the teachers and through them the schools, were the teachers' institutes, conducted by the county superintendent, with the aid of a conductor sent by the state. Local teachers' associations were organized in different parts of the county and regular meetings held. There was no outside assistance from any source whatever and the program was entirely rendered by the members themselves. These meetings were always held on Saturdays and those attending them came on foot and a walk of ten or fifteen miles back and forth was nothing unusual, in those days and there was neither allowance for time or expense of any kind. You walked and you worked, and like virtue, the work done was its own reward.

The old time text book is another noteworthy item in the history of education. There were a few different authors and among the readers used, McGuffy's were the most common and by far superior to some of the others. They were not used in the school that I attended, I am sorry to say, but in their stead we were saddled with a set of readers gotten up by a couple of learned professors who were cranks on diacritical markings and every reading lesson in the two first grades, was grouped around a few words having the same vowel sound. For instance, the words: go, no, so made one story, then on, of, ox, box, fox; next hay, may, lay and also lass, lad, nag, the three last named being a great help to children not capable of speaking one word of English. Imagine what thrilling stories could be made up of a list of words grouped around one vowel sound. They were so dry that we really never knew whether the gig was before the nag or vice versa. One advantage was that they never created laughter, which was absolutely taboo with some of the stern, early day masters. One redeeming feature of the series was that the advanced books were largely devoted to classic literature, but alas, that was over the heads of children of foreign descent who had been taught such words as lad, lass, nag, gig and hundreds of other almost obsolete words just because they were grouped around a certain vowel sound. With absolutely no supplementary reading matter in the shape of either library, magazine or newspaper our opportunities were certainly limited.

Spelling, in all but a very few schools, was the paramount issue. Here again the words were grouped according to diacritical marks and not half of them were ever used in common conversation but that was neither here nor there and I know that it never occurred to either teacher or parent to ask of what use the spelling exercises were, the only object being to be able to spell the others down. To accomplish this some ambitious pupils devoted so much time, both in school and at home, to this game that nothing else mattered. To be the champion speller of the school was the height of the pupil's ambition and to spell down the others when a number of schools met, at a spelling bee or spelling school was an honor much to be coveted. Sad to relate, however, when it came to express their thoughts in writing many of these champions were the most wretched spellers, for in those spelling matches small common words were not used and in a letter they had little use for words like, ichneumon, plesiosaurus, phthisis, charivari, etc.

The text books on history and geography were also hopeless. The geography books were evidently prepared for teachers licensed by a town superintendent, for outside of the maps, the text consisted of a series of questions and answers read by the teacher and answered by the pupil. For instance; Q. What are products of Colorado? A. Gold and silver. Q. For what is Italy famous? A. Painting, sculpture, and music, and so on, ad libitum infinitum. All that was necessary to teach such geography was that the teacher could read. Such were some of the early day text books and I am happy to say that early in my school days, there was a general housecleaning and these books were replaced by more useful ones, which by no means measured up to present day text books nor to the school books that my mother had brought from

Switzerland, which were the one bright spot in my early day education. However, when I took over, my first school, I was horrified to meet up with every single one of my old friends-the enemy. An energetic protest to an open minded school board authorized me to clean house and what a housecleaning it was. After the first few months "Italy was no longer famous" in that school nor were there any dry, dead words to be spelled. We had a set of new books.

Every school was furnished a copy of Webster's unabridged dictionary by the state but precious little use was made of it in most cases, especially where it was most necessary.

There is very much that I could relate regarding conditions that were so different from what they are now but time and space forbid. I will, however, mention the fact that the teachers under the regime of the town superintendent earned every cent they got and more, for I have heard salaries of ten and twenty dollars a month mentioned and even in my day fifty dollars a month was about the maximum and a school of fifty pupils of all ages was not an exception. So you see that the "good old times" were not always "What they are cracked up to be."

Lawrence Kessinger

Buffalo County's Historian…..

His Work and Character Briefly Reviewed

Before there were any newspapers in the county, there was not even a record of current events and even after the advent of those mediums for recording local happenings, those records were, of necessity, piecemeal and unreliable, owing to the lack of communication. Mail service was slow and irregular and so was communication of all kinds, between the widely scattered settlements. They often had to depend on rumors and often when they were published, as reported, those concerned did not even go to the trouble of giving the papers the correct version. On the other hand, events of even more than local importance were never reported to the papers and that also mitigated against the keeping of an accurate record of current events and later on added to the difficulties confronting a local historian.

In 1878 was published "The Historical Atlas of Buffalo and Pepin Counties". While as an atlas, this publication was a success, the maps and plats being well executed and accurate, historically it was of little or no value. In fact its only redeeming feature was its brevity. Like sporadic efforts were repeatedly made but the only one who ever did anything worth-while and tangible, along those lines, was Lawrence Kessinger and the only authentic work on this subject is Kessinger's History of Buffalo County.

Lawrence Kessinger, a native of Gottmadingen, in the Grand-duchy of Baden Germany, enjoyed the, privileges and educational advantages afforded by the excellent German colleges, whose reputation, even at that time, was world wide. He came to Buffalo City in 1859 and taught school there the same year. To him was intrusted the job of drawing the plans and specifications of the proposed court house, which never materialized, as well as other work of a like nature.

In 1865 he moved onto a farm in the town of Belvidere and in 1867 he represented the district of which his town was a unit, as county commissioner. I think that during that period he also taught school, as well as, occasionally after that time, when not otherwise employed.

In 1870 he moved to Alma and was elected to the office of county superintendent of schools, holding that office for six consecutive years, with another term of five years from 1881 to 1886. It was while serving in this capacity, which took him to all parts of the county and afforded him contact with all classes of people, that the plan of writing a history of the county first took shape. He planned and gathered material, consulted the old settlers and in various ways made preparations for this undertaking, which proved a stupendous one, indeed, so much so that anyone not endowed with the enthusiasm, willpower and tenacity of purpose, possessed by Mr. Kessinger, would ever have ventured to undertake it. The work he devoted to this undertaking did, however, in no way interfere with the faithful performance of his official duties, as all who worked under his supervision can truthfully say. Neither raging blizzards nor roads that were almost impassable could long deter him from making his rounds, for the surmounting of such obstacles was all in the day's work. Plowing through snowdrifts in winter and wallowing in muddy roads in the spring was a task that confronted anyone who was compelled to travel the country roads of that day. Rain or shine, heat or cold Mr. Kessinger and his faithful old nag were bound to turn up, sooner or later.

Right here let me say that whenever Mr. Kessinger entered a schoolroom he did so with dignity decorum and due respect to himself, the teacher and the pupils. During his entire official career, I was either a pupil or teacher in the schools, visited by him but never did I see him enter a school and perforce take charge of the class in vocal music, using the bow of his violin to enforce discipline. In fact I never saw him with a violin and diligent inquiry has not divulged the fact that he ever played that instrument. He was a surveyor but never did I see him enter a schoolroom, terrorizing the pupils with a transit, strapped to his back.

He had his idiosincrasies but in the performance of his duties and in his intercourse with his fellowmen he was always a gentleman. I am impelled to interpolate these remarks, owing to the fact that in a recent newspaper interview, granted by one who neither knew Mr. Kessinger nor was well informed about him and his work, these freakish acts and others of alike nature were attributed to him. So much in defense of one who can no longer speak for himself.

He worked at this self-imposed task until it became an obsession with him and on retiring from the superintendency all his time and energy was concentrated upon it. And who was better qualified for it than he and who could have acquitted himself of it as he did? An eminent scholar well versed not only in history, both ancient and modern, but likewise in geology, zoology, botany and all phases of natural history, he embodied all this and more in his work and treated every subject comprehensibly as related to local conditions. The aborigines, both Mound Builders and Indians, their mode of living, manners and customs, religious beliefs and rites are ably discussed. The early explorers of this region receive proper attention as do those who were pioneers locally. The leading industries and above all agriculture are ably discussed and statistics are given on this and other subjects. Political History, Education, Religion, Civic Societies, Fraternal Orders are all discussed. River traffic including rafting, as well as other matters pertaining to transportation come in for their share of attention. The soldiers of the civil war are listed and classified, in short, everything that goes to make up real history receives consideration at his hands. Much time and labor was expended in getting information of the county's first, settler, Thomas A. Holmes, whose peregrinations he traced from one location, where he pioneered, to another. The organization of the state, county and the different towns is traced from the very beginning. In short, nothing worth while was overlooked, while non-essentials received no attention.

The history was now completed without one biographical sketch except of the very early pioneers, most of whom were dead and gone. If the author had done this work "for revenue only", as has since repeatedly been the case, he would have never overlooked this appeal to the vanity of the masses but I can hear him snort had anyone suggested to him that the way to make the thing pay was to flatter the vanity of would-be purchasers of the book. I can imagine him saying "This is a history and not a mutual admiration affair". It is a history but it did not sell and the main reason, I think, was because it did not speak of the hundreds who were expected to buy it, as prominent farmers, distinguished citizens, enterprising business men or something equally flattering. Farthermore, the publication having been left to a concern not well equipped for such work, the book was poorly bound, printed on cheap paper and the text teemed with typographical errors, which we know that the author was not responsible for, being a fine penman and excellent grammarian and linguist.

The books were put on sale in 1888 and the author patiently waited for the public to come and get them but the demand was not great. It soon became evident that while Mr. Kessinger was a great scholar and able writer, he was no salesman and did not know how to play up to the galleries or rather he had not fathomed the mystery of appealing to the human element that yields to persuasion and I think he would not have done it had he known how. He was too independent to curry favor and when he offered something for sale he wanted to give value received in exchange. He came to this country to be independent and independent he remained.

That the outcome of this venture, for in a business way it proved to be a venture indeed, should have disappointed the author is selfevident for again the saying, that a prophet is not appreciated in his own land proved true. Accordingly Lawrence Kessinger, although not a young man, took the advice of Horace Greeley and went West. Selling his home here in 1890, he went with his family to Mount Vernon, Washington, where his declining years were spent in peace and contentment. In communion with nature, accompanied by a grandson, to whom he revealed and explained all the mysteries of growth and decay, as well as the beauties hidden in the fauna and flora, aye in the inanimate rocks, he relived the happy days of his childhood but again the bitter cup was not to pass by him and when that relentless arbiter and grim reaper, Death, called from his side his companion and disciple, his gallant spirit was broken and he too followed him to that realm where there is neither toll nor sorrow but eternal peace and rest. Thus passed Buffalo County's historian and eminent scholar.

Besides the accomplishments above enumerated, he was a mathematician of parts and an excellent draughtsman and his handwriting was a thing of beauty and a joy forever, especially to those of us who were deficient in that art. No doubt others besides myself, who held teacher's certificates signed by him, gazed with due admiration upon that artistic scroll with which he signed the name "L. Kessinger" to those documents. He dearly loved an argument and his intellectual and educational superiority, almost invariably crowned him victor in such contests. Well do I remember how, on these occasions, he would draw himself erect, a triumphant smile pursing his lips, as much as to say, in the present day vernacular, "And that is that". Money, outside of its practical needs, held no charm for him otherwise he might have held positions that carried with them remuneration and emolument. He loved the simple life and preferred being a big fish in small pond to being a small fish in a big pond. He was congenial and helpful and never did he refuse aid to anyone, especially his teachers, who appealed to him for assistance. When the time shall have come that the efforts of our forebears will be appreciated and I trust that in due season it will come, the name of Lawrence Kessinger will be found in the front ranks.

In Memoriam of Edwin F. Ganz

Born at Waumandee, Wis.,
June 13th, 1859

Died at Wabasha, Minn.,
January 20th, 1946

"The benevolence of the good and the courage of the undefeated remain, like the creative achievements of the richly gifted, a part of the heritage of humanity forever. As such they attain their own shining immortality, though it is not without tears that we see them pass from our individual experience."

EDWIN F. GANZ

(Written for the Journal by Theo. Buehler.)

Edwin F. Ganz, for many years one of the foremost citizens of Buffalo county, both in business and in public life, has been called to his reward. At the advanced age of 86 years, the life of this well known resident of this county came to a close Sunday evening, January 20, in the St. Elizabeth hospital at Wabasha where he had been taken Jan. 3 for special care. Death was due to acute leukemia.

Few there are who could make better claim to be designated a leading citizen of this county, for in the course of his life he did creditable service to his fellow men as teacher, editor and publisher, postmaster, school officer, assemblyman, member of the county board and Republican committee chairman, besides other activities.

199

It was inevitable that these columns of the Journal must in the relentless course of time bring to its readers the news of the death and the account of the life of the one who so many times had, with such feeling and fidelity, used these pages to pay a final tribute to a departed friend or relative. In his long and fruitful career which saw activity in such various fields he gained the respect and affection of a wide circle of acquaintances and friends. But it is probable none of his work brought him warmer personal gratitude than the carefully composed obituaries written during the more than a score of years when he was publisher of the Journal, and afterward quite frequently as a contributor. And in them, far more faithfully than another can here set down, he himself, quite unwittingly, revealed his own strong yet gentle character his own recognition and appreciation of the dignity of labor, the virtues of hospitality, of character, of Nature and her mysteries of life and growth, the soil and its bounties, the need for loyalty and devotion to home and country.

This subject is covered first, and dwelt upon, because over the years so many families were drawn nearer to the warmly human side of the man, his sympathetic understanding of those in sorrow or trouble.

But this has to do only with one phase of his works. Much more may be gathered from even a brief account of his life, so closely woven into the story of the growth and development of this county, beginning after its early settlement and up to and including the vast changes of modern times. For as his parents were early settlers and pioneers of this county, so was he proud to be classed as one of the Wisconsin author, Hamlin Garland's, "Sons of the Middle Border" who valiantly carried on the ambitious task the pioneers had begun – the building of a new country of freedom and opportunity.

Edwin Ferdinand Ganz was born in the town of Waumandee on June 13, 1859, a son of Johann Kasper and Louise (Kuerderli) Ganz, both of the canton of Zurich, Switzerland, who came to America in 1857 and settled in the Waumandee valley. In the rural school there he received his elementary education. When Edwin was a lad of 16 years, his father died, leaving upon the mother the responsibility of maintaining the farm and bringing up the family of seven children, most of them quite young. Nevertheless she urged him, her oldest son, to attend the state normal school at Platteville. On his completion of the course there he took charge of the Mill Creek school and taught there ten years.

At that time this school had only a six months' school year, and so he spent a great part of each year working at home on the farm. But one season, in 1881, he left in the spring for the west and worked near Sentinel Butte, Mont., on the Northern Pacific railroad which was being built; later that season he worked in the Red River valley harvest fields. Also, for three summer seasons he drove the Bangor Woolen Mills wagon, buying up wool and he credited this experience for a better knowledge of Buffalo county roads and people.

During the summer of 1886 he attended business college at La Crosse. It was about this time that he applied for the position of principal of the grade school at Waumandee, which had a nine months' school term, and he taught the home school three years.

His marriage to Kunigunde Wald, who had been one of his pupils in Mill Creek, occurred Sept. 1, 1887, and they began their life together in the teacherage, which consisted of dwelling rooms upstairs over the schoolroom.

He had thirteen years of teaching experience when he made the decision which launched him on his new field of work, that of journalism. He learned that the Buffalo County Journal at Alma was to be sold, and he bought the paper, of which he was editor and publisher for 23 years.

Before he came to Alma he became interested in politics and took an active part in Republican party affairs, and after he had used his editorial influence effectively in the service of his party he was made chairman of the county committee, and in 1897 was appointed postmaster; this office he also held until he retired from the newspaper business, a term of 16 years.

He had purchased a tract of land just east of Alma near the crest of the bluffs overlooking the Mississippi river and had built a modern farm home and buildings, and there. On "Buena Vista" farm, he moved with his family in 1913 to spend the remainder of his life.

While he lived in Alma, as publisher of the Journal, he consistently worked in the interest of agriculture and education, besides taking an active part in local and county government. He served as a member of the local school district board, with the office of treasurer. In 1901, when it was proposed that a teachers training school for Buffalo county be established, he became one of the most ardent promoters, and after success was achieved and the school built here at Alma he was a member of the training school board from its beginning in 1902 until 1934.

He served on the city council for a time as alderman, and for five years represented the second ward on the county board, the last year as chairman of the board.

Appointed a court commissioner in the early nineties by Circuit Judge E. W. Helms, he held that office more than 40 years, and as such he performed many marriage ceremonies, besides presiding at and conducting hearings in legal actions.

When the first World War involved this country in 1917 he did patriotic service on the home front, as chairman of the County Council of Defense; and as a member of the Selective Service Board, in which capacity he served through the war.

He left a valuable heritage in the numerous historical writings on local and county events of which he had accurate personal knowledge. These he had printed and bound in book form and they provide a permanent source of reliable information.

His transition from business life in the city to life on the farm was by no means a retirement, but a response to a call of the land, for his real interest at heart was always in agriculture, and since 1913 he and his son Armin, as E. F. Ganz & Son have operated Buena Vista farm with eminent success. They specialized in beef cattle, and from the beginning have had an exceptionally fine herd of Aberdeen-Angus – the first accredited herd of that breed in the state and the first of any breed in Buffalo County. His outstanding work in the interest of agriculture was recognized when in 1930 he was one of the ten farmers of the state selected by the Wisconsin Agriculturist as Master Farmers for that year.

Another honor accorded him after he moved on the farm was his election as assemblyman in 1918, and he represented the Buffalo-Pepin district in the Wisconsin legislature for one term.

Besides his ability as a writer, Mr. Ganz was also an able and forceful public speaker, and on many occasions was called upon to take a leading place on public programs, of a political, educational, or agricultural nature, or just a pleasant social affair. His keen powers of observation, his remarkable retentive memory, his ready wit and sense of humor, all added to these gifts of writing and speaking-powers he never hesitated to use in voicing the approval of what he believed to be right and commendable, or condemn what to him seemed inadvisable or wrong.

He was a member of one fraternal society, Alma Lodge No. 48 of the Knights of Pythias.

All these various activities were secondary to his one great central interest, his home and family, which they only served to provide for and protect. His supreme desire was to surround the family with those things most worthwhile, and to assure for his children the means toward useful and happy lives. Always very fond of small children, his greatest joy in his later years was in the companionship of his two grandchildren, Robert and David McClyman, and the attachment was mutual.

The married life of Mr. and Mrs. Ganz was a most happy one, as nearly ideal as man can hope for, and was interrupted only by the death of Mrs. Ganz on Jan. 29, 1940. The pair had, however, been granted that rare privilege – the celebration of their golden wedding, on Sept. 1, 1937.

Many of his relatives and friends from the neighboring country attended the funeral.

Surviving members of the family are three daughters and a son, namely: Rosalie, former principal of the Buffalo County Normal and county superintendent of schools, now at home; Olga, also at home; Armin Edwin, who has been operating the farm with his father, at Alma, Mrs. C. A. McClyman of Wisconsin Dells. The first-born, a son, Armin Arnold, died in infancy. He leaves two brothers and a sister, J. C. Ganz, Arcadia; Arnoldina, Mrs. F. L. Mattausch, Rosalia, Wash.; and J. Adolf Ganz, this city. Those deceased are Louisa (Mrs. John Schmitz), Alwina, (Mrs. Conrad Farner), and Lydia; and four half-brothers and sisters – Arnold, Annetta (Mrs. Joel Doenier), Paulina (Mrs. John Farner), and Alfred.

Funeral services were held Wednesday, Jan. 23. Rev. Harvey Schweppe delivered the funeral sermon at the Stohr funeral chapel, and Miss Gloria Miller sang three beautiful solos, accompanied on the organ by Mrs. Darrell Breitung.

Members of the Knights of Pythias attended in a body, and participated in the services at the cemetery. The pallbearers were T. C. Beckmire, Carl Ritland. H. F. Ibach, Theodore Buehler, Frank Stroebel and Adolph Brunstad.

TRIBUTES

Dr. J. S. Tenney, Alma, one of his closest friends-

Mr. Ganz was one of several men who befriended me when as a young man I first came to Alma to practice medicine. All these years we have been very firm friends. He possessed many fine qualities, and foremost among them was his capacity for being a staunch and true friend. This, of course, conformed with his unwavering sense of justice and honesty by which his every act was guided whether in his own business, in public office, or in his social relations. Of himself and his employees he demanded strict attention to duty and the best of workmanship, and yet he was always considerate and kind and deeply interested in the welfare of his men.

If I were to be allowed but one word to describe Mr. Ganz, I should say that he was "honorable", – with sterling honesty, unimpeachable morals, kindness, and sense of duty.

Dr. J. S. Tenney.

Hon. Merlin Hull, Black River Falls, Member of Congress:

In the passing of our good friend, Honorable Edwin F. Ganz, the long and useful career of one of Wisconsin's best citizens was brought to a close. It has fallen to the lot of but few people to have been of such firm and lasting influence in his home community and in his state as well over a period of more than 70 years. And few, indeed, of any age have exemplified such influence in so many fields of endeavor. From his boyhood days on the farm of his pioneer parents he had a warm interest in people, and sought to do his full part in every capacity in which he was called upon.

My first acquaintance with my good friend was from reading the Buffalo County Journal, of which he was editor and publisher in the long ago. I came to anticipate that pleasure as the years passed. He wrote ably and forcibly in expressing his opinions upon current problems and with sincere and sympathetic interest in portraying the activities of those whom his publication served. When there came the real opportunity of personal acquaintance we found ourselves in touch with common ideas upon many subjects, particularly regarding the rural school problem of that earlier time with which he was thoroughly informed from his long and successful contact and experience.

When his district elected him to the Wisconsin Assembly, I was in a state position at Madison. The first World War ended, and then as now, many new problems of vast import were thrust upon our nation and our state. Loyal to the best interest of both, he was an earnest and industrious legislator. He quickly had gained that confidence of his fellow-members which was his in any circle at home or elsewhere. He was respected by all for his honesty, integrity and fine ability. Even those who were not in accord with his views upon public questions shared the esteem of those who were. Careful and conscientious, the sincerity of his convictions carried weight and influence.

He was often a visitor in my office while serving in the Assembly. Independent in thought and action, he based his judgment upon the facts of any situation, and he was not one who swerved from his conclusions by the pressure of passing events. Frequently he would form one of a circle of his legislative friends and they studied important legislative proposals and sought departmental information upon which to rely. My high estimate of Mr. Ganz as a legislator was fully shared by others at the State Capitol who became acquainted with him. He formed friendships which endured.

It was my pleasure in later years to visit him at his home at Buena Vista, a beautiful place. I always found there the warm welcome and hearty greetings which characterized our meetings in earlier years. He retained all his interest in public affairs and in the activities of his friends even though he had reached a great age. His faculties seemed unaffected and unabated by his long activities. I never left Buena Vista after such a visit but that I hoped and fully expected to return again at the earliest opportunity. My recollections of Mr. Ganz and his hospitable home and family never become dim. They never will.

A great man has passed to his reward – great in character, in service to his people and in the experience of a long, successful and highly influential career, dating from his boyhood and ending only as he heard the final summons. He had a host of friends. They share with his son and daughters and other relatives a loss felt by all.

Merlin Hull

Hon. Grover L. Broadfoot, Mondovi, assemblyman for the Buffalo-Pepin district:

The activities and leadership of men of a community are reflected in its development and progress. Buffalo County had produced and, in its progress, has enjoyed many distinguished men – forward looking men whose ideals and accomplishments have left their mark upon our history. One of our most distinguished leaders in thought and action was E. F. Ganz, of Alma. In his passing, we have lost a patriotic citizen, a good neighbor, a true friend.

By his ways, his cheery words, and his good deeds, he made his reputation as one who loved his community and his fellow man. His genuineness and simplicity of character, combined with his kindness and understanding, won him friends. Everyone who had the privilege of an intimate acquaintanceship with him not only respected him but loved him. Our friendship was his reward.

The lesson of his life is one for all to learn. He will live in our memories, but we will always miss him.

G. L. Broadfoot.

Edward M. Bardill, publisher of the Spooner Advocate, former Alma boy who began his career as a printer in the Journal office with Mr. Ganz is now president of the Wisconsin Press Association:

News of the passing of E. F. Ganz was received with mixed emotions on my part, for his death removes from this sphere one of Buffalo County's most prominent citizens, a community leader, a man devoted to his family circle, and a true friend to many of us.

He has lived to a ripe age, leaving this world a better place in which to live, for his years were fruitful as the result of his labors among us.

Sentiment no doubt moves us to express our mutual friendship in no uncertain words, for under his guidance we were first initiated into newspaper work, and it was probably through our early training under his guidance that we carried on in our field to such success as may have come to us. His kindly interest in our work was ever appreciated and proved encouraging at all times.

A man of high principles whose courage ever matched his convictions has passed to his eternal reward. A good friend has passed on. His friendship enriched us, his passing is a distinct loss.

E. M. Bardill.

Emil W. Zingg, Vancouver, B. C., Canada, former Alma boy, one of many who appreciates the fatherly aid and counsel from Mr. Ganz that helped him through life, sent the following telegram:

Edwin F. Ganz lived a truly useful life and gave inspiration and direction to many of us, as a writer. He was unexcelled in writing tributes to the dead. His righteous praise in honoring pioneers inspired everyone.

In spirit I stand at the foot of his grave and say "My distinguished friend, well done." His freed soul as it moves hither and yon will guide and direct us.

E. W. Zingg.

M. L. Fugina, Fountain City, former county judge:

Honorable Edwin F. Ganz, familiarly called "E. F." by his close friends and associates, was an outstanding and distinguished citizen of his community. During my fifty years' of acquaintance and association with Mr. Ganz, in many public affairs and interests of the community, I have had an excellent opportunity to estimate his capabilities, and to acquire his friendship and loyalty.

Throughout his entire business career he served in many responsible positions of honor and trust in public life, and in civic affairs pertaining to his city, county, State and Country.

To those who sought his advice and counsel he was an able, willing and conscientious advisor and counselor; he never hesitated to aid and assist those who sought his aid and advice; those of us who have known and worked with him over a long period of years have well learned to appreciate his friendship, counsel and advice; these qualities together with his high standard of ethics, his sense of fairness to friend and adversary alike; his sense of responsibility and duty to every responsibility entrusted to him, all made him one of the outstanding citizens of the community.

Mr. Ganz was endowed with sterling manhood; with an abundance of common sense and sound judgment; with a keen mind and wealth of learning and experience; with unquestionable honesty and integrity, and with a kind heart and sympathetic nature; he looked upon and regarded everyone as his equal; he was considerate of his fellow men and his friendship was lasting and sincere.

As a citizen, public servant, newspaper editor and publisher, Mr. Ganz never sought to be in the lime-light and rather preferred the quiet seclusion of his home, office or study, to the strife and conflict of the forum. In every matter entrusted to him he was careful and conscientious and ever solicitous of the welfare of his friends and associates; as a citizen, newspaper man and public official he was regarded highly.

He modestly, carefully and studiously gave the best efforts of which he was capable to the performance and discharge of every duty or task entrusted to him, and never approached such a duty or task with a view or purpose of attracting the attention of the public or winning public acclaim.

All those who worked with Mr. Ganz knew him as a man of kind and gentle disposition; as one rather reserved, yet one, who during his entire lifetime and career held the complete confidence and respect of others. He had the courage of his convictions and he never left a doubt as to where he stood on any question or responsibility.

A life and career like that of the late EDWIN F. GANZ, writes its own history in the life and records of the community in which he lived and labored.

I know that the public generally recognizes and appreciates the services and wholesome influences of the late Edwin F. Ganz, in the community in which he was so prominent and active.

I am confident that his good deeds and accomplishments will "Forever" stand as a "Memorial" to him.

M. L. Fugina.

Oliver R. Weinandy, Cochrane attorney and postmaster:

A warm bond of friendship has existed between the Ganz and Weinandy families since the pioneer days when E. F. Ganz was teaching in Mill Creek valley and the Weinandy family resided there. Mr. Ganz and my father were both sons of the Middle Border and worked shoulder to shoulder to improve the condition which existed at that time. They believed that a better educational system and better lines of communications would be the solution of the pioneer problems and advocated these measures with unrelenting zeal.

Mr. Ganz was a man of strong personality, of high personal integrity. His friendships were based upon absolute sincerity and unfailing loyalty. He was devoted to the welfare of his immediate family but always had a profound interest in the progress and success of every boy and girl that grew up in his community. From his lips came words of wisdom and helpful encouragement. Those lips have now been silenced forever, but the memory of this grand old gentleman will linger with me, throughout the years to come.

Oliver R. Weinandy.

Loving and kind in all his ways
Upright and just to the end of his days
Sincere and true in his heart and mind
Beautiful memories he has left behind.
Edna A. Haase.

Index

212

H

I

213